Mastering Cloud Technologies

Your Path to CompTIA Cloud+ Certification

Rob Chubbuck

Mastering Cloud Technologies: Your Path to CompTIA Cloud+ Certification

Table of Contents

Dedication

To my amazing wife, Maria—your unwavering love and belief in me have been the cornerstone of all I've achieved. Your encouragement and steadfast support have made this book a reality, and for that, I am forever grateful.

To my children, their partners, and my grandchildren—you are my daily inspiration, filling my life with strength, love, and purpose. Your unwavering support and encouragement, and your constant presence through every challenge and triumph, have been my greatest source of motivation. Thank you for always being there for me.

To my extended family and cherished friends—your wisdom, support, and encouragement have been a guiding light. Your presence in my life has provided endless strength and motivation, reminding me of the incredible power of community and connection.

Rob Chubbuck

Chapter 1: Introduction to CompTIA Cloud+ Certification (CV0-004)

Chapter 1 lays the foundation for understanding cloud computing and its significance in modern IT environments. It provides a detailed overview of cloud computing models (public, private, and hybrid) and service models (IaaS, PaaS, and SaaS), emphasizing their applications and benefits. This chapter highlights the transformative impact of cloud technologies on businesses, focusing on scalability, cost efficiency, and flexibility. It also introduces the vendor-neutral CompTIA Cloud+ Certification, explaining its relevance in equipping professionals with the skills needed to manage diverse cloud environments.

This chapter sets the stage for the certification journey by outlining the core competencies required for success, including virtualization, networking, and security fundamentals. It emphasizes the importance of hands-on practice and real-world application, encouraging readers to engage with cloud platforms and virtual labs. By the end of Chapter 1, readers gain a clear understanding of the certification's objectives and how it prepares them to address challenges in hybrid and multi-cloud deployments, making it a vital step for career advancement in cloud computing.

Overview of the CompTIA Cloud+ Certification (CV0-004)

Purpose and Relevance of the Cloud+ Certification

The CompTIA Cloud+ Certification is a globally recognized credential that validates an IT professional's expertise in cloud-based infrastructure and services. Unlike vendor-specific certifications, Cloud+ is vendor-neutral, making it versatile for professionals working in various cloud environments. The certification bridges the gap between foundational IT skills and advanced cloud competencies, ensuring that certified individuals can design, deploy, secure, and optimize cloud solutions across multiple platforms.

Cloud+ plays a pivotal role in addressing the challenges of modern IT environments. As organizations increasingly adopt hybrid and multi-cloud models, the need for professionals who can seamlessly manage and integrate these environments grows exponentially. The certification emphasizes practical skills, making it particularly valuable for professionals involved in managing cloud resources, security, and troubleshooting.

Key Objectives and Areas of Focus for the CV0-004 Exam

The CV0-004 exam is structured around five key domains, each addressing critical aspects of cloud infrastructure and operations:

1. **Cloud Architecture and Design (13%)**
    - Understanding cloud models (public, private, hybrid)
    - Evaluating cloud design considerations, such as cost, performance, and scalability
    - Incorporating business continuity and disaster recovery into cloud architectures
2. **Security (20%)**
    - Implementing security controls for cloud environments
    - Managing identity and access management (IAM) within cloud solutions
    - Applying compliance and regulatory requirements
3. **Deployment (23%)**
    - Configuring cloud resources for high availability and fault tolerance
    - Implementing and managing virtual environments
    - Automating cloud provisioning and management tasks
4. **Operations and Support (22%)**
    - Performing cloud environment monitoring and maintenance
    - Troubleshooting connectivity and performance issues
    - Managing cloud service performance metrics
5. **Troubleshooting (22%)**
    - Diagnosing and resolving cloud-related issues
    - Optimizing cloud environments for improved performance
    - Ensuring system reliability and uptime

Each domain includes performance-based questions, testing the candidate's ability to apply theoretical knowledge to real-world scenarios.

Industry Demand for Cloud Professionals

The demand for cloud computing expertise continues to grow as businesses accelerate their digital transformation initiatives. According to industry reports, global cloud spending is projected to reach $1 trillion by 2030. This surge is driven by the need for scalable, cost-effective, and secure IT solutions.

Cloud+ certification holders are well-positioned to meet this demand. Their skills are sought after in various roles, including:

- **Cloud Engineers:** Responsible for designing and managing cloud-based systems.
- **Systems Administrators:** Ensuring seamless operation of hybrid IT environments.
- **Cloud Security Specialists:** Safeguarding sensitive data in the cloud.

The CV0-004 certification is particularly relevant for mid-level professionals, such as network and system administrators, who are transitioning into cloud-focused roles. By earning the Cloud+ certification, these professionals demonstrate their ability to work with complex cloud environments, making them invaluable to organizations leveraging cloud technologies.

Benefits of Achieving the Cloud+ Certification

Career Advancement Opportunities in Cloud Computing

Achieving the CompTIA Cloud+ Certification is a significant step for IT professionals aiming to advance their careers in cloud computing. As organizations transition from on-premises solutions to cloud-based environments, the demand for skilled cloud professionals has surged. Certified individuals have the credentials to fill roles that require expertise in cloud architecture, operations, and security.

Key career advancement opportunities include:

- **Higher-paying roles:** Professionals with the Cloud+ certification often qualify for advanced roles, such as Cloud Systems Engineer, Cloud Architect, and Cloud Operations Specialist, which command competitive salaries.
- **Broader career options:** With its vendor-neutral approach, Cloud+ certification equips candidates to work with diverse cloud platforms, such as AWS, Microsoft Azure, Google Cloud, and private cloud solutions.
- **Global opportunities:** The certification is recognized internationally, enabling professionals to pursue roles in organizations worldwide.

Recognition of Expertise in Cloud Infrastructure and Security

The Cloud+ certification signals a high level of competence in managing cloud infrastructure and ensuring its security. The certification's emphasis on practical skills, such as deploying, managing, and securing cloud environments, sets professionals apart in a competitive job market.

Key areas where expertise is recognized include:

- **Cloud deployment and integration:** Certified professionals demonstrate proficiency in deploying cloud solutions that align with business objectives, ensuring seamless integration with existing infrastructure.
- **Security best practices:** The certification validates an understanding of advanced security measures, including identity and access management (IAM), data encryption, and compliance with regulatory standards.
- **Problem-solving capabilities:** Cloud+ professionals are skilled in troubleshooting complex cloud environments, ensuring reliability, scalability, and performance.

Employers value Cloud+ certification holders for their ability to apply these competencies to real-world challenges, positioning them as experts in the field.

Employer Benefits of Hiring Certified Professionals

Organizations that invest in hiring or training employees with the Cloud+ certification gain significant benefits, including:

1. **Enhanced Operational Efficiency**
   - Certified professionals bring a deep understanding of cloud technologies, enabling streamlined deployment and management of cloud resources. This reduces downtime and improves overall efficiency.
2. **Increased Security Posture**
   - With a strong focus on cloud security, Cloud+ professionals implement robust measures to safeguard data and prevent unauthorized access. This is particularly critical for organizations handling sensitive or regulated information.
3. **Cost Optimization**
   - Certified professionals understand how to optimize cloud environments for performance and cost-efficiency. They can identify opportunities for scaling resources appropriately, eliminating waste, and ensuring maximum ROI on cloud investments.
4. **Competitive Advantage**
   - Hiring certified staff demonstrates a commitment to maintaining a knowledgeable and skilled workforce, which can be a significant differentiator in competitive markets. It also instills confidence in clients and stakeholders regarding the organization's technical capabilities.
5. **Future-Proofing the Workforce**
   - As cloud technologies evolve, professionals with foundational certifications like Cloud+ are better equipped to adapt and upskill, ensuring the organization stays ahead of technological advancements.

By earning the CompTIA Cloud+ Certification, IT professionals position themselves as indispensable assets in the cloud computing space, while organizations benefit from their expertise in building and maintaining secure, efficient, and scalable cloud environments.

Understanding the Cloud+ Certification Exam Format

Breakdown of Exam Structure: Multiple-Choice and Performance-Based Questions

The CompTIA Cloud+ (CV0-004) exam combines theoretical knowledge with practical problem-solving skills to evaluate a candidate's ability to manage real-world cloud environments. The exam is designed to ensure that certified professionals possess both the foundational understanding and hands-on experience needed to succeed in cloud computing roles.

- **Multiple-Choice Questions (MCQs):**
  These questions test conceptual knowledge of cloud infrastructure, security, deployment, operations, and troubleshooting. Each question typically includes one correct answer or requires selecting multiple correct options.
- **Performance-Based Questions (PBQs):**
  PBQs are scenario-based tasks where candidates demonstrate their ability to perform specific technical actions. For example:
  - Configuring cloud resources
  - Troubleshooting network connectivity in a cloud environment
  - Applying security controls to virtual machines

PBQs simulate real-world challenges and require candidates to interact with a virtualized environment or follow specific steps to resolve a problem. These questions assess practical skills, emphasizing the certification's focus on hands-on expertise.

Number of Questions, Time Limit, and Passing Score

To adequately prepare for the Cloud+ exam, understanding its logistical details is crucial:

- **Number of Questions:**
  The exam contains up to 90 questions, which may include a mix of multiple-choice and performance-based questions.
- **Time Limit:**
  Candidates have 90 minutes to complete the exam. Managing time effectively is critical, particularly for performance-based questions, which can be more time-intensive than multiple-choice questions.
- **Passing Score:**
  The minimum passing score is **750** on a scale of 100–900. The scoring system weights performance-based questions more heavily, reflecting their emphasis on practical skills.

Tips for Navigating Performance-Based Scenarios

Performance-based questions can be challenging but are also an excellent opportunity to showcase your expertise. Below are strategies to effectively tackle these scenarios:

1. **Familiarize Yourself with Virtual Environments**
   Practice interacting with cloud management tools, virtual machines, and network

configurations. Simulated labs, such as those offered by CompTIA or other training platforms, provide valuable experience.

2. **Read the Instructions Carefully**
   PBQs often contain detailed instructions outlining the task. Carefully review the requirements before taking any actions to avoid missing critical steps.
3. **Prioritize Time Management**
   - Allocate sufficient time for PBQs but avoid getting stuck on one scenario. If a task is taking too long, move on and revisit it if time permits.
   - Complete easier multiple-choice questions first to build confidence and leave more time for complex PBQs.
4. **Focus on Practical Solutions**
   While PBQs are designed to test specific skills, they also reward logical thinking and problem-solving. Even if unsure, applying basic troubleshooting steps or configurations can lead to partial credit.
5. **Leverage Exam Preparation Resources**
   - Practice using CompTIA-approved materials, such as labs and exam simulators, to gain confidence in performing technical tasks under exam conditions.
   - Review cloud-related concepts, such as virtual networking, storage provisioning, and security controls, which are frequently tested in PBQs.

Understanding the Cloud+ exam format and structure is a crucial step in achieving certification success. With a clear strategy and ample practice, candidates can approach the exam confidently, demonstrating both theoretical knowledge and practical expertise.

Preparing for the Certification Exam

Recommended Study Strategies

Success in the CompTIA Cloud+ Certification exam requires a well-structured study plan tailored to the exam's objectives. Below are effective strategies to prepare:

1. **Develop a Study Schedule**
   - Break the exam content into manageable sections based on the five domains.
   - Allocate specific times for studying each domain, ensuring coverage of all topics.
   - Reserve time for review and practice tests closer to the exam date.
2. **Leverage Multiple Learning Resources**
   - Use official CompTIA study guides and third-party textbooks aligned with the CV0-004 exam objectives.
   - Explore video tutorials to reinforce complex concepts, such as configuring virtual environments or understanding disaster recovery strategies.
3. **Practice Active Recall and Spaced Repetition**
   - Regularly quiz yourself on key concepts to solidify retention.
   - Use flashcards for quick review of cloud terminology, deployment methods, and security protocols.
4. **Take Practice Exams**
   - Attempt full-length practice exams under timed conditions to simulate the test environment.

   - Review incorrect answers to identify knowledge gaps and revisit those topics in your studies.
5. **Join Study Groups or Forums**
   - Engage with peers preparing for the same certification to share insights and resources.
   - Participate in discussions on forums like Reddit, LinkedIn groups, or CompTIA's online community to clarify doubts and gain different perspectives.

Importance of Hands-On Practice with Cloud Technologies

The CompTIA Cloud+ exam emphasizes practical skills, particularly through performance-based questions. Gaining hands-on experience is essential to prepare effectively:

1. **Work with Cloud Platforms**
   - Practice using popular cloud platforms, such as Amazon Web Services (AWS), Microsoft Azure, and Google Cloud. These environments provide real-world scenarios to enhance your understanding of cloud deployment, management, and security.
2. **Set Up a Virtual Lab**
   - Use virtualization software like VirtualBox, VMware Workstation, or Hyper-V to create and manage virtual machines. This helps develop skills in configuring and troubleshooting virtual environments.
3. **Simulate Common Cloud Scenarios**
   - Practice tasks like creating virtual networks, scaling resources, applying access controls, and implementing disaster recovery strategies.
   - Use sandbox environments or free-tier cloud subscriptions to experiment with different configurations safely.
4. **Explore Training Platforms**
   - Leverage training labs from CompTIA or third-party providers that simulate real-world scenarios. These labs often align with the CV0-004 objectives, offering a targeted approach to skill-building.

Using the CompTIA Cloud+ Exam Objectives as a Study Guide

The CompTIA Cloud+ Exam Objectives are an invaluable resource, outlining the precise topics covered on the CV0-004 exam. Here's how to make the most of this guide:

1. **Familiarize Yourself with the Exam Domains**
   - Review the five main domains and their subtopics. Focus on areas where you feel less confident, allocating extra time to those topics.
2. **Align Study Materials with the Objectives**
   - Cross-reference your study resources with the official objectives to ensure comprehensive coverage of all required knowledge and skills.
3. **Track Your Progress**
   - Use the objectives as a checklist. Mark topics as "complete" as you review and practice them to monitor your readiness.

4. **Integrate Objectives into Practice**
   - When performing hands-on exercises, align tasks with specific objectives. For example:
     - While configuring a virtual machine, tie the task to the **Deployment** domain.
     - Practice applying IAM roles to address the **Security** domain.
5. **Stay Updated**
   - Regularly check CompTIA's website for updates to the exam objectives or additional resources, ensuring your preparation reflects the latest requirements.

Preparing for the CompTIA Cloud+ certification exam requires a balance of theoretical knowledge, practical experience, and strategic planning. By following these recommendations, candidates can approach the exam with confidence, equipped with the skills needed to excel.

Building a Strong Foundation for Cloud+ Success

Prerequisite Knowledge and Recommended Experience

The CompTIA Cloud+ Certification (CV0-004) is designed for IT professionals with a foundational understanding of system administration and networking. Before attempting the certification, candidates should meet these prerequisites:

1. **Recommended Experience**
   - **Two to three years of IT experience:** Candidates should have experience in roles such as systems administrator, network administrator, or cloud specialist.
   - Familiarity with maintaining and troubleshooting IT systems in environments that integrate cloud-based resources.
2. **Prior Certifications or Training**
   - While not mandatory, certifications like CompTIA Network+ or CompTIA Server+ are helpful. They provide foundational knowledge in networking and server administration, which are essential for success in Cloud+.
3. **Basic Understanding of Cloud Concepts**
   - Candidates should have a working knowledge of cloud computing models (public, private, and hybrid), service models (IaaS, PaaS, SaaS), and the general benefits and challenges of cloud adoption.

Key Technical Skills to Focus On

The Cloud+ exam evaluates candidates on several technical competencies. Building a strong foundation in the following areas is critical:

1. **Virtualization**
   - **Skill Focus:**
     - Creating and managing virtual machines (VMs)
     - Configuring virtual networks and storage
     - Understanding hypervisors, such as VMware ESXi, Microsoft Hyper-V, and KVM

- **Why It Matters:**
  - Virtualization forms the backbone of cloud infrastructure, enabling resource scalability and efficient utilization.

2. **Networking**
   - **Skill Focus:**
     - Configuring virtual networks, including subnets, VLANs, and routing
     - Understanding protocols like TCP/IP, DNS, and DHCP
     - Troubleshooting network connectivity in hybrid and cloud environments
   - **Why It Matters:**
     - Networking ensures seamless communication between cloud resources and on-premises systems, making it a vital skill for cloud professionals.
3. **Security**
   - **Skill Focus:**
     - Implementing identity and access management (IAM)
     - Applying encryption techniques for data at rest and in transit
     - Managing compliance and regulatory requirements
   - **Why It Matters:**
     - Security is a top priority for organizations leveraging cloud environments, and certified professionals are expected to safeguard data and resources against evolving threats.
4. **Cloud Deployment and Management**
   - **Skill Focus:**
     - Deploying and configuring cloud resources
     - Implementing backup, redundancy, and disaster recovery solutions
     - Automating cloud workflows using tools like Terraform, Ansible, or AWS CloudFormation
   - **Why It Matters:**
     - Efficient deployment and management of resources are critical for maintaining reliable and cost-effective cloud environments.

Setting Realistic Timelines and Goals for Exam Preparation

Establishing a structured and achievable preparation plan is essential for success. Below are steps to create a timeline that aligns with your schedule and goals:

1. **Assess Your Current Knowledge**
   - Take a diagnostic practice test to identify your strengths and areas that need improvement.
   - Use the results to prioritize topics in your study plan.
2. **Create a Study Timeline**
   - For candidates with moderate IT experience, allocate **8–12 weeks** for preparation.
   - Break the study period into phases:
     - **Weeks 1–4:** Build foundational knowledge in networking, virtualization, and cloud security.
     - **Weeks 5–8:** Focus on advanced topics like troubleshooting and performance-based tasks.

    - **Weeks 9–10:** Take practice exams, review weak areas, and solidify key concepts.
    - **Weeks 11–12:** Perform final reviews and practice performance-based scenarios.

3. **Set Specific Goals**
    - Define measurable goals for each study session, such as completing a chapter, configuring a virtual machine, or achieving a target score on a practice test.
4. **Schedule Regular Practice**
    - Dedicate time each week to hands-on activities, such as setting up virtual labs or using cloud platform free tiers.
    - Practice troubleshooting common cloud issues to build confidence in real-world scenarios.
5. **Incorporate Flexibility**
    - Leave buffer days in your schedule for unplanned delays or additional review time.

By understanding the prerequisites, honing key technical skills, and setting a realistic preparation plan, candidates can lay a solid foundation for Cloud+ success. This approach not only helps with exam readiness but also ensures long-term competency in cloud environments.

Chapter 2: Introduction to Cloud Concepts

Chapter 2 provides a comprehensive introduction to cloud computing, covering its definition, historical evolution, and modern applications. It examines key characteristics such as on-demand self-service, broad network access, and the deployment models—public, private, hybrid, and community clouds—highlighting their unique features, advantages, and challenges to guide organizational decision-making.

The chapter also explains cloud service models, including Infrastructure as a Service (IaaS), Platform as a Service (PaaS), and Software as a Service (SaaS), with examples of their functionalities and use cases. Core principles like elasticity, scalability, high availability, and resiliency are discussed, emphasizing their importance in building efficient and reliable cloud systems. Lastly, it addresses the benefits and challenges of cloud adoption, focusing on cost-efficiency, security considerations, and compliance, providing readers with a balanced perspective on leveraging cloud computing effectively.

Overview of Cloud Computing

Definition and Evolution of Cloud Computing

Cloud computing refers to the delivery of computing services—including servers, storage, databases, networking, software, and more—over the internet ("the cloud"). This model allows users to access and manage resources on a pay-as-you-go basis, eliminating the need for physical infrastructure and enabling scalability, flexibility, and cost efficiency.

The Evolution of Cloud Computing:

1. **Mainframe Computing (1950s–1970s):**
   The concept of shared resources began with mainframes, where multiple users accessed computing resources through terminals. This laid the groundwork for resource centralization and multi-user access.
2. **Virtualization (1970s–1990s):**
   Virtualization technologies, such as VMware and Microsoft Hyper-V, revolutionized computing by enabling multiple operating systems to run on a single physical machine. This innovation paved the way for modern cloud computing by improving resource utilization and scalability.
3. **The Internet and Web Services (1990s–2000s):**
   The growth of the internet allowed applications to be delivered via the web. Early Software as a Service (SaaS) solutions, such as Salesforce, demonstrated the viability of cloud-based software delivery.
4. **The Rise of Cloud Providers (2000s–Present):**
   Companies like Amazon, Google, and Microsoft launched cloud platforms (AWS, Google Cloud, and Azure), offering Infrastructure as a Service (IaaS), Platform as a Service (PaaS), and SaaS. These platforms made cloud computing accessible to businesses of all sizes.
5. **Hybrid and Multi-Cloud Models:**
   Organizations increasingly adopt hybrid (combining on-premises and cloud resources) and multi-cloud (utilizing multiple cloud providers) strategies to optimize performance, cost, and compliance.

Core Characteristics of Cloud Computing

Cloud computing is defined by several essential characteristics that differentiate it from traditional IT models. Below are two foundational traits:

1. **On-Demand Self-Service**
   - **Definition:**
     On-demand self-service allows users to provision and manage computing resources, such as virtual machines, storage, and applications, without requiring human interaction from the service provider.
   - **Key Features:**
     - Resources are available via an intuitive interface or API.

    - Users can scale resources up or down as needed, ensuring flexibility and cost efficiency.
  - **Example Use Case:**
    A developer can spin up a virtual machine on AWS to test an application within minutes, paying only for the time the resource is active.
2. **Broad Network Access**
  - **Definition:**
    Cloud resources are accessible over a network (typically the internet) using standard protocols and platforms, including laptops, smartphones, and tablets.
  - **Key Features:**
    - Availability on diverse devices ensures accessibility across geographic locations.
    - Standardized access protocols, such as HTTP/HTTPS, enable seamless integration with existing applications.
  - **Example Use Case:**
    An organization using a SaaS solution like Google Workspace allows employees to collaborate on documents in real-time, regardless of their location or device.

These characteristics highlight how cloud computing transforms the way IT resources are delivered and consumed. They provide the foundation for the scalable, flexible, and accessible nature of modern cloud environments.

Cloud Deployment Models

Cloud computing offers various deployment models tailored to meet the diverse needs of organizations. These models define how cloud resources are hosted, accessed, and managed, enabling businesses to choose the most appropriate setup based on their operational requirements.

Public, Private, Hybrid, and Community Clouds

1. **Public Cloud**
  - **Definition:**
    A public cloud is owned and operated by a third-party provider that delivers computing resources over the internet. Examples include Amazon Web Services (AWS), Microsoft Azure, and Google Cloud Platform.
  - **Characteristics:**
    - Shared infrastructure among multiple tenants.
    - Highly scalable and cost-effective, with a pay-as-you-go pricing model.
    - Minimal management responsibilities for the user.
  - **Advantages:**
    - Easy to scale resources up or down based on demand.
    - Lower upfront costs, as there's no need for on-premises infrastructure.
    - Accessibility from any location with internet access.
  - **Challenges:**
    - Limited customization options.

        - Potential security concerns due to shared infrastructure.

2. **Private Cloud**
    - **Definition:**
      A private cloud is dedicated to a single organization, either hosted on-premises or managed by a third-party provider. It offers exclusive access to cloud resources.
    - **Characteristics:**
        - Greater control and customization of resources.
        - Enhanced security and compliance capabilities.
    - **Advantages:**
        - Tailored to meet specific business and regulatory requirements.
        - Provides greater data security and control over sensitive information.
    - **Challenges:**
        - Higher initial and ongoing costs compared to public clouds.
        - Requires in-house expertise for setup and maintenance.
3. **Hybrid Cloud**
    - **Definition:**
      A hybrid cloud integrates public and private cloud environments, allowing data and applications to move seamlessly between the two.
    - **Characteristics:**
        - Combines the scalability of public clouds with the security of private clouds.
        - Allows organizations to run workloads in the most appropriate environment.
    - **Advantages:**
        - Flexibility to optimize workloads based on performance, cost, or compliance needs.
        - Enables gradual cloud adoption without fully abandoning on-premises infrastructure.
    - **Challenges:**
        - Complex to manage and integrate.
        - Requires robust network connectivity and monitoring tools.
4. **Community Cloud**
    - **Definition:**
      A community cloud is shared among multiple organizations with similar goals, security requirements, or compliance needs. It can be hosted by one of the participating organizations or a third party.
    - **Characteristics:**
        - Tailored to specific industries or sectors, such as healthcare or education.
        - Encourages collaboration while maintaining shared governance.
    - **Advantages:**
        - Cost-effective compared to private clouds.
        - Focused on addressing specific industry challenges.
    - **Challenges:**
        - Limited scalability compared to public clouds.
        - Potential for conflicting governance or management requirements among participants.

Use Cases and Selection Criteria

1. **Public Cloud Use Cases**
   - Hosting web applications or websites.
   - Running development and testing environments.
   - Analyzing large datasets using high-performance computing.
   - Scaling resources for short-term or seasonal workloads.
   - **Selection Criteria:**
     - Cost sensitivity.
     - Need for rapid deployment and scalability.
     - Minimal customization or regulatory requirements.
2. **Private Cloud Use Cases**
   - Hosting mission-critical applications or sensitive workloads.
   - Managing compliance-heavy industries (e.g., finance, healthcare).
   - Supporting legacy systems requiring high levels of customization.
   - **Selection Criteria:**
     - Need for strict control over data and resources.
     - Industry-specific compliance requirements.
     - Desire for long-term operational control.
3. **Hybrid Cloud Use Cases**
   - Maintaining business continuity and disaster recovery.
   - Balancing workloads between public and private environments.
   - Keeping sensitive data on-premises while leveraging public cloud scalability for less critical workloads.
   - **Selection Criteria:**
     - Flexibility to optimize resource placement.
     - Seamless integration between on-premises and cloud environments.
     - Support for fluctuating or unpredictable workloads.
4. **Community Cloud Use Cases**
   - Sharing resources among organizations with similar goals, such as non-profits or research institutions.
   - Complying with industry-specific standards like HIPAA or GDPR.
   - Collaborating within sectors like government or education.
   - **Selection Criteria:**
     - Common needs and compliance requirements among participants.
     - Shared goals and governance frameworks.

By understanding the unique characteristics, advantages, and challenges of each cloud deployment model, organizations can select the approach that aligns best with their operational needs, budget, and compliance requirements.

Cloud Service Models

Cloud computing services are categorized into three primary models: Infrastructure as a Service (IaaS), Platform as a Service (PaaS), and Software as a Service (SaaS). These models define how cloud resources are delivered and managed, catering to various organizational needs and levels of control.

Infrastructure as a Service (IaaS)

Definition:
IaaS provides virtualized computing resources, such as servers, storage, and networking, over the internet. It offers the foundational building blocks for IT infrastructure, enabling organizations to deploy and manage their applications without the need for physical hardware.

Key Features:

- On-demand provisioning of virtual machines, storage, and networks.
- Pay-as-you-go pricing models for cost flexibility.
- High scalability to adjust resources based on workload demands.

Benefits:

- **Cost Efficiency:** Eliminates the need for upfront hardware investments.
- **Control:** Users manage the operating systems, applications, and configurations while the provider manages the underlying hardware.
- **Scalability:** Resources can be quickly scaled up or down to meet business needs.

Challenges:

- Requires expertise in managing and configuring IT infrastructure.
- Responsibility for securing applications and data lies with the user.

Examples of IaaS Providers:

- Amazon Web Services (AWS): Elastic Compute Cloud (EC2)
- Microsoft Azure: Virtual Machines
- Google Cloud Platform: Compute Engine

Use Cases:

- Hosting websites and applications.
- Development and testing environments.
- Disaster recovery and backup solutions.

Platform as a Service (PaaS)

Definition:
PaaS provides a managed environment for developing, testing, and deploying applications. It abstracts infrastructure management, enabling developers to focus on writing code and building software.

Key Features:

- Pre-configured environments for application development.
- Integration with development tools and APIs.
- Automated infrastructure management, including scaling, patching, and backups.

Benefits:

- **Developer Productivity:** Simplifies application deployment and reduces time to market.
- **Cost Savings:** Developers can focus on coding without worrying about hardware or infrastructure maintenance.
- **Integration:** Seamlessly integrates with APIs and third-party services.

Challenges:

- Limited control over the underlying infrastructure.
- Dependency on the platform provider for availability and compatibility.

Examples of PaaS Providers:

- AWS: Elastic Beanstalk
- Microsoft Azure: App Services
- Google Cloud Platform: App Engine

Use Cases:

- Building web and mobile applications.
- Creating APIs and microservices.
- Prototyping and developing new software products.

Software as a Service (SaaS)

Definition:
SaaS delivers fully managed applications over the internet, allowing users to access software without installation or maintenance. The provider manages everything, including infrastructure, platforms, and software.

Key Features:

- Accessible through a web browser or dedicated client.
- Subscription-based pricing, often per user or usage.
- Automatic updates and patches handled by the provider.

Benefits:

- **Ease of Use:** Users can quickly access applications without setup or technical expertise.

- **Cost Predictability:** Subscription pricing eliminates large upfront costs.
- **Accessibility:** Applications are available from anywhere with an internet connection.

Challenges:

- Limited customization compared to self-hosted solutions.
- Dependency on the provider for uptime and data security.

Examples of SaaS Providers:

- Google Workspace (Docs, Sheets, Drive)
- Microsoft 365 (Word, Excel, Teams)
- Salesforce (CRM software)

Use Cases:

- Email and collaboration tools.
- Customer relationship management (CRM).
- Enterprise resource planning (ERP) systems.

Comparing the Models: IaaS, PaaS, SaaS

Feature	IaaS	PaaS	SaaS
User Responsibility	Infrastructure setup and application management	Application development	Application use
Control	High	Moderate	Low
Scalability	High	High	Moderate
Target Audience	IT administrators and system architects	Developers	End users and business teams

---

By understanding the distinctions and advantages of these service models, organizations can select the best-fit solution for their technical requirements, operational goals, and budgetary

Key Concepts: Elasticity, Scalability, On-Demand, and Resiliency

Cloud computing is built upon fundamental principles that enable efficient resource management and ensure the availability and reliability of services. This section explores core concepts—**elasticity, scalability, on-demand provisioning, and resiliency**—and their importance in modern cloud environments.

Differentiating Elasticity and Scalability

Elasticity and scalability are often discussed together, but they represent distinct aspects of cloud resource management.

1. **Elasticity**
   - **Definition:**
     Elasticity refers to the ability of a system to automatically adjust resources in response to fluctuating demand. Resources are dynamically added or removed as needed to meet workload requirements.
   - **Key Characteristics:**
     - Real-time resource adjustment.
     - Cost efficiency, as organizations only pay for what they use.
     - Ideal for variable workloads, such as e-commerce websites during seasonal sales.
   - **Example Use Case:**
     An online retailer experiences a surge in traffic during a flash sale. The cloud system automatically scales up server capacity to handle the increased load and scales down when the traffic subsides.
2. **Scalability**
   - **Definition:**
     Scalability refers to a system's ability to handle increased workload by adding resources, either vertically (adding more power to existing resources) or horizontally (adding more resources to the system).
   - **Types of Scalability:**
     - **Vertical Scalability:** Increasing the capacity of a single resource, such as upgrading a server's CPU or memory.
     - **Horizontal Scalability:** Adding more resources, such as deploying additional servers in a cluster.
   - **Example Use Case:**
     A company adds more virtual machines to its infrastructure to support the long-term growth of its customer base.

Key Difference:
Elasticity focuses on dynamic, real-time adjustments to meet short-term changes in demand, while scalability addresses the system's ability to grow and handle long-term or sustained increases in demand.

Importance of High Availability and Fault Tolerance

In cloud environments, ensuring uninterrupted service and minimizing the impact of failures are critical. High availability and fault tolerance are two essential components that address these goals:

1. **High Availability**
    - **Definition:**
      High availability (HA) ensures that a system remains operational and accessible for as long as possible, minimizing downtime.
    - **Key Features:**
        - Redundant resources are deployed across multiple zones or regions.
        - Monitoring systems detect and resolve issues proactively.
        - Load balancers distribute traffic to healthy resources.
    - **Benefits:**
        - Enhances user experience by ensuring continuous access to services.
        - Reduces financial and reputational losses caused by outages.
    - **Example Use Case:**
      A global content delivery network (CDN) ensures that users can access website content even if one data center experiences an outage.
2. **Fault Tolerance**
    - **Definition:**
      Fault tolerance is the system's ability to continue functioning despite the failure of one or more components.
    - **Key Features:**
        - Built-in redundancy at hardware, software, and network levels.
        - Failover mechanisms automatically redirect traffic to backup resources.
        - Data replication ensures data consistency across multiple locations.
    - **Benefits:**
        - Prevents single points of failure from disrupting operations.
        - Ensures critical applications and services remain available during failures.
    - **Example Use Case:**
      A database cluster uses replication to maintain copies of data. If the primary database fails, the system automatically switches to a replica without affecting users.

High Availability vs. Fault Tolerance:

- High availability focuses on minimizing downtime and ensuring service continuity, often achieved through redundancy and proactive monitoring.
- Fault tolerance emphasizes the ability to sustain failures without service disruption, typically requiring more robust and complex infrastructure.

On-Demand Provisioning and Resiliency

1. **On-Demand Provisioning**
    - **Definition:**
      On-demand provisioning allows users to access and allocate resources as needed, without requiring manual intervention from the provider.
    - **Benefits:**
        - Rapid deployment of infrastructure and applications.
        - Cost savings by eliminating the need for overprovisioning.

- **Example Use Case:**
  A development team provisions virtual machines to test a new application and deprovisions them after testing is complete.

2. **Resiliency**
   - **Definition:**
     Resiliency refers to a system's ability to recover quickly from failures and maintain service continuity.
   - **Key Features:**
     - Disaster recovery plans, such as backup and replication.
     - Geographic distribution of resources to mitigate regional failures.
   - **Example Use Case:**
     A company uses a multi-region deployment strategy to ensure its web application remains accessible even if one region experiences an outage.

By understanding and leveraging concepts such as elasticity, scalability, high availability, and fault tolerance, organizations can design cloud systems that are efficient, reliable, and capable of meeting both short-term and long-term demands.

Benefits and Challenges of Cloud Computing

Cloud computing offers transformative benefits for organizations but also presents challenges that must be carefully managed. Understanding these advantages and obstacles helps organizations maximize the value of cloud adoption while mitigating risks.

Benefits of Cloud Computing

1. **Cost Efficiency and Resource Optimization**
   - **Pay-As-You-Go Model:**
     Cloud computing eliminates the need for upfront investments in hardware, software, and maintenance. Instead, organizations pay for the resources they consume, optimizing costs and reducing financial risk.
   - **Scalability:**
     Resources can be scaled up or down based on demand, ensuring that businesses only pay for what they need. This is particularly advantageous for handling fluctuating workloads or seasonal spikes.
   - **Reduced IT Overhead:**
     By outsourcing infrastructure management to cloud providers, businesses can reallocate IT staff to strategic initiatives rather than routine maintenance tasks.
   - **Optimized Resource Utilization:**
     Cloud platforms enable organizations to efficiently allocate computing resources, avoiding underutilization or overprovisioning common in traditional data centers.

   Example Use Case:
   A startup launches a mobile app using cloud resources, avoiding the significant capital expense of setting up its own data center. The app's cloud infrastructure scales automatically as the user base grows, ensuring performance and cost efficiency.

Challenges of Cloud Computing

1. **Security Considerations**
    - **Data Breaches and Unauthorized Access:**
      Moving data to the cloud introduces risks of exposure, especially if the provider's security measures are insufficient or improperly configured.
    - **Shared Responsibility Model:**
      Cloud providers are responsible for securing the underlying infrastructure, but customers are responsible for securing data, applications, and access controls. Mismanagement in these areas can lead to vulnerabilities.
    - **Mitigation Strategies:**
        - Encrypt data at rest and in transit.
        - Use multi-factor authentication (MFA) and identity and access management (IAM) policies.
        - Regularly audit and monitor cloud environments for anomalies.

   Example Challenge:
   A misconfigured cloud storage bucket results in the exposure of sensitive customer data. Implementing proper access controls and encryption could have prevented the breach.

2. **Latency and Performance Issues**
    - **Network Dependency:**
      Cloud services rely heavily on internet connectivity. Latency issues can arise if users are located far from the provider's data centers or if there is insufficient bandwidth.
    - **Mitigation Strategies:**
        - Use content delivery networks (CDNs) to cache content closer to end users.
        - Leverage cloud regions and zones strategically to minimize latency.
        - Invest in direct connectivity options, such as AWS Direct Connect or Azure ExpressRoute, for high-performance workloads.

   Example Challenge:
   A video streaming platform experiences buffering issues for users in remote areas due to high latency. Using CDNs and strategically placed data centers can improve delivery speed.

3. **Compliance Considerations**
    - **Regulatory Requirements:**
      Organizations in industries such as finance, healthcare, and government must adhere to stringent regulations like GDPR, HIPAA, or PCI DSS. Non-compliance can lead to legal penalties and reputational damage.
    - **Data Sovereignty:**
      Cloud providers may store data in regions outside the customer's jurisdiction, potentially violating local data residency laws.
    - **Mitigation Strategies:**

- Choose cloud providers that offer region-specific compliance options.
- Regularly review provider compliance certifications and align configurations with regulatory requirements.
- Implement governance frameworks to ensure adherence to internal and external policies.

Example Challenge:
A European company using a global cloud provider discovers that its data is stored outside the EU, violating GDPR requirements. Selecting an EU-based region or provider could address this issue.

Balancing Benefits and Challenges

While cloud computing delivers unparalleled flexibility, cost savings, and scalability, success requires proactive planning and management of its inherent challenges. Organizations must:

- Conduct thorough risk assessments before migrating to the cloud.
- Invest in training IT staff to manage cloud environments effectively.
- Select providers and services aligned with their operational and compliance needs.

By leveraging the benefits while addressing security, latency, and compliance considerations, businesses can harness the full potential of cloud computing to drive innovation and efficiency.

Chapter 3: Virtualization and Cloud Infrastructure

Chapter 3 explores virtualization as the foundation of modern cloud infrastructure, detailing its role in enabling scalable, efficient, and cost-effective cloud services. It examines core concepts such as resource abstraction, isolation, and elasticity while highlighting how virtualization underpins service models like IaaS, PaaS, and SaaS. Key advancements, including containerization, hyperconverged infrastructure, and edge computing, demonstrate the evolving landscape of virtualization technologies.

The chapter also contrasts virtual machines and containers, outlining their architectures, benefits, and use cases to help organizations choose the right technology for their needs. Additionally, hypervisors, their types, and use cases are discussed alongside cloud storage and networking solutions, including SDN, VPNs, and resource optimization strategies. By understanding these technologies, organizations can harness virtualization to build robust, scalable, and efficient cloud environments that align with modern business demands.

Introduction to Virtualization Technologies

Virtualization is the backbone of modern cloud computing, enabling the efficient use of physical resources by abstracting hardware into virtual environments. This section explores the role of virtualization in enabling cloud services and highlights recent trends and advancements that continue to shape the landscape.

Role of Virtualization in Enabling Cloud Services

Virtualization allows multiple operating systems and applications to run on a single physical server by creating virtual instances of resources like CPUs, memory, and storage. This technology is critical to the scalability, flexibility, and efficiency that define cloud computing.

1. **Resource Abstraction and Optimization**
   - Virtualization abstracts the physical hardware layer, enabling the creation of virtual machines (VMs) that operate independently of the underlying hardware.
   - This abstraction optimizes resource utilization by allowing multiple workloads to share the same physical infrastructure.
2. **Scalability and Elasticity**
   - Virtual machines can be quickly created, resized, or removed based on workload demands, making them ideal for dynamic cloud environments.
   - Cloud providers leverage virtualization to deliver on-demand scalability, ensuring resources are available as needed.
3. **Isolation and Security**
   - Virtualization creates isolated environments for each VM, enhancing security by preventing one instance from affecting others.
   - This isolation supports multi-tenant cloud environments where multiple customers share the same physical infrastructure without compromising security or performance.
4. **Cost Efficiency**
   - Virtualization reduces the need for dedicated hardware, leading to significant cost savings in data centers.
   - By consolidating workloads onto fewer servers, organizations lower energy consumption, cooling costs, and maintenance overhead.
5. **Enabling Cloud Service Models**
   - Virtualization underpins all three primary cloud service models:
     - **Infrastructure as a Service (IaaS):** Virtual machines and storage are the foundation of IaaS offerings.
     - **Platform as a Service (PaaS):** Virtualization supports application development platforms by managing the underlying infrastructure.
     - **Software as a Service (SaaS):** Virtualized environments host the applications delivered through SaaS solutions.

Virtualization Trends and Advancements

As cloud computing continues to evolve, virtualization technologies are advancing to meet the growing demands for performance, security, and efficiency. Below are key trends and innovations shaping the field:

1. **Containerization**
    - **Definition:** Containers provide lightweight, portable environments for running applications, sharing the host operating system kernel instead of requiring a full OS for each instance.
    - **Advantages:** Faster startup times, improved resource efficiency, and better application portability compared to traditional VMs.
    - **Key Technologies:** Docker, Kubernetes, OpenShift.
    - **Impact on Cloud:** Containers have become essential for cloud-native applications, enabling microservices architectures and simplifying DevOps workflows.
2. **Hyperconverged Infrastructure (HCI)**
    - **Definition:** HCI integrates compute, storage, and networking into a single, software-defined system.
    - **Benefits:** Simplifies deployment and management, improves scalability, and reduces hardware footprint.
    - **Relevance:** HCI is widely used in private and hybrid cloud environments for its ease of integration and cost efficiency.
3. **Bare-Metal Virtualization**
    - **Definition:** Bare-metal virtualization runs directly on physical hardware without requiring a host operating system.
    - **Advantages:** Provides better performance and lower latency compared to traditional virtualization.
    - **Use Cases:** Ideal for high-performance workloads such as big data analytics, AI, and machine learning.
4. **Virtualization for Edge Computing**
    - **Trend:** Virtualization is expanding to edge computing environments, where data is processed closer to the source rather than in centralized cloud data centers.
    - **Benefits:** Reduces latency, enhances real-time processing, and supports IoT applications.
    - **Examples:** VMware Edge Compute Stack, Azure Stack Edge.
5. **Security Enhancements in Virtualization**
    - **Advancements:** Virtualization technologies now incorporate advanced security features, such as hardware-based encryption, secure boot, and trusted execution environments.
    - **Impact:** These features help mitigate risks in multi-tenant cloud environments and protect sensitive workloads.
6. **Serverless and Function-as-a-Service (FaaS)**
    - **Evolution:** While serverless computing abstracts virtualization entirely from the end user, it relies on advanced virtualization at the provider level to dynamically allocate resources.

- **Significance:** Serverless architectures are revolutionizing cloud computing by enabling developers to focus solely on code, with the cloud provider managing resource provisioning.

Virtualization remains a cornerstone of cloud computing, driving innovations that enhance scalability, flexibility, and efficiency. By understanding the role of virtualization and staying informed about emerging trends, organizations can better leverage cloud technologies to meet their operational needs.

Virtual Machines vs. Containers

Virtual machines (VMs) and containers are both critical technologies in cloud computing, providing isolation and efficiency for workloads. However, they differ significantly in architecture, performance, and use cases. This section explores the differences, benefits, limitations, and practical applications of both technologies.

Differences Between Virtual Machines and Containers

Aspect	Virtual Machines (VMs)	Containers
Definition	Emulates a complete operating system and hardware environment.	Runs lightweight, portable applications in isolated environments using a shared OS kernel.
Architecture	Requires a hypervisor to manage multiple VMs on a single physical machine.	Uses a container runtime (e.g., Docker, containerd) and shares the host OS kernel.
Size	Larger, typically includes an entire operating system.	Smaller, contains only the application and dependencies.
Startup Time	Slower due to the need to boot a full operating system.	Faster since no OS boot is required.
Isolation	Strong isolation with dedicated resources per VM.	Process-level isolation with shared kernel.
Resource Utilization	Requires more resources per instance (CPU, memory, storage).	More efficient, allowing higher density of workloads.
Portability	Limited portability across environments without significant configuration.	Highly portable and consistent across environments.

Benefits and Limitations

Virtual Machines

- **Benefits:**
  - **Strong Isolation:** Each VM runs its own OS, ensuring complete separation between environments.

  - **Broad Compatibility:** Can run any OS, including legacy systems, on the same physical hardware.
  - **Mature Ecosystem:** Proven technology with established tools and support for complex workloads.
- **Limitations:**
  - **Resource Intensive:** Requires significant memory, CPU, and storage for each VM.
  - **Slower Performance:** Longer startup times and less efficient resource utilization compared to containers.
  - **Overhead:** Each VM includes a full OS, increasing overall resource requirements.

Containers

- **Benefits:**
  - **Efficiency:** Minimal overhead with shared kernel, enabling higher density on the same hardware.
  - **Portability:** Containers can run consistently across development, testing, and production environments.
  - **Speed:** Rapid startup times, ideal for dynamic workloads and microservices.
  - **Simplified DevOps:** Seamless integration with CI/CD pipelines and orchestration tools like Kubernetes.
- **Limitations:**
  - **Weaker Isolation:** Containers share the host OS kernel, making them less isolated than VMs.
  - **OS Dependency:** Limited to environments where the same OS kernel can be shared.
  - **Security Concerns:** Kernel vulnerabilities can potentially affect all containers on the host.

Use Cases for Virtual Machines and Containers

Virtual Machines

1. **Use Cases:**
   - **Legacy Applications:** Running older software that requires a specific OS or configuration.
   - **Multi-OS Environments:** Hosting different operating systems on a single server for diverse workloads.
   - **Dedicated Workloads:** Applications needing strong isolation, such as financial systems or government workloads.
   - **Hybrid Cloud Deployments:** Bridging on-premises infrastructure with cloud environments.
2. **Example:**
   An organization uses VMs to run both Linux-based and Windows-based enterprise applications on the same physical server for cost savings and operational simplicity.

Containers

1. **Use Cases:**
    - **Microservices Architecture:** Building scalable, modular applications with loosely coupled services.
    - **DevOps and CI/CD:** Streamlining development workflows by ensuring consistent environments across stages.
    - **Cloud-Native Applications:** Deploying lightweight and portable applications optimized for cloud environments.
    - **Edge Computing:** Running lightweight applications on resource-constrained devices.
2. **Example:**
   A software company deploys a microservices-based application using Docker containers, orchestrated with Kubernetes, to scale individual services based on demand.

Choosing Between Virtual Machines and Containers

- **When to Use VMs:**
    - Workloads requiring strong isolation or multi-OS environments.
    - Legacy applications that cannot run in containerized environments.
    - Scenarios where resource utilization is less of a concern.
- **When to Use Containers:**
    - Applications requiring rapid deployment, scaling, and portability.
    - Development workflows needing consistent environments across teams.
    - Cloud-native and edge workloads demanding high efficiency and minimal overhead.

By understanding the differences, benefits, and use cases of virtual machines and containers, organizations can make informed decisions about the best technology to support their workloads, ensuring optimal performance, scalability, and cost efficiency.

Hypervisors: Types and Use Cases

A hypervisor is a critical component of virtualization, enabling multiple virtual machines (VMs) to run on a single physical machine by abstracting the hardware. Hypervisors come in two primary types—Type 1 and Type 2—each suited to different workloads and deployment scenarios. This section examines the differences between these types and provides guidance on selecting the right hypervisor based on workload requirements.

Type 1 vs. Type 2 Hypervisors

Feature	Type 1 Hypervisor	Type 2 Hypervisor
Definition	Runs directly on the host's physical hardware, bypassing the operating system.	Runs on top of a host operating system, relying on it for resource management.

Feature	Type 1 Hypervisor	Type 2 Hypervisor
Alternate Name	Bare-metal hypervisor	Hosted hypervisor
Performance	High performance with minimal overhead due to direct hardware access.	Lower performance due to the additional layer of the host OS.
Complexity	Requires advanced setup and management.	Easier to set up and manage, especially for non-enterprise users.
Use Case	Enterprise environments and data centers.	Personal or small-scale environments, such as development and testing.
Examples	VMware ESXi, Microsoft Hyper-V, Xen, KVM	VMware Workstation, Oracle VirtualBox, Parallels Desktop

Type 1 Hypervisors: Features and Use Cases

Features:

- Direct interaction with hardware, offering enhanced performance and scalability.
- Enhanced security due to the absence of a host operating system, reducing attack surface.
- Built for enterprise-grade virtualization and workload consolidation.

Use Cases:

1. **Data Centers and Cloud Environments:**
    - Consolidating multiple workloads onto fewer physical servers.
    - Supporting Infrastructure as a Service (IaaS) platforms with high availability and fault tolerance.
2. **High-Performance Applications:**
    - Running resource-intensive applications, such as big data analytics, machine learning, or real-time financial systems.
3. **Scalable Multi-Tenant Systems:**
    - Hosting multiple VMs with strict resource isolation, ensuring consistent performance across tenants.

Example Scenario: A large enterprise deploys VMware ESXi in its data center to consolidate servers, reduce costs, and support its private cloud infrastructure.

Type 2 Hypervisors: Features and Use Cases

Features:

- Installed as software on an existing operating system, making it easier to deploy.
- Ideal for use on personal computers or small-scale environments.
- Typically, less resource-efficient compared to Type 1 hypervisors.

Use Cases:

1. **Development and Testing:**
   - Creating isolated environments for developers to test applications without affecting the host system.
   - Running multiple operating systems on a single machine for compatibility testing.
2. **Personal or Educational Use:**
   - Learning and experimenting with virtualization technologies in non-production environments.
3. **Lightweight Virtualization Needs:**
   - Supporting small businesses or home labs where enterprise-grade features are unnecessary.

Example Scenario: A developer uses Oracle VirtualBox on their laptop to test a Linux-based application while running Windows as the host operating system.

Selecting a Hypervisor Based on Workload

When choosing a hypervisor, consider the following factors:

1. **Performance Requirements:**
   - For high-performance workloads or enterprise environments, Type 1 hypervisors are preferred.
   - For less resource-intensive tasks, Type 2 hypervisors provide sufficient performance.
2. **Scale and Complexity:**
   - Type 1 hypervisors are ideal for large-scale environments with multiple servers and complex virtualization needs.
   - Type 2 hypervisors are suitable for smaller-scale setups, such as individual developer machines or educational use.
3. **Cost and Licensing:**
   - Type 1 hypervisors often involve higher licensing costs but offer enterprise-grade features.
   - Type 2 hypervisors are typically free or low-cost, making them accessible for personal use.
4. **Ease of Deployment and Management:**
   - Type 2 hypervisors are easier to deploy for quick and simple virtualization needs.
   - Type 1 hypervisors may require specialized knowledge and tools for setup and management.

Example Comparison of Workloads

Workload	Recommended Hypervisor	Rationale
Hosting a private cloud	Type 1	Requires high performance, scalability, and robust management.

Workload	Recommended Hypervisor	Rationale
Testing software across multiple OS types	Type 2	Quick setup for isolated test environments.
Running high-availability applications	Type 1	Supports fault tolerance and resource isolation.
Personal experimentation with virtualization	Type 2	Low-cost and user-friendly.

By understanding the differences between Type 1 and Type 2 hypervisors and evaluating workload requirements, organizations can select the most appropriate technology to optimize performance, scalability, and cost efficiency.

Storage Types

Cloud storage solutions offer various methods to store and manage data, each suited to specific workloads and use cases. This section explores three primary storage types—**block, object, and file storage**—along with their underlying concepts, advantages, and practical applications in cloud environments.

Block Storage

Concept:
Block storage divides data into fixed-size blocks and stores them independently, each with a unique identifier. These blocks can be accessed and modified directly, making block storage highly efficient for structured workloads.

Key Features:

- High performance for read/write operations.
- Data is stored in blocks that can be assembled by the operating system into files or databases.
- Often used as the underlying storage for virtual machines and databases.

Advantages:

- **Performance:** Optimized for low-latency and high-throughput workloads.
- **Scalability:** Easily scales to support growing workloads.
- **Flexibility:** Works with a variety of operating systems and applications.

Limitations:

- **Complexity:** Requires a file system or database to manage data structure.
- **Cost:** Generally more expensive than object storage.

Use Cases:

- Hosting virtual machine disk images (e.g., AWS Elastic Block Store [EBS]).
- Storing transactional databases requiring high performance.
- Applications needing low-latency storage.

Object Storage

Concept:
Object storage stores data as discrete objects, each accompanied by metadata and a unique identifier. It is designed for scalability and accessibility, making it ideal for unstructured data.

Key Features:

- Data is accessed via APIs, rather than through traditional file systems.
- Metadata associated with each object enhances searchability and organization.
- Supports massive scalability for large datasets.

Advantages:

- **Scalability:** Handles petabytes of data with ease.
- **Cost-Effective:** Lower cost compared to block storage for large volumes of data.
- **Durability:** Designed for high fault tolerance, often with redundancy across multiple data centers.

Limitations:

- **Latency:** Higher latency compared to block storage, making it unsuitable for real-time applications.
- **Limited Write Performance:** Primarily designed for write-once, read-many (WORM) use cases.

Use Cases:

- Storing large amounts of unstructured data like images, videos, and backups (e.g., AWS S3, Azure Blob Storage).
- Data archiving and disaster recovery.
- Content delivery via CDNs.

File Storage

Concept:
File storage organizes data into a hierarchical structure of directories and files. It is widely used for applications requiring shared access to data.

Key Features:

- Accessible via standard file system protocols like NFS or SMB.
- Familiar directory and file structure for ease of use.
- Supports simultaneous access by multiple users or applications.

Advantages:

- **Simplicity:** Easy to use and integrate with existing applications.
- **Collaboration:** Ideal for shared access across teams or systems.
- **Compatibility:** Works with legacy applications requiring file systems.

Limitations:

- **Scalability:** Limited scalability compared to object storage.
- **Performance:** Less performant than block storage for high IOPS workloads.

Use Cases:

- File sharing and collaboration platforms (e.g., Dropbox, Google Drive).
- Shared directories in hybrid cloud environments (e.g., Amazon Elastic File System [EFS], Azure Files).
- Application logs and configuration files.

Cloud Storage Services and Their Use Cases

Cloud providers offer storage services tailored to these storage types, ensuring organizations can select the best option for their needs:

1. **Block Storage Services**
   - **Examples:** AWS EBS, Azure Disk Storage, Google Persistent Disk.
   - **Use Cases:** Virtual machine storage, transactional databases, and low-latency workloads.
2. **Object Storage Services**
   - **Examples:** AWS S3, Azure Blob Storage, Google Cloud Storage.
   - **Use Cases:** Media hosting, backup and archiving, big data analytics, and static website hosting.
3. **File Storage Services**
   - **Examples:** AWS EFS, Azure Files, Google Filestore.
   - **Use Cases:** Shared directories, team collaboration, and application configurations.

Choosing the Right Storage Type

When selecting a storage type, consider the following factors:

- **Performance Needs:** Choose block storage for high IOPS or low-latency applications, and object storage for scalable but less time-sensitive data.
- **Data Structure:** Use file storage for hierarchical data and object storage for unstructured data.
- **Scalability Requirements:** Opt for object storage for large-scale, unstructured datasets.
- **Cost Sensitivity:** Object storage is generally more cost-effective for large volumes of data, while block and file storage may incur higher costs.

By understanding block, object, and file storage concepts, along with their respective use cases, organizations can design efficient and cost-effective storage solutions that meet their operational needs.

Networking in Virtualized Environments

Networking plays a crucial role in virtualized environments, enabling communication between virtual machines (VMs), containers, and other resources. Advanced networking technologies like Software-Defined Networking (SDN) and Virtual Private Networks (VPNs) form the backbone of modern cloud and hybrid infrastructures. This section explores these technologies and their role in cloud networking setups.

Software-Defined Networking (SDN)

Definition:
Software-Defined Networking (SDN) is an approach to networking that decouples the control plane (decision-making) from the data plane (traffic forwarding). This separation enables centralized management and programmability, making networks more agile and responsive to changing demands.

Key Components of SDN:

1. **Control Plane:**
    - Centralized controller that defines network policies and manages traffic flow.
2. **Data Plane:**
    - Physical or virtual network devices (e.g., switches, routers) that forward traffic based on policies set by the control plane.
3. **Application Plane:**
    - Interfaces and applications that interact with the SDN controller to configure and monitor the network.

Benefits of SDN:

- **Centralized Management:** Provides a single point of control for network resources, simplifying administration.
- **Agility:** Enables rapid deployment of new applications and services without reconfiguring physical hardware.
- **Cost Efficiency:** Reduces dependency on proprietary hardware by leveraging software-based controls.
- **Enhanced Security:** Facilitates network segmentation and dynamic security policies.

Use Cases of SDN:

1. **Cloud Data Centers:**
   Dynamic management of traffic between VMs and containers.
2. **Hybrid Cloud Environments:**
   Seamless integration of on-premises and cloud networks.
3. **Network Automation:**
   Automating routine tasks like provisioning and configuration updates.
4. **Microsegmentation:**
   Enforcing security policies at a granular level to isolate workloads.

Example Technology:
VMware NSX enables SDN in virtualized environments, offering features like microsegmentation, network automation, and multi-cloud connectivity.

Virtual Private Networks (VPNs) and Cloud Networking Setups

Virtual Private Networks (VPNs):

Definition:
A Virtual Private Network (VPN) creates a secure and encrypted connection over the internet, enabling private communication between devices or networks.

Types of VPNs in Cloud Environments:

1. **Site-to-Site VPN:**
   Connects entire networks (e.g., on-premises data center to a cloud provider).
    - **Use Case:** Hybrid cloud setups where organizations extend their internal network into the cloud.
    - **Example:** AWS Site-to-Site VPN, Azure VPN Gateway.
2. **Client-to-Site VPN:**
   Allows individual users to connect securely to a remote network.
    - **Use Case:** Remote employees accessing cloud resources securely.
    - **Example:** OpenVPN, Cisco AnyConnect.

Benefits of VPNs:

- **Security:** Encrypts data in transit, ensuring privacy and protection from interception.
- **Remote Access:** Enables secure connections to resources from any location.
- **Cost-Effective:** Provides secure connectivity without requiring expensive dedicated lines.

Limitations of VPNs:

- **Latency:** May introduce latency due to encryption and routing.
- **Complexity:** Configuration and maintenance can be challenging in large-scale environments.

Cloud Networking Setups:

1. **Virtual Private Cloud (VPC):**
   - **Definition:** A logically isolated section of a public cloud where organizations can define their network topology.
   - **Features:**
     - Subnet creation with defined IP ranges.
     - Configurable routing tables, firewalls, and NAT gateways.
   - **Example:** AWS VPC, Azure Virtual Network (VNet), Google Cloud VPC.
   - **Use Case:** Hosting applications in isolated environments with customized networking.
2. **Direct Connectivity Solutions:**
   - **Definition:** Dedicated connections between on-premises infrastructure and cloud providers for high-performance networking.
   - **Examples:** AWS Direct Connect, Azure ExpressRoute.
   - **Use Case:** Organizations requiring low-latency, high-bandwidth connections for hybrid cloud environments.
3. **Load Balancing:**
   - **Definition:** Distributes incoming traffic across multiple resources to ensure high availability and performance.
   - **Examples:** Elastic Load Balancing (AWS), Azure Load Balancer, Google Cloud Load Balancing.
   - **Use Case:** Ensuring reliable access to applications under varying loads.
4. **Cloud Gateways:**
   - **Definition:** Act as entry points for managing traffic between on-premises networks and cloud environments.
   - **Example:** Cloud VPN gateways, NAT gateways.
   - **Use Case:** Providing secure access to cloud resources.

Comparing SDN and VPN in Cloud Networking

Feature	SDN	VPN
Purpose	Centralized management of network traffic.	Secure communication between networks or users.

Feature	SDN	VPN
Scalability	High; ideal for dynamic, large-scale environments.	Moderate; dependent on network size and configuration.
Security	Built-in segmentation and access control.	Encrypted tunnels for secure data transmission.
Use Case	Multi-cloud and hybrid cloud environments.	Remote access and hybrid cloud connectivity.

By leveraging SDN, VPNs, and tailored cloud networking setups, organizations can create efficient, secure, and scalable virtualized environments that support modern application demands.

Cloud Resource Allocation and Optimization

Efficient allocation and optimization of cloud resources are critical for ensuring performance, cost efficiency, and scalability in cloud environments. This section explores the management of compute, memory, and storage resources, as well as tools for monitoring and optimizing resource usage.

Managing Compute, Memory, and Storage Resources

1. **Compute Resources**
   - **Definition:** Compute resources include virtual CPUs (vCPUs) and other processing capabilities needed to run applications and workloads.
   - **Key Considerations:**
     - **Right-Sizing:** Choose appropriate instance types or VM configurations to match workload requirements.
     - **Autoscaling:** Use cloud-native autoscaling services to dynamically adjust compute capacity based on demand.
     - **Workload Placement:** Optimize the placement of workloads across regions or availability zones to balance performance and cost.
   - **Best Practices:**
     - Regularly monitor CPU utilization to identify over-provisioned or underutilized instances.
     - Use spot or preemptible instances for non-critical workloads to reduce costs.
2. **Memory Resources**
   - **Definition:** Memory (RAM) is used for temporarily storing data that applications or workloads process.
   - **Key Considerations:**
     - **Monitoring Usage Patterns:** Track memory utilization to ensure that workloads are neither memory-constrained nor over-provisioned.
     - **Choosing Memory-Optimized Instances:** For applications like in-memory databases or analytics, select memory-optimized instance types (e.g., AWS R5, Azure M-Series).

- **Best Practices:**
  - Enable memory monitoring alerts to detect potential bottlenecks.
  - Configure caching mechanisms to reduce memory pressure.

3. **Storage Resources**
   - **Definition:** Storage resources include block, object, and file storage used for data persistence.
   - **Key Considerations:**
     - **Storage Tiers:** Use different storage tiers (e.g., hot, cool, or archive) to optimize cost and performance.
     - **Capacity Planning:** Ensure adequate storage capacity while avoiding excessive provisioning.
     - **Data Redundancy:** Leverage redundancy mechanisms, such as replication and snapshots, to enhance reliability.
   - **Best Practices:**
     - Regularly analyze storage usage to identify unused or redundant data.
     - Compress and deduplicate data to optimize storage utilization.

Tools for Resource Monitoring and Optimization

1. **Native Cloud Monitoring Tools**
   - **Amazon CloudWatch (AWS):**
     - Monitors resources like EC2 instances, RDS databases, and Lambda functions.
     - Provides metrics, alarms, and logs for performance tracking.
   - **Azure Monitor (Microsoft Azure):**
     - Offers insights into Azure resources with logs, metrics, and alerts.
     - Integrates with Azure Advisor for optimization recommendations.
   - **Google Cloud Operations Suite (formerly Stackdriver):**
     - Tracks resource usage and performance metrics across GCP services.
     - Features dashboards and alerts for anomaly detection.
2. **Third-Party Optimization Tools**
   - **Datadog:**
     - A comprehensive monitoring platform for cloud environments.
     - Provides dashboards, alerts, and integrations with major cloud providers.
   - **New Relic:**
     - Focuses on application and infrastructure performance monitoring.
     - Tracks resource utilization and offers optimization insights.
   - **CloudHealth by VMware:**
     - Specializes in cost optimization, governance, and performance management.
     - Identifies underutilized resources and recommends rightsizing actions.
3. **Resource Optimization Techniques**
   - **Cost Analysis and Alerts:**
     - Use cost management tools like AWS Cost Explorer, Azure Cost Management, or GCP Cost Management to track and predict expenses.
   - **Autoscaling and Load Balancing:**

- Configure autoscaling groups to handle variable workloads efficiently.
- Implement load balancers to distribute traffic across resources and prevent bottlenecks.

- **Lifecycle Policies:**
  - Automate the lifecycle of resources, such as deleting unused snapshots or transitioning data to cheaper storage tiers.
- **Performance Tuning:**
  - Optimize application configurations (e.g., thread pools, database connections) to minimize resource consumption.

4. **AI and ML for Optimization**
   - Modern cloud platforms integrate AI and ML algorithms to suggest and automate resource optimization:
     - **AWS Compute Optimizer:** Provides recommendations for instance types and configurations based on workload history.
     - **Google Cloud Recommender:** Offers suggestions for VM rightsizing, storage optimization, and IAM policy improvements.

Example Workflow for Resource Optimization

1. **Assess Current Usage:**
   - Use monitoring tools to collect data on CPU, memory, and storage usage.
2. **Identify Bottlenecks and Wastage:**
   - Look for underutilized or overprovisioned resources.
3. **Apply Optimization Strategies:**
   - Scale resources dynamically with autoscaling.
   - Move workloads to more cost-effective instance types or regions.
4. **Continuously Monitor:**
   - Set up alerts and dashboards to track ongoing performance and cost trends.

Efficient management of compute, memory, and storage resources, combined with the use of robust monitoring and optimization tools, ensures that cloud environments remain cost-effective, scalable, and high-performing.

Chapter 4: Resource Management and Performance

Chapter 4 provides a comprehensive guide to managing and optimizing cloud resources for performance, cost-efficiency, and reliability. It covers critical aspects of cloud resource monitoring, including key performance indicators (KPIs) such as compute, memory, network, and storage metrics, alongside tools like AWS CloudWatch, Azure Monitor, and third-party solutions for effective oversight. Performance tuning techniques are discussed to identify and resolve bottlenecks, improve application efficiency, and leverage best practices like right-sizing, autoscaling, and caching.

The chapter further explores capacity planning and scaling strategies, emphasizing the use of horizontal and vertical scaling, predictive autoscaling, and redundancy planning to handle peak demand and ensure availability. It highlights the role of automation and orchestration tools, such as Infrastructure as Code (IaC) frameworks, Kubernetes, and Terraform, to streamline cloud management. Finally, strategies for managing workloads across multi-cloud and hybrid environments focus on ensuring portability, interoperability, and unified management, enabling organizations to build scalable, cost-effective, and resilient cloud infrastructures.

Monitoring Cloud Resources and Metrics

Effective monitoring is essential to ensure the performance, security, and cost-efficiency of cloud environments. This section explores the **key performance indicators (KPIs)** for monitoring cloud resources and highlights popular **tools for cloud monitoring** to help organizations maintain optimal operations.

Key Performance Indicators for Cloud Environments

KPIs provide measurable metrics to assess the health and performance of cloud resources. Below are some critical categories of KPIs:

1. **Compute Performance Metrics**
    - **CPU Utilization:** Measures the percentage of CPU resources in use. High utilization indicates potential bottlenecks, while low utilization may signal over-provisioning.
    - **Memory Usage:** Tracks the percentage of allocated memory being used. Spikes in memory usage can lead to application crashes if not addressed.
    - **Disk I/O:** Monitors read/write operations on disk storage, critical for storage-intensive applications.
2. **Network Performance Metrics**
    - **Network Throughput:** Measures data transfer rates (e.g., Mbps). Ensures sufficient bandwidth for workloads.
    - **Packet Loss:** Tracks the percentage of lost data packets, which can degrade application performance.
    - **Latency:** Measures the time it takes for data to travel from the source to the destination. Low latency is vital for real-time applications.
3. **Storage Metrics**
    - **Disk Space Utilization:** Tracks the percentage of used storage capacity. Helps avoid capacity-related service interruptions.
    - **Storage Read/Write Latency:** Measures the time taken for storage operations. High latency indicates potential performance issues with storage resources.
4. **Application and Service Metrics**
    - **Response Time:** Monitors the time it takes for an application or API to respond to user requests.
    - **Error Rate:** Tracks the percentage of failed requests or operations. Indicates issues in application logic or configuration.
    - **Availability/Uptime:** Measures the percentage of time a service is operational. Critical for assessing high availability.
5. **Security Metrics**
    - **Unauthorized Access Attempts:** Monitors failed login attempts or suspicious activity.
    - **Compliance Metrics:** Tracks adherence to regulatory or organizational security policies.
    - **Encryption Coverage:** Ensures that sensitive data is encrypted both in transit and at rest.

6. **Cost and Usage Metrics**
   - **Resource Utilization:** Measures how efficiently resources are used to avoid over-provisioning.
   - **Cost per Resource:** Tracks spending on individual resources or services.
   - **Reserved Instances vs. On-Demand Usage:** Analyzes the balance of reserved capacity to ensure cost-effectiveness.

Tools for Monitoring Cloud Resources

1. **Cloud Provider Native Tools**
   - **Amazon CloudWatch (AWS):**
     - Offers real-time monitoring of AWS resources like EC2, RDS, and Lambda.
     - Provides alarms, dashboards, and log analytics.
   - **Azure Monitor (Microsoft Azure):**
     - Tracks performance metrics and logs for Azure services and resources.
     - Integrates with Azure Advisor for optimization recommendations.
   - **Google Cloud Operations Suite (formerly Stackdriver):**
     - Monitors Google Cloud services with dashboards, logs, and alerts.
     - Offers insights into network, application, and service performance.
2. **Third-Party Monitoring Tools**
   - **Datadog:**
     - Provides end-to-end monitoring of cloud infrastructure, applications, and logs.
     - Features AI-driven alerts and anomaly detection.
   - **New Relic:**
     - Monitors application performance and resource usage in hybrid and multi-cloud environments.
     - Offers insights into transaction traces and error rates.
   - **Dynatrace:**
     - Delivers AI-powered full-stack monitoring for applications, networks, and infrastructure.
     - Supports root cause analysis for performance issues.
   - **SolarWinds AppOptics:**
     - Focuses on infrastructure and application monitoring.
     - Provides pre-configured integrations with popular cloud services.
3. **Open-Source Monitoring Tools**
   - **Prometheus:**
     - An open-source system for monitoring and alerting, optimized for time-series data.
     - Integrates well with containerized environments like Kubernetes.
   - **Grafana:**
     - A visualization tool that works alongside Prometheus to create custom dashboards and monitor metrics.
   - **Nagios:**
     - Monitors servers, applications, and networks.

        - Supports plugins for cloud environments.
4. **Cost and Resource Optimization Tools**
    - **CloudHealth by VMware:**
        - Tracks cloud resource usage and provides cost optimization recommendations.
    - **AWS Trusted Advisor:**
        - Offers real-time guidance on best practices for cost optimization, performance, and security.
    - **Azure Cost Management and Billing:**
        - Monitors Azure resource spending and provides recommendations for savings.

Monitoring Strategies

1. **Set Baselines and Alerts:**
    - Establish baseline metrics for key resources and configure alerts for deviations.
    - Example: Set a CPU utilization alert threshold at 80% to detect potential bottlenecks.
2. **Implement Dashboards:**
    - Use monitoring tools to create real-time dashboards displaying critical KPIs.
    - Example: A dashboard showing CPU, memory, and network metrics for virtual machines.
3. **Leverage Automation:**
    - Automate responses to specific events, such as autoscaling during high traffic or restarting failing services.
    - Example: Use AWS Auto Scaling policies based on CloudWatch alarms.
4. **Adopt Multi-Cloud Monitoring:**
    - Use unified tools like Datadog or New Relic to monitor resources across multiple cloud platforms.
    - Example: Monitor workloads running on both AWS and Azure from a single interface.
5. **Focus on Security Monitoring:**
    - Continuously monitor for unauthorized access, misconfigurations, and compliance violations.
    - Example: Enable logging for IAM activities and analyze them for suspicious behavior.

Effective monitoring and proactive management of KPIs are essential for maintaining reliable, secure, and cost-efficient cloud environments. By leveraging the right tools and strategies, organizations can ensure that their cloud resources are optimized for performance and aligned with business goals.

Performance Tuning for Cloud Environments

Performance tuning in cloud environments ensures applications and resources operate efficiently, delivering optimal performance while minimizing costs. This section focuses on identifying and addressing performance bottlenecks and explores best practices for optimizing workloads.

Identifying and Addressing Performance Bottlenecks

1. **Identifying Performance Bottlenecks**
   - **CPU Bottlenecks:**
     - **Symptoms:** High CPU utilization, slow application response times.
     - **Tools:** Amazon CloudWatch, Azure Monitor, Google Cloud Operations Suite.
     - **Causes:** Overloaded virtual machines, inefficient application code, or high user demand.
   - **Memory Bottlenecks:**
     - **Symptoms:** Excessive memory usage, frequent crashes, or "out-of-memory" errors.
     - **Tools:** Resource monitoring tools such as Datadog or New Relic.
     - **Causes:** Memory leaks, improper configuration of caches, or insufficient RAM allocation.
   - **Storage Bottlenecks:**
     - **Symptoms:** High disk I/O latency, slow database queries, or storage space depletion.
     - **Tools:** AWS EBS metrics, Azure Disk metrics, Google Persistent Disk monitoring.
     - **Causes:** Inadequate storage performance tier, fragmented data, or poorly optimized queries.
   - **Network Bottlenecks:**
     - **Symptoms:** High latency, packet loss, or reduced throughput.
     - **Tools:** Network performance monitoring tools, such as SolarWinds or Cloudflare Analytics.
     - **Causes:** Insufficient bandwidth, misconfigured virtual networks, or high traffic volume.
2. **Addressing Bottlenecks**
   - **CPU Optimization:**
     - Scale up by selecting higher-performance instance types.
     - Optimize application code to reduce CPU load (e.g., parallel processing or optimized algorithms).
   - **Memory Optimization:**
     - Increase RAM allocation or migrate to memory-optimized instances.
     - Fix memory leaks by profiling and debugging applications.
     - Implement caching mechanisms using services like Redis or Memcached.
   - **Storage Optimization:**
     - Upgrade to faster storage tiers (e.g., NVMe-backed volumes).

        - Optimize database queries and implement indexing for faster data retrieval.
        - Use lifecycle management policies to move infrequently accessed data to cheaper storage tiers.
    - **Network Optimization:**
        - Use Content Delivery Networks (CDNs) to reduce latency for end-users.
        - Leverage multi-region deployments to reduce data travel distances.
        - Implement load balancing to distribute traffic across multiple resources.

Best Practices for Optimizing Workloads

1. **Right-Sizing Resources**
    - Analyze resource usage patterns to identify under- or over-provisioned resources.
    - Use tools like AWS Compute Optimizer, Azure Advisor, or Google Cloud Recommender for rightsizing suggestions.
    - Example: Downgrade an oversized EC2 instance to save costs without affecting performance.
2. **Autoscaling**
    - Configure autoscaling policies to dynamically adjust compute and memory resources based on workload demands.
    - Example: Use AWS Auto Scaling to scale application servers during peak traffic and scale them down during off-peak hours.
3. **Leverage Caching**
    - Use caching to store frequently accessed data in memory, reducing the load on primary databases or storage.
    - Example: Implement Amazon ElastiCache or Azure Cache for Redis for high-speed data retrieval.
4. **Implement Load Balancing**
    - Use cloud-native load balancers to evenly distribute traffic across multiple resources, ensuring high availability and performance.
    - Example: AWS Elastic Load Balancing or Azure Load Balancer for application servers.
5. **Optimize Application Code**
    - Profile and optimize code to reduce resource consumption.
    - Use asynchronous processing, reduce API call dependencies, and optimize database queries.
6. **Optimize Storage and Database Performance**
    - Use the appropriate storage tier based on workload needs (e.g., SSD for high IOPS workloads, HDD for archival data).
    - Optimize database schema, implement partitioning, and index frequently queried fields.
    - Consider using managed database services like Amazon RDS or Google Cloud SQL for automated tuning.
7. **Use Multi-Region Deployments**
    - Deploy workloads across multiple regions to reduce latency and enhance fault tolerance.

- Example: Use AWS Global Accelerator to route traffic to the nearest region for low-latency access.

8. **Enable Monitoring and Alerts**
   - Continuously monitor resource metrics and set alerts for thresholds.
   - Example: Configure alerts in Azure Monitor for CPU usage exceeding 80%.
9. **Adopt Cost and Performance Trade-Offs**
   - Identify workloads that can tolerate lower performance (e.g., non-critical batch jobs) and run them on cost-efficient resources like spot instances.
   - Example: Use AWS Spot Instances or Google Preemptible VMs for temporary, fault-tolerant workloads.
10. **Optimize Networking**
    - Use private connections like AWS Direct Connect or Azure ExpressRoute to improve network performance.
    - Enable compression for data in transit to reduce bandwidth usage.

Example Workflow for Performance Tuning

1. **Analyze Metrics:**
   - Use monitoring tools to collect data on CPU, memory, storage, and network usage.
2. **Identify Hotspots:**
   - Determine which resources are underperforming or overutilized.
3. **Implement Solutions:**
   - Apply appropriate optimizations, such as scaling, caching, or code refactoring.
4. **Test Changes:**
   - Validate performance improvements through stress testing or load testing.
5. **Monitor Continuously:**
   - Set up dashboards and alerts to ensure ongoing performance and scalability.

By identifying and addressing performance bottlenecks and adopting best practices for workload optimization, organizations can ensure their cloud environments are cost-effective, high-performing, and resilient to demand fluctuations.

Capacity Planning and Scaling Strategies

- Autoscaling techniques
- Planning for peak demand and redundancy

Capacity Planning and Scaling Strategies

Effective capacity planning and scaling are essential for ensuring that cloud environments can meet demand while remaining cost-efficient. This section explores **autoscaling techniques** and strategies for **planning for peak demand and redundancy** to maintain optimal performance and availability.

Autoscaling Techniques

Autoscaling allows cloud environments to dynamically adjust resources based on workload demands, ensuring efficient utilization without over- or under-provisioning.

1. **Horizontal Scaling (Scale Out/In)**
   - **Definition:** Involves adding or removing instances of resources, such as virtual machines (VMs) or containers.
   - **Benefits:**
     - Easily handles fluctuating workloads.
     - Reduces the risk of single points of failure by distributing traffic across multiple instances.
   - **Use Case:** Scaling out web servers during high traffic periods and scaling in during off-peak hours.
   - **Example Technology:** AWS Auto Scaling, Azure Virtual Machine Scale Sets, Kubernetes Horizontal Pod Autoscaler.
2. **Vertical Scaling (Scale Up/Down)**
   - **Definition:** Increases or decreases the capacity of a single instance, such as adding more CPU, memory, or storage.
   - **Benefits:**
     - Provides a quick solution for resource-constrained applications.
     - No need for changes to the application architecture.
   - **Use Case:** Upgrading a database server to handle increased query loads.
   - **Example Technology:** AWS EC2 instance resizing, Azure VM resizing.
3. **Predictive Autoscaling**
   - **Definition:** Uses historical usage patterns and machine learning to anticipate future demand and adjust resources proactively.
   - **Benefits:**
     - Minimizes latency by scaling resources before spikes occur.
     - Reduces cost by avoiding unnecessary over-provisioning.
   - **Use Case:** E-commerce platforms preparing for seasonal sales events.
   - **Example Technology:** AWS Predictive Scaling, Azure Auto Scale with Machine Learning.
4. **Event-Driven Autoscaling**
   - **Definition:** Triggers resource scaling based on specific events or thresholds, such as CPU utilization or queue length.
   - **Benefits:**
     - Provides granular control over scaling decisions.
     - Ensures resources match immediate workload demands.
   - **Use Case:** Automatically scaling compute resources when a message queue exceeds a defined threshold.
   - **Example Technology:** AWS Lambda with Amazon SQS triggers, Kubernetes Event-Driven Autoscaling (KEDA).

Planning for Peak Demand and Redundancy

1. **Understanding Peak Demand**
    - **Definition:** Peak demand refers to periods of unusually high resource utilization, often caused by seasonal events, marketing campaigns, or unforeseen spikes in traffic.
    - **Challenges:**
        - Sudden demand spikes can lead to degraded performance or outages.
        - Over-provisioning to handle peaks can result in wasted resources during normal operations.
2. **Strategies for Planning Peak Demand**
    - **Capacity Buffering:**
        - Maintain a buffer of idle resources to accommodate sudden spikes.
        - Use reserved instances or burstable instances for predictable workloads.
    - **Load Testing:**
        - Perform regular stress tests to evaluate how the system performs under peak conditions.
        - Example: Use tools like Apache JMeter or AWS CloudFormation Stress Test Templates.
    - **Elastic Resource Pools:**
        - Implement elastic pools for databases or storage systems to handle variable loads.
        - Example: Azure SQL Elastic Pool for managing database performance during peak times.
3. **Redundancy Planning**
    - **Geographic Redundancy:**
        - Deploy resources across multiple regions or availability zones to ensure service continuity during regional failures.
        - Example: Use AWS Global Accelerator or Azure Traffic Manager for cross-region failover.
    - **Active-Active and Active-Passive Architectures:**
        - **Active-Active:** All instances are live and handle traffic, providing maximum availability.
        - **Active-Passive:** One instance is active while the other remains on standby, ready to take over during a failure.
    - **Data Redundancy:**
        - Implement replication and backups to ensure data availability.
        - Example: Use AWS RDS Multi-AZ for database redundancy or Azure Blob Storage with geo-redundancy.
4. **Cost Management for Peak Planning**
    - Use spot instances or preemptible VMs for non-critical workloads to save costs.
    - Example: AWS Spot Instances or Google Cloud Preemptible VMs for temporary workloads.
    - Leverage savings plans or reserved instances for predictable resource usage.
5. **Implementing Disaster Recovery Plans**
    - **Definition:** A strategy to recover from major outages while maintaining business continuity.
    - **Components:**

        - Backups: Regularly back up data to a separate region or provider.
        - Replication: Use real-time replication to keep data synchronized.
        - Recovery Time Objectives (RTO): The target time to restore service.
        - Recovery Point Objectives (RPO): The maximum acceptable data loss in a failure scenario.
    - **Example Plan:** Set up AWS Elastic Disaster Recovery to replicate workloads across regions.

Example Scaling Workflow

1. **Baseline Analysis:**
    - Monitor and analyze historical usage data to understand typical and peak demand patterns.
2. **Define Scaling Policies:**
    - Establish thresholds for autoscaling, such as CPU usage exceeding 70% or disk I/O latency surpassing 5 ms.
3. **Test Scaling Scenarios:**
    - Simulate traffic spikes using load testing tools to ensure scaling policies function as intended.
4. **Deploy and Monitor:**
    - Implement scaling policies and continuously monitor performance metrics for optimization opportunities.

By leveraging autoscaling techniques and carefully planning for peak demand and redundancy, organizations can ensure their cloud environments remain reliable, cost-effective, and scalable. These strategies not only enhance performance during demand fluctuations but also safeguard against failures and disruptions.

Cloud Capacity Planning & Workload Balancing

Cloud capacity planning ensures that workloads receive optimal resource allocation while preventing performance bottlenecks and cost overruns. It involves strategic decision-making in workload placement, scaling, and forecasting resource needs based on performance metrics. A well-planned capacity strategy enhances efficiency, cost savings, and system reliability.

Workload Placement Considerations

When deploying workloads in the cloud, several factors must be considered to ensure optimal performance and compliance:

- **Regional Constraints:** Workloads must be placed in regions that comply with **data sovereignty laws** (e.g., GDPR in Europe, CCPA in California). Choosing the correct region also minimizes latency and improves performance.
- **Scalability:** Applications should be placed in regions that support **auto-scaling features** to handle fluctuating demands.

- **Compliance:** Industries such as healthcare and finance require workloads to comply with standards like **HIPAA, PCI-DSS, and FedRAMP**.
- **Cost Considerations:** Pricing varies by region; selecting the appropriate region can **reduce cloud expenses**.

Example: A financial services company running workloads on **AWS GovCloud** to comply with U.S. federal regulations.

Auto-Scaling vs. Manual Scaling Trade-Offs

Auto-Scaling dynamically adjusts cloud resources based on demand, while **manual scaling** involves adjusting resources manually.

Feature	Auto-Scaling	Manual Scaling
Resource Allocation	Automatic based on metrics	Manually adjusted
Performance	Responds in real-time to traffic spikes	Can result in over/under-provisioning
Cost Efficiency	Avoids idle resources, saving costs	May lead to wasted spending
Use Case	Web applications, e-commerce, SaaS	Batch processing, static workloads

Best Practice: Use auto-scaling for unpredictable workloads and manual scaling for workloads with **consistent demand patterns**.

Right-Sizing Cloud Resources

Right-sizing ensures workloads use **appropriately-sized compute instances** to optimize performance without unnecessary costs. Over-provisioning leads to **wasted resources**, while under-provisioning causes **performance issues**.

Right-Sizing Considerations:

- **Monitor Resource Utilization:** Use cloud monitoring tools to assess CPU, memory, and disk usage.
- **Choose Instance Types Wisely:** Select instances based on workload requirements (e.g., **memory-optimized vs. compute-optimized instances**).
- **Identify Underutilized Resources:** Deallocate idle instances or resize them to lower-cost options.

Example: Using **AWS Compute Optimizer** to resize an **over-provisioned EC2 instance** running at only **20% CPU utilization**.

Cost-Benefit Analysis: Reserved vs. Spot Instances

Choosing between **reserved and spot instances** can optimize costs for cloud workloads.

Instance Type	Cost Savings	Best Use Case
Reserved Instances	Up to 72% discount for long-term commitment	Predictable, always-on workloads (e.g., databases)
Spot Instances	Up to 90% savings on unused capacity	Non-critical, fault-tolerant workloads (e.g., batch processing)

Best Practice: Use a mix of **reserved instances for core workloads** and **spot instances for non-critical jobs** to maximize cost savings.

Capacity Forecasting with Cloud-Native Tools

Cloud providers offer tools to help predict future capacity needs based on historical data and workload trends.

Cloud Provider	Capacity Planning Tool	Functionality
AWS	**Compute Optimizer**	Recommends right-sized EC2 instances and Auto Scaling policies
Azure	**Azure Advisor**	Analyzes VM performance and suggests cost optimizations
Google Cloud	**Recommender**	Identifies underutilized resources and suggests optimizations

Example: Using **Azure Advisor** to identify **underutilized VMs** and recommending **downsizing or auto-scaling policies**.

Automation and Orchestration Tools

Automation and orchestration are key to efficiently managing modern cloud environments, enabling teams to deploy, configure, and scale resources with speed and precision. This section explores the **benefits of Infrastructure as Code (IaC)** and introduces **popular automation tools and platforms** used in cloud environments.

Benefits of Infrastructure as Code (IaC)

Definition:
Infrastructure as Code (IaC) is a practice where infrastructure configurations are defined in machine-readable files (e.g., YAML, JSON, or HCL). These configurations can be versioned, tested, and deployed automatically, enabling consistent and repeatable infrastructure management.

Key Benefits:

1. **Consistency and Reliability**
    - IaC ensures that infrastructure deployments are consistent across environments (e.g., development, testing, production).
    - Reduces the risk of human error by automating repetitive tasks.
2. **Version Control**
    - IaC files can be stored in version control systems (e.g., Git), enabling teams to track changes, roll back to previous configurations, and collaborate effectively.
    - Example: Using Git to manage Terraform scripts for cloud infrastructure.
3. **Faster Deployment**
    - Automated scripts eliminate manual configuration steps, speeding up the provisioning and deployment of resources.
    - Example: A developer can use an IaC tool to deploy a new environment in minutes instead of hours.
4. **Scalability**
    - IaC enables rapid scaling by automating the provisioning of additional resources during peak demand.
    - Example: Autoscaling groups can be defined in IaC templates to handle variable workloads.
5. **Improved Testing and Validation**
    - Infrastructure configurations can be tested in isolated environments before deployment, reducing the risk of errors.
    - Tools like HashiCorp Sentinel can enforce policy compliance during IaC execution.
6. **Cost Efficiency**
    - Automating resource provisioning and decommissioning ensures that resources are used efficiently, avoiding unnecessary costs.
    - Example: Using IaC scripts to terminate unused resources during non-peak hours.

Popular Automation Tools and Platforms

Automation and orchestration tools simplify cloud management, improve consistency, and enhance operational efficiency. Below are popular tools categorized by their primary use cases:

1. **Infrastructure Provisioning and Management**
    - **Terraform:**
        - Developed by HashiCorp, Terraform is an open-source IaC tool that allows the creation, modification, and deletion of infrastructure across multiple providers (e.g., AWS, Azure, GCP).
        - **Key Features:**
            - Declarative syntax using HashiCorp Configuration Language (HCL).
            - Supports multi-cloud and hybrid environments.
        - **Use Case:** Provisioning a multi-tier application with servers, databases, and load balancers.

- **AWS CloudFormation:**
  - A native AWS service that enables users to define and manage AWS infrastructure using JSON or YAML templates.
  - **Key Features:**
    - Integration with AWS services for seamless resource management.
    - Stack updates and rollback capabilities.
  - **Use Case:** Deploying a scalable web application in AWS using predefined templates.
- **Azure Resource Manager (ARM) Templates:**
  - Microsoft Azure's IaC tool for deploying and managing Azure resources.
  - **Key Features:**
    - Declarative syntax with integration into Azure DevOps pipelines.
    - Support for nested and linked templates for complex deployments.
  - **Use Case:** Setting up an Azure Kubernetes Service (AKS) cluster with associated resources.

2. **Configuration Management**
   - **Ansible:**
     - A simple, agentless automation tool that uses YAML-based playbooks to configure and manage servers.
     - **Key Features:**
       - Wide compatibility with cloud platforms, on-premises systems, and containers.
       - Declarative and idempotent configurations.
     - **Use Case:** Installing and configuring a LAMP stack on multiple VMs.
   - **Chef:**
     - A configuration management tool that uses Ruby-based cookbooks to automate infrastructure configuration.
     - **Key Features:**
       - Supports hybrid and multi-cloud environments.
       - Focus on compliance and auditability.
     - **Use Case:** Managing application updates across a fleet of servers.
   - **Puppet:**
     - An enterprise-grade tool for automating infrastructure configuration and management.
     - **Key Features:**
       - Centralized management with a master-agent architecture.
       - Strong integration with CI/CD pipelines.
     - **Use Case:** Ensuring consistent configuration of cloud and on-premises servers.

3. **Orchestration and Workflow Automation**
   - **Kubernetes:**
     - An open-source orchestration platform for automating the deployment, scaling, and management of containerized applications.
     - **Key Features:**

        - Manages workloads using declarative YAML files.
        - Supports rolling updates, autoscaling, and self-healing.
    - **Use Case:** Deploying and scaling a microservices architecture across a cluster.
  - **Jenkins:**
    - A widely used CI/CD automation tool for building, testing, and deploying applications.
    - **Key Features:**
      - Integration with IaC tools and cloud platforms.
      - Plugins for automating infrastructure workflows.
    - **Use Case:** Automating the testing and deployment of Terraform scripts.
  - **AWS Step Functions:**
    - A serverless orchestration service for automating workflows across AWS services.
    - **Key Features:**
      - Visual workflows with conditional logic.
      - Integration with Lambda, ECS, S3, and other AWS services.
    - **Use Case:** Orchestrating a data processing pipeline with S3, Lambda, and DynamoDB.

4. **Monitoring and Compliance**
   - **HashiCorp Sentinel:**
     - A policy-as-code framework for enforcing compliance during IaC deployments.
     - **Use Case:** Ensuring that all deployed resources meet organizational security policies.
   - **CloudHealth by VMware:**
     - A cost and performance optimization platform for multi-cloud environments.
     - **Use Case:** Monitoring IaC deployments for cost and performance efficiency.

Choosing the Right Automation and Orchestration Tools

- **Single-Cloud Environments:**
  - Use native tools like AWS CloudFormation or Azure Resource Manager for seamless integration.
- **Multi-Cloud Environments:**
  - Leverage Terraform for cross-cloud provisioning and Ansible for configuration management.
- **Containerized Workloads:**
  - Kubernetes is the go-to solution for orchestrating and scaling containerized applications.
- **Compliance-Focused Organizations:**
  - Use tools like HashiCorp Sentinel or Chef InSpec for policy enforcement.

By adopting Infrastructure as Code and leveraging robust automation tools, organizations can streamline cloud management, ensure consistency, and achieve operational agility.

Managing Workloads Across Cloud Platforms

As organizations increasingly adopt multi-cloud and hybrid cloud strategies, managing workloads across platforms becomes crucial. This section explores strategies for **ensuring portability and interoperability** and managing **multi-cloud and hybrid environments** effectively.

Ensuring Portability and Interoperability

Portability and interoperability are essential for seamlessly moving workloads between platforms and ensuring compatibility across diverse environments.

1. **Workload Portability**
    - **Definition:** The ability to move applications and data across cloud platforms without requiring extensive reconfiguration.
    - **Challenges:**
        - Dependency on proprietary tools or APIs.
        - Inconsistent configurations between environments.
    - **Best Practices:**
        - Use containerization technologies like **Docker** to package applications and dependencies into portable containers.
        - Adopt **Infrastructure as Code (IaC)** tools like Terraform to define infrastructure configurations that work across multiple cloud platforms.
        - Implement platform-agnostic frameworks and tools (e.g., Kubernetes for container orchestration).
2. **Interoperability**
    - **Definition:** The ability of different systems and platforms to work together, exchanging data and services seamlessly.
    - **Challenges:**
        - Differences in APIs, protocols, and data formats.
        - Limited support for standardized tools across providers.
    - **Best Practices:**
        - Leverage open standards for APIs, protocols, and data formats (e.g., RESTful APIs, JSON, or YAML).
        - Use cloud-agnostic middleware or orchestration layers to abstract platform-specific complexities.
        - Ensure network connectivity between environments using solutions like **AWS Direct Connect** or **Azure ExpressRoute**.

Strategies for Multi-Cloud and Hybrid Environments

1. **Multi-Cloud Strategies**

- **Definition:** A multi-cloud approach involves using two or more cloud providers to meet diverse organizational needs.
- **Advantages:**
  - Reduces vendor lock-in by allowing flexibility in choosing providers.
  - Enhances reliability by distributing workloads across multiple platforms.
  - Optimizes cost and performance by leveraging each provider's strengths.
- **Best Practices:**
  - **Unified Management Tools:** Use platforms like **HashiCorp Consul**, **CloudHealth by VMware**, or **RightScale** for centralized management of multi-cloud environments.
  - **Application Design:** Develop applications using microservices and containers for greater portability.
  - **Data Strategy:** Use distributed databases (e.g., **CockroachDB**, **Amazon DynamoDB Global Tables**) to ensure consistency across regions and providers.
  - **Compliance:** Ensure data residency and regulatory compliance when working with providers in different regions.

2. **Hybrid Cloud Strategies**
   - **Definition:** Hybrid cloud integrates on-premises infrastructure with public and/or private clouds to create a unified environment.
   - **Advantages:**
     - Maintains control over sensitive workloads while leveraging cloud scalability for non-sensitive tasks.
     - Supports legacy systems alongside modern applications.
   - **Best Practices:**
     - **Seamless Integration:** Use hybrid platforms like **AWS Outposts**, **Azure Arc**, or **Google Anthos** to bridge on-premises and cloud environments.
     - **Unified Identity Management:** Implement single sign-on (SSO) and unified access controls using tools like **Azure Active Directory** or **Okta**.
     - **Consistent Networking:** Use virtual private networks (VPNs) or private connectivity options like **AWS Direct Connect** for secure and reliable communication.

Key Tools and Technologies for Managing Workloads Across Platforms

1. **Orchestration and Automation**
   - **Kubernetes:** Portable container orchestration for managing workloads across platforms.
   - **Terraform:** Infrastructure as Code for multi-cloud resource provisioning.
   - **Ansible:** Configuration management for ensuring consistent deployments across environments.
2. **Monitoring and Optimization**
   - **Datadog:** Centralized monitoring of multi-cloud environments.
   - **New Relic:** Application and infrastructure performance monitoring across clouds.
   - **CloudHealth by VMware:** Cost and performance optimization for multi-cloud deployments.

3. **Networking and Connectivity**
    - **AWS Transit Gateway:** Simplifies network management across multiple VPCs and on-premises networks.
    - **Azure Virtual WAN:** Provides a unified connectivity solution for hybrid and multi-cloud architectures.
    - **Software-Defined Networking (SDN):** Solutions like VMware NSX provide network abstraction and centralized control.

Example Workflow for Managing Multi-Cloud and Hybrid Environments

1. **Assess Workload Requirements:**
    - Identify workloads that require high availability, low latency, or compliance with specific regulations.
    - Classify workloads into categories: cloud-native, legacy, and sensitive data.
2. **Design a Portable Architecture:**
    - Use containers and orchestration tools like Kubernetes to abstract workload dependencies.
    - Define infrastructure using IaC templates that work across providers.
3. **Implement Connectivity and Security:**
    - Set up secure and reliable network connections between platforms.
    - Apply consistent security policies across environments using unified identity and access management tools.
4. **Monitor and Optimize:**
    - Use centralized monitoring tools to track performance, cost, and resource utilization.
    - Regularly review configurations and policies to ensure efficiency and compliance.
5. **Leverage Automation:**
    - Automate scaling, failover, and routine tasks to reduce operational overhead.
    - Use policy-as-code tools to enforce compliance and governance.

By focusing on portability, interoperability, and unified management strategies, organizations can effectively manage workloads across cloud platforms, ensuring flexibility, performance, and cost-efficiency.

Chapter 5: Security in the Cloud

Chapter 5 explores the critical aspects of securing cloud environments, emphasizing principles like the shared responsibility model, least privilege, and zero trust. It discusses key strategies for safeguarding data, applications, and infrastructure, including encryption, identity and access management (IAM), and multi-factor authentication (MFA). Readers will learn about effective implementation of IAM policies, encryption methods for data at rest and in transit, and managing encryption keys and certificates.

The chapter also covers the use of cloud-native and third-party security tools for monitoring, threat detection, and compliance with frameworks like GDPR, HIPAA, and PCI-DSS. Additionally, it provides insights into robust incident response processes, including detection, investigation, mitigation, and recovery, while highlighting the importance of lessons learned to continuously enhance security posture. By adopting these best practices and leveraging the right tools, organizations can build secure, compliant, and resilient cloud environments.

Cloud Security Principles and Best Practices

As organizations move workloads to the cloud, maintaining robust security becomes a top priority. This section focuses on the **shared responsibility model** and the importance of **least privilege** and **zero trust principles** in securing cloud environments.

Shared Responsibility Model in Cloud Security

Definition:
The shared responsibility model defines the division of security responsibilities between the cloud provider and the customer. While providers secure the infrastructure, customers are responsible for securing their data, applications, and configurations.

Key Aspects:

1. **Cloud Provider Responsibilities:**
   - **Infrastructure Security:**
     - Physical security of data centers.
     - Security of hardware, networking, and foundational software (e.g., hypervisors).
   - **Compliance:**
     - Meeting regulatory requirements (e.g., GDPR, HIPAA, PCI DSS) for the underlying cloud environment.
   - **Service Availability:**
     - Ensuring uptime through fault-tolerant infrastructure and disaster recovery.
2. **Customer Responsibilities:**
   - **Data Security:**
     - Encrypting data at rest and in transit.
     - Implementing secure data storage policies.
   - **Application Security:**
     - Configuring access controls and application firewalls.
     - Securing APIs and integrating secure development practices.
   - **Identity and Access Management (IAM):**
     - Managing user accounts, roles, and permissions.
     - Enforcing multi-factor authentication (MFA).

Shared Responsibilities:

- **Patch Management:**
  - Providers patch infrastructure, but customers are responsible for application and operating system patches in Infrastructure as a Service (IaaS).
- **Monitoring and Logging:**
  - Providers supply tools (e.g., AWS CloudTrail, Azure Monitor), but customers must actively use them to monitor for security incidents.

Example:
In AWS, while Amazon secures the physical servers and storage, the customer must ensure proper configuration of S3 bucket permissions to prevent data leaks.

Importance of Least Privilege and Zero Trust Principles

1. **Least Privilege Principle**
   - **Definition:**
     The principle of least privilege ensures that users, applications, and systems are granted only the minimum permissions required to perform their tasks.
   - **Benefits:**
     - Reduces the attack surface by limiting access to sensitive resources.
     - Minimizes the impact of compromised accounts or systems.
   - **Implementation Strategies:**
     - **Role-Based Access Control (RBAC):** Assign permissions based on roles rather than individuals.
     - **Granular Policies:** Use fine-grained access policies for resources (e.g., IAM policies in AWS, Azure, or GCP).
     - **Periodic Reviews:** Regularly audit and revoke unnecessary permissions.
   - **Example Use Case:**
     A developer is granted read-only access to an S3 bucket instead of full access, preventing accidental or malicious data deletion.
2. **Zero Trust Principle**
   - **Definition:**
     Zero trust is a security model that assumes no user, device, or application is inherently trustworthy, even within the network perimeter.
   - **Core Tenets:**
     - **Verify Explicitly:** Authenticate and authorize every request based on all available context (e.g., user identity, device state, location).
     - **Least Privilege Access:** Limit access based on necessity and enforce dynamic policies.
     - **Assume Breach:** Design systems with the expectation that breaches may occur, and limit their impact.
   - **Benefits:**
     - Protects against insider threats and lateral movement by attackers.
     - Enhances security for remote and hybrid workforces.
   - **Implementation Strategies:**
     - **Identity-Centric Security:** Use IAM tools like AWS IAM, Azure Active Directory, or Okta to enforce strict access controls.
     - **Network Microsegmentation:** Restrict traffic between resources using virtual network rules and firewalls.
     - **Continuous Monitoring:** Monitor user and device behavior for anomalies using tools like AWS GuardDuty or Azure Sentinel.
   - **Example Use Case:**
     A cloud-based application allows access only to verified users connecting from managed devices, with all traffic encrypted and monitored.

Best Practices for Cloud Security

1. **Identity and Access Management:**
    - Use MFA for all accounts, especially administrative accounts.
    - Regularly rotate access keys and passwords.
    - Use conditional access policies based on device and location.
2. **Data Protection:**
    - Encrypt sensitive data at rest using services like AWS KMS or Azure Key Vault.
    - Encrypt data in transit using protocols like TLS/SSL.
    - Implement backup and disaster recovery plans to ensure data resilience.
3. **Network Security:**
    - Use virtual private networks (VPNs) or private connectivity solutions like AWS Direct Connect.
    - Implement network security groups or firewall rules to restrict traffic.
    - Leverage intrusion detection and prevention systems (IDS/IPS) for enhanced visibility.
4. **Monitoring and Logging:**
    - Enable logging services such as AWS CloudTrail, Azure Monitor, or GCP Cloud Logging.
    - Centralize logs for better visibility and analysis using SIEM tools.
    - Set up real-time alerts for critical events, such as unauthorized access attempts.
5. **Compliance and Governance:**
    - Use tools like AWS Config, Azure Policy, or GCP Policy Analyzer to enforce compliance.
    - Conduct regular security assessments and audits.
    - Maintain an inventory of all cloud resources to ensure consistent governance.

By adhering to the shared responsibility model and implementing least privilege and zero trust principles, organizations can build resilient and secure cloud environments. These practices not only mitigate security risks but also align with regulatory and compliance standards.

Identity and Access Management (IAM)

Identity and Access Management (IAM) is a critical component of cloud security, enabling organizations to control who can access resources, under what conditions, and to what extent. This section covers the implementation of **IAM policies and permissions** and the role of **multi-factor authentication (MFA)** in enhancing security.

Implementing IAM Policies and Permissions

Definition:
IAM policies and permissions define the actions a user, group, or role can perform on specific cloud resources. Proper implementation ensures secure and controlled access across cloud environments.

Key Components of IAM Policies:

1. **Users:**
   Individual accounts representing people or applications needing access to cloud resources.
2. **Groups:**
   Collections of users with shared permissions. Example: Developers or Administrators.
3. **Roles:**
   Assigned permissions used by users or applications temporarily. Example: An EC2 instance assuming a role to access an S3 bucket.
4. **Policies:**
   JSON-based documents specifying allowed or denied actions. They define:
   - **Actions:** API operations the entity can perform (e.g., `s3:PutObject`).
   - **Resources:** The target resource (e.g., an S3 bucket).
   - **Effect:** Allow or Deny.

Best Practices for Implementing IAM Policies:

1. **Use Least Privilege:**
   - Grant users only the permissions they need to perform their job.
   - Example: A read-only user for S3 should have the `s3:GetObject` permission but not `s3:PutObject`.
2. **Assign Permissions to Groups or Roles:**
   - Avoid directly attaching policies to individual users. Instead, assign permissions to groups or roles for consistency and scalability.
   - Example: Developers have access to deploy applications, while administrators manage infrastructure.
3. **Define Resource-Specific Policies:**
   - Scope policies to specific resources using ARNs (Amazon Resource Names).
   - Example: Restrict an IAM user's access to a specific S3 bucket.
4. **Enable Fine-Grained Permissions:**
   - Use condition keys to enforce granular controls.
   - Example: Allow actions only from specific IP ranges or during specific times.
5. **Monitor and Audit IAM Usage:**
   - Use IAM Access Analyzer (AWS), Identity Protection (Azure), or Cloud Identity (Google) to audit and validate policies.
   - Regularly review permissions to detect unused or excessive access.
6. **Enforce Temporary Credentials:**
   - Use short-lived tokens for services requiring dynamic access.
   - Example: Use AWS STS (Security Token Service) for temporary credentials.

Multi-Factor Authentication (MFA)

Definition:
MFA is a security measure that requires users to provide two or more authentication factors to verify their identity. These factors typically include:

- **Something You Know:** Password or PIN.
- **Something You Have:** Security token, smartphone, or hardware device.
- **Something You Are:** Biometric verification like fingerprint or facial recognition.

Benefits of MFA:

1. **Enhanced Security:**
    - Prevents unauthorized access even if passwords are compromised.
    - Thwarts phishing and social engineering attacks.
2. **Compliance:**
    - Meets regulatory requirements such as GDPR, HIPAA, and PCI DSS.
3. **Reduced Risk of Account Takeover:**
    - Limits the impact of weak or stolen credentials.

Implementing MFA in Cloud Environments:

1. **Enable MFA for All Privileged Accounts:**
    - Apply MFA to IAM accounts with administrative privileges.
    - Example: Use AWS MFA for root accounts and high-privilege IAM users.
2. **Integrate with Single Sign-On (SSO):**
    - Use SSO providers like Okta, Azure AD, or Google Workspace with MFA to streamline authentication.
3. **Enforce Conditional MFA:**
    - Require MFA based on context, such as accessing resources from outside the corporate network.
    - Example: Azure Conditional Access policies.
4. **Use Adaptive MFA:**
    - Implement risk-based MFA to challenge users only when anomalies are detected (e.g., new location or device).
    - Example: Google Identity-Aware Proxy.
5. **Choose MFA Methods:**
    - **Hardware Tokens:** Physical devices like YubiKeys or RSA tokens.
    - **Soft Tokens:** Authenticator apps like Google Authenticator or Microsoft Authenticator.
    - **Biometrics:** Fingerprint or face recognition on supported devices.

Example IAM Policy for S3 with MFA Requirement (AWS):

```
json
Copy code
{
  "Version": "2012-10-17",
  "Statement": [
    {
      "Sid": "RequireMFAForS3Access",
      "Effect": "Deny",
      "Action": "s3:*",
      "Resource": "arn:aws:s3:::example-bucket/*",
```

```
        "Condition": {
          "BoolIfExists": {
            "aws:MultiFactorAuthPresent": "false"
          }
        }
      },
      {
        "Sid": "AllowAllS3Actions",
        "Effect": "Allow",
        "Action": "s3:*",
        "Resource": "arn:aws:s3:::example-bucket/*"
      }
    ]
}
```

- This policy ensures that S3 actions are allowed only when MFA is enabled.

Best Practices for MFA Deployment:

1. **Educate Users:**
   Provide training on setting up and using MFA devices or apps.
2. **Backup Methods:**
   Offer backup options (e.g., SMS codes or backup codes) to avoid locking out users.
3. **Regularly Update MFA Policies:**
   Monitor and enforce the use of strong MFA methods, phasing out older or less secure options.

IAM policies and MFA together form the foundation of a secure access management strategy in cloud environments. By implementing these measures effectively, organizations can safeguard their resources and minimize the risk of unauthorized access.

Encryption and Data Protection

Encryption is fundamental to protecting data in cloud environments, ensuring confidentiality and compliance with regulatory standards. This section discusses **encrypting data at rest and in transit** and **managing encryption keys and certificates** to secure cloud resources.

Encrypting Data at Rest and In Transit

1. **Encrypting Data at Rest**
   - **Definition:** Encryption of data stored on physical media, such as disks or databases, to prevent unauthorized access in case of breaches or physical theft.
   - **Techniques:**
     - **Full Disk Encryption:** Encrypts the entire storage disk, protecting all data stored on it.
     - **File-Level Encryption:** Encrypts individual files, offering granular protection.
     - **Database Encryption:** Encrypts specific fields or tables within a database for sensitive information.

- **Cloud Provider Features:**
  - **AWS:** Amazon S3 default encryption, Amazon RDS encryption, and EBS volume encryption.
  - **Azure:** Storage Service Encryption (SSE) for Azure Storage, Azure SQL Database encryption.
  - **Google Cloud:** Customer-managed encryption keys (CMEK) or Google-managed encryption keys.
- **Best Practices:**
  - Use provider-managed encryption for simplicity and compliance.
  - Encrypt backup files and snapshots to maintain data security.

2. **Encrypting Data in Transit**
   - **Definition:** Encryption of data as it moves between systems, devices, or networks to prevent interception or tampering.
   - **Techniques:**
     - **Transport Layer Security (TLS):** Ensures secure communication over HTTPS, securing APIs, and web traffic.
     - **IPsec VPNs:** Encrypts traffic between on-premises networks and cloud environments.
     - **End-to-End Encryption (E2EE):** Encrypts data from the source to the destination, with no intermediate party able to decrypt it.
   - **Cloud Provider Features:**
     - **AWS:** AWS Certificate Manager (ACM) for managing TLS/SSL certificates.
     - **Azure:** Azure Front Door and Application Gateway for TLS termination.
     - **Google Cloud:** Cloud Load Balancer with SSL/TLS termination.
   - **Best Practices:**
     - Enforce HTTPS for all web traffic using strong TLS protocols (TLS 1.2 or higher).
     - Use secure VPN connections or private links for sensitive traffic.

Managing Encryption Keys and Certificates

Encryption keys and certificates are critical for implementing and managing encryption effectively.

1. **Encryption Key Management**
   - **Key Management Services (KMS):**
     - Cloud-native services for creating, storing, and managing encryption keys.
     - Examples:
       - **AWS:** AWS Key Management Service (KMS).
       - **Azure:** Azure Key Vault.
       - **Google Cloud:** Cloud Key Management.
   - **Best Practices:**
     - **Customer-Managed Keys (CMK):** Maintain control over keys for critical workloads.

        - **Automatic Rotation:** Configure regular key rotation to minimize the risk of key compromise.
        - **Access Control:** Use IAM policies to restrict who can create, delete, or use keys.
        - **Audit and Monitoring:** Enable logging for key usage events to detect unauthorized access.
2. **Certificate Management**
    - **Definition:** Certificates enable secure communication via protocols like HTTPS by providing authentication and encryption.
    - **Certificate Authorities (CAs):**
        - Providers that issue and validate digital certificates.
        - Examples: Let's Encrypt, DigiCert, AWS Certificate Manager.
    - **Best Practices:**
        - Use automated certificate management tools to handle renewals and updates.
        - Deploy wildcard certificates to simplify certificate management for multiple subdomains.
        - Regularly audit certificate validity to prevent expired certificates from disrupting services.
3. **Hybrid and Multi-Cloud Key Management**
    - Use centralized key management solutions for consistent control across environments.
    - Example: HashiCorp Vault for managing keys in hybrid and multi-cloud setups.

Best Practices for Encryption and Data Protection

1. **Classify and Prioritize Data:**
    - Identify sensitive data (e.g., PII, financial data) and apply stronger encryption measures to critical assets.
2. **Use Strong Encryption Standards:**
    - Adopt industry-standard algorithms like AES-256 for data at rest and TLS 1.2+ for data in transit.
3. **Minimize Key Exposure:**
    - Avoid embedding keys in code repositories.
    - Use environment variables or secure key management services instead.
4. **Implement Dual Control and Separation of Duties:**
    - Require multiple individuals to approve key generation or usage for sensitive operations.
5. **Enable Logging and Alerts:**
    - Monitor key and certificate usage to detect anomalies.
    - Integrate with SIEM tools to analyze encryption-related events.
6. **Regularly Test Encryption Mechanisms:**
    - Conduct penetration tests and audits to validate the strength and implementation of encryption.

Example Workflow: Encrypting Data at Rest in AWS

1. **Enable S3 Default Encryption:**
   - Configure Amazon S3 to use AES-256 or AWS KMS keys for automatic encryption of uploaded objects.
2. **Manage KMS Keys:**
   - Create and configure a CMK in AWS KMS with policies restricting access to specific IAM roles.
3. **Monitor Key Usage:**
   - Enable CloudTrail logs to track key access and usage patterns.
4. **Validate Security:**
   - Periodically review S3 bucket policies and ensure encryption settings are not overridden.

By encrypting data at rest and in transit and employing robust key and certificate management practices, organizations can secure sensitive information and meet compliance requirements, ensuring a resilient and trustworthy cloud environment.

Cloud Security Tools and Services

Cloud environments demand robust security measures to protect data, applications, and infrastructure from threats. This section explores **cloud-native security tools** and **third-party security solutions** to safeguard cloud resources.

Cloud-Native Security Tools

Cloud providers offer built-in security services to help customers monitor, protect, and manage their resources. These tools are tailored to the provider's ecosystem, providing seamless integration and ease of use.

1. **AWS Security Tools**
   - **AWS Security Hub:**
     - Provides a centralized view of security alerts across AWS accounts.
     - Aggregates findings from services like Amazon GuardDuty, AWS Config, and AWS Firewall Manager.
     - **Use Case:** Continuous monitoring of security compliance and alert aggregation.
   - **Amazon GuardDuty:**
     - Detects threats using machine learning and threat intelligence.
     - Monitors for unauthorized activity, such as compromised instances or unusual API calls.
     - **Use Case:** Identifying and responding to malicious activity.
   - **AWS Shield:**
     - Protects against Distributed Denial of Service (DDoS) attacks.
     - Two tiers: Standard (free) and Advanced (enhanced mitigation for critical resources).

        - **Use Case:** DDoS protection for web applications.
    - **AWS Config:**
        - Tracks resource configurations and ensures compliance with predefined rules.
        - **Use Case:** Auditing infrastructure changes for compliance violations.
2. **Azure Security Tools**
    - **Azure Security Center:**
        - Unified infrastructure security management for Azure and hybrid environments.
        - Features include vulnerability scanning, advanced threat protection, and security recommendations.
        - **Use Case:** Securing virtual machines, databases, and other Azure resources.
    - **Azure Sentinel:**
        - A cloud-native Security Information and Event Management (SIEM) tool.
        - Uses AI for threat detection and response automation.
        - **Use Case:** Aggregating and analyzing security data across Azure and third-party services.
    - **Azure Defender (formerly Advanced Threat Protection):**
        - Provides proactive protection for Azure resources, including VMs, containers, and SQL databases.
        - **Use Case:** Detecting and mitigating vulnerabilities.
3. **Google Cloud Security Tools**
    - **Google Cloud Security Command Center (SCC):**
        - A centralized platform for security management and monitoring in Google Cloud.
        - Integrates with tools like Cloud Armor and Event Threat Detection.
        - **Use Case:** Identifying and mitigating risks across Google Cloud resources.
    - **Cloud Armor:**
        - Provides DDoS protection and WAF (Web Application Firewall) capabilities.
        - **Use Case:** Protecting applications from malicious traffic and attacks.
    - **Cloud Data Loss Prevention (DLP):**
        - Identifies and protects sensitive data, such as PII and credit card numbers.
        - **Use Case:** Compliance with data privacy regulations.

Third-Party Security Solutions for Cloud Environments

Third-party tools extend the capabilities of cloud-native services, offering enhanced flexibility, multi-cloud compatibility, and advanced features.

1. **SIEM and Threat Detection**
    - **Splunk:**
        - A powerful SIEM tool for aggregating and analyzing logs from diverse sources.

        - **Use Case:** Detecting anomalies and generating actionable insights across multi-cloud environments.
    - **Rapid7 InsightIDR:**
        - Combines SIEM, user behavior analytics, and endpoint detection.
        - **Use Case:** Real-time threat detection and response.
2. **Cloud Workload Protection Platforms (CWPPs)**
    - **Prisma Cloud (by Palo Alto Networks):**
        - Secures workloads across AWS, Azure, and Google Cloud.
        - Features include vulnerability management, runtime protection, and compliance monitoring.
        - **Use Case:** Securing containers, serverless functions, and VMs.
    - **Trend Micro Cloud One:**
        - Provides security for workloads, networks, containers, and applications.
        - **Use Case:** Comprehensive protection for hybrid and multi-cloud environments.
3. **Cloud Security Posture Management (CSPM)**
    - **Check Point CloudGuard:**
        - Automates security policy management and ensures compliance across cloud platforms.
        - **Use Case:** Identifying misconfigurations and compliance risks.
    - **Orca Security:**
        - Provides agentless security for detecting vulnerabilities and threats in cloud environments.
        - **Use Case:** Rapid deployment and continuous security assessment.
4. **Endpoint and Identity Protection**
    - **CrowdStrike Falcon:**
        - Endpoint detection and response (EDR) platform with strong integration into cloud environments.
        - **Use Case:** Protecting virtual machines and containers from advanced threats.
    - **Okta:**
        - Identity and access management (IAM) tool with multi-cloud compatibility.
        - **Use Case:** Implementing secure single sign-on (SSO) and MFA for cloud users.
5. **Network Security**
    - **Zscaler:**
        - Provides secure internet access and private application access for cloud users.
        - **Use Case:** Enabling zero trust for remote and hybrid workforces.
    - **Fortinet FortiGate:**
        - Delivers advanced firewall capabilities for cloud environments.
        - **Use Case:** Securing network traffic and implementing virtual private cloud firewalls.

Best Practices for Cloud Security Tools and Services

1. **Adopt a Defense-in-Depth Approach:**
   - Combine cloud-native tools with third-party solutions for layered security.
   - Example: Use AWS GuardDuty for threat detection and CrowdStrike Falcon for endpoint protection.
2. **Integrate Monitoring and Alerts:**
   - Centralize security alerts from multiple tools using SIEM solutions like Azure Sentinel or Splunk.
3. **Ensure Multi-Cloud Compatibility:**
   - Choose tools that provide visibility and control across multiple cloud platforms.
4. **Automate Compliance Monitoring:**
   - Use CSPM tools like Prisma Cloud or AWS Config to enforce compliance policies.
5. **Regularly Evaluate Security Posture:**
   - Conduct periodic vulnerability assessments and penetration tests.

By leveraging a combination of cloud-native and third-party security tools, organizations can achieve comprehensive protection for their cloud environments while addressing unique needs like compliance, multi-cloud support, and advanced threat detection.

Compliance and Regulatory Requirements

Compliance with regulatory frameworks is essential for organizations operating in cloud environments, particularly those handling sensitive or personal data. This section provides an overview of **common compliance frameworks** and discusses **auditing and reporting for regulatory compliance** in the cloud.

Overview of Common Frameworks

1. **General Data Protection Regulation (GDPR)**
   - **Scope:**
     - Applies to organizations processing personal data of individuals in the European Union (EU) and the European Economic Area (EEA), regardless of the organization's location.
   - **Key Requirements:**
     - **Data Protection by Design:** Ensure that systems are designed to safeguard personal data.
     - **Right to Access and Erasure:** Allow individuals to access and request deletion of their personal data.
     - **Data Breach Notification:** Notify regulatory authorities of data breaches within 72 hours.
     - **Cross-Border Data Transfers:** Restrict data transfer outside the EU unless compliance mechanisms are in place (e.g., Standard Contractual Clauses).

   - **Relevance in Cloud:** Ensure cloud providers meet GDPR standards for data protection and secure data transfer.
2. **Health Insurance Portability and Accountability Act (HIPAA)**
   - **Scope:**
     - U.S.-based regulation governing the security and privacy of Protected Health Information (PHI).
   - **Key Requirements:**
     - **Privacy Rule:** Limits the use and disclosure of PHI.
     - **Security Rule:** Mandates safeguards for the confidentiality, integrity, and availability of electronic PHI (ePHI).
     - **Business Associate Agreements (BAAs):** Requires cloud providers to sign agreements outlining their responsibilities in handling PHI.
   - **Relevance in Cloud:** Use HIPAA-compliant cloud services for storing and processing PHI, such as AWS HIPAA-eligible services or Azure HIPAA-compliant offerings.
3. **Payment Card Industry Data Security Standard (PCI-DSS)**
   - **Scope:**
     - Applies to organizations handling cardholder data for credit card transactions.
   - **Key Requirements:**
     - **Access Control:** Restrict access to cardholder data to authorized personnel.
     - **Data Encryption:** Encrypt cardholder data at rest and in transit.
     - **Vulnerability Management:** Regularly test systems for vulnerabilities.
     - **Monitoring:** Maintain logging and monitoring of all access to network resources and cardholder data.
   - **Relevance in Cloud:** Ensure cloud providers comply with PCI-DSS standards, especially for services used in e-commerce or payment processing.

Auditing and Reporting for Regulatory Compliance

1. **Auditing Cloud Environments**
   - **Purpose:** Ensure that the cloud environment adheres to regulatory frameworks and organizational policies.
   - **Steps in Cloud Auditing:**
     1. **Inventory Assessment:**
        - Identify all resources, services, and data stored in the cloud.
        - Categorize sensitive data, such as PHI, PII, or financial data.
     2. **Policy Verification:**
        - Validate that access controls, encryption, and monitoring policies meet regulatory standards.
        - Example: Ensure encryption algorithms comply with AES-256 for GDPR and PCI-DSS.
     3. **Configuration Audits:**
        - Use tools like AWS Config, Azure Policy, or GCP Policy Analyzer to detect misconfigurations.

4. **Log Review:**
    - Audit logs for unauthorized access attempts, data breaches, or policy violations.
    - Example: Use SIEM tools like Splunk or Azure Sentinel for centralized log analysis.

2. **Compliance Reporting**
    - **Key Elements of Compliance Reports:**
        - **Executive Summary:** Overview of compliance status and key findings.
        - **Detailed Findings:** Identify areas of non-compliance, such as misconfigured resources or unencrypted data.
        - **Remediation Plan:** Provide actionable steps to address gaps and improve compliance.
        - **Supporting Evidence:** Include audit logs, configuration snapshots, and policy reports.
    - **Reporting Tools:**
        - **CloudHealth by VMware:** Offers compliance dashboards and automated reporting.
        - **AWS Artifact:** Provides access to compliance reports and certifications for AWS services.
        - **Azure Compliance Manager:** Assesses and tracks compliance status for Azure resources.
3. **Automation in Compliance Auditing**
    - **Benefits:**
        - Reduces the time and effort required for audits.
        - Ensures continuous monitoring for real-time compliance.
    - **Tools:**
        - **Prisma Cloud:** Automates compliance assessments for multi-cloud environments.
        - **Qualys Cloud Platform:** Conducts vulnerability scans and compliance audits.
        - **AWS Security Hub:** Aggregates findings from multiple tools to identify compliance violations.

Best Practices for Ensuring Regulatory Compliance

1. **Adopt a Compliance-First Mindset:**
    - Incorporate compliance requirements into the design of cloud architectures.
    - Example: Use encryption by default for all storage and data transfer processes.
2. **Leverage Cloud Provider Compliance Certifications:**
    - Verify that your cloud provider holds certifications for relevant frameworks (e.g., ISO 27001, SOC 2, HIPAA).
3. **Implement Role-Based Access Control (RBAC):**
    - Restrict access to sensitive data based on user roles and responsibilities.
4. **Conduct Regular Training:**
    - Train employees on compliance requirements and best practices to reduce human error.

5. **Stay Updated on Regulatory Changes:**
   - Monitor updates to frameworks and adjust policies accordingly.

By adhering to regulatory frameworks like GDPR, HIPAA, and PCI-DSS and employing robust auditing and reporting processes, organizations can ensure compliance in cloud environments while protecting sensitive data and maintaining trust.

Incident Response in Cloud Environments

Incident response in cloud environments requires a structured approach to detecting, investigating, and mitigating security incidents while ensuring minimal disruption to business operations. This section covers the processes of **detecting, investigating, and responding to security incidents** and emphasizes **recovery and lessons learned** to strengthen security postures.

Detecting, Investigating, and Responding to Security Incidents

1. **Detection**

   Goal: Identify potential security incidents as early as possible to minimize their impact.

   - **Common Indicators of Compromise (IoCs):**
     - Unusual spikes in resource usage (e.g., CPU, memory, or network traffic).
     - Unauthorized configuration changes.
     - Suspicious API calls or access attempts.
     - Unexpected data exfiltration activities.
   - **Detection Tools:**
     - **AWS:** Amazon GuardDuty for threat detection, CloudTrail for logging and monitoring.
     - **Azure:** Azure Security Center for threat alerts, Azure Sentinel for SIEM capabilities.
     - **Google Cloud:** Security Command Center (SCC) for centralized alerting, VPC Flow Logs for network monitoring.
     - **Third-Party Tools:** Splunk, Datadog, or Rapid7 for multi-cloud threat detection and monitoring.
   - **Best Practices for Detection:**
     - Enable real-time monitoring for all critical resources.
     - Use anomaly detection and machine learning-based tools to identify unusual patterns.
     - Set up alerting thresholds for key metrics, such as login failures or unauthorized API activity.

2. **Investigation**

   Goal: Analyze the incident to understand its scope, impact, and root cause.

- **Steps in Investigation:**
  1. **Collect Evidence:**
     - Review logs, such as access logs, application logs, and network flow logs.
     - Example: Use AWS CloudTrail or Azure Monitor to trace API activity and identify unauthorized actions.
  2. **Correlate Data:**
     - Correlate events across multiple logs and monitoring tools to identify attack patterns.
     - Example: Correlate a suspicious login with subsequent data exfiltration via S3.
  3. **Assess Impact:**
     - Determine the affected resources, data, and users.
     - Identify whether the incident is isolated or part of a larger attack.
- **Tools for Investigation:**
  - SIEM Tools: Azure Sentinel, Splunk, or Elastic Security for log correlation and threat hunting.
  - Forensic Tools: Volatility or AWS Forensics Framework for memory and system analysis.
- **Best Practices for Investigation:**
  - Preserve evidence by isolating affected systems and creating snapshots of compromised instances.
  - Use IAM policies to temporarily restrict access to compromised resources.

3. **Response**

Goal: Mitigate the immediate threat and prevent further damage.

- **Mitigation Steps:**
  - **Containment:**
    - Isolate affected resources or accounts.
    - Example: Detach a compromised EC2 instance from the network.
  - **Eradication:**
    - Remove malicious code, terminate unauthorized sessions, or delete compromised accounts.
  - **Remediation:**
    - Patch vulnerabilities, update security configurations, or implement additional controls.
- **Response Tools:**
  - **Automation:** Use AWS Lambda or Azure Logic Apps to automate containment and remediation.
  - **Network Controls:** Update security group rules or firewall policies to block malicious traffic.
  - **Identity Controls:** Rotate credentials, enforce MFA, or revoke compromised tokens.
- **Best Practices for Response:**

- Implement automated playbooks for rapid containment and remediation.
- Communicate effectively with stakeholders, including internal teams and external partners.

Recovery and Lessons Learned

1. **Recovery**

   Goal: Restore normal operations while ensuring that systems are secure and reliable.

   - **Steps for Recovery:**
     1. **Restore Services:**
        - Rebuild or replace affected systems using backups or predefined IaC templates.
        - Example: Use an Amazon Machine Image (AMI) to quickly redeploy a compromised instance.
     2. **Verify Security:**
        - Conduct post-recovery scans to ensure the absence of malicious artifacts.
        - Example: Use Trend Micro Cloud One to perform a comprehensive security assessment.
     3. **Validate Functionality:**
        - Test restored systems to confirm normal operations and performance.
     4. **Monitor for Recurrence:**
        - Enable enhanced monitoring to detect residual threats or repeat attacks.
2. **Lessons Learned**

   Goal: Use insights from the incident to strengthen security posture and prevent future occurrences.

   - **Post-Incident Review (PIR):**
     - Conduct a detailed analysis of the incident, including:
       - Root cause.
       - Timeline of events.
       - Gaps in detection, response, or policies.
     - Document findings and share them with relevant stakeholders.
   - **Update Security Policies:**
     - Revise access controls, network rules, and incident response plans based on the PIR.
   - **Implement Preventive Measures:**
     - Patch vulnerabilities, enhance monitoring thresholds, and adopt new security tools as needed.
   - **Key Metrics to Track:**
     - Mean Time to Detect (MTTD): The average time to identify an incident.

- Mean Time to Respond (MTTR): The average time to mitigate and resolve an incident.
- Number of Repeated Incidents: Indicates the effectiveness of preventive measures.

Example Incident Response Workflow

1. **Detection:**
    - GuardDuty detects anomalous API activity in AWS, triggering an alert in Security Hub.
2. **Investigation:**
    - Analyze CloudTrail logs to trace unauthorized actions and identify the compromised user account.
3. **Response:**
    - Disable the compromised account, revoke all associated keys, and block malicious IP addresses.
4. **Recovery:**
    - Use an AMI to restore the affected instance and rotate sensitive credentials.
5. **Lessons Learned:**
    - Update IAM policies to enforce stricter least-privilege access.
    - Conduct team training on recognizing phishing emails, which led to the initial compromise.

By implementing robust incident detection, investigation, response, and recovery processes, organizations can mitigate the impact of security incidents and continuously improve their cloud security practices.

Chapter 6: Deployment and Configuration

Chapter 6 examines the key strategies and tools for deploying and configuring applications in cloud environments, focusing on techniques that enhance scalability, reliability, and operational efficiency. It begins by comparing manual and automated deployment approaches, highlighting the benefits of automation for consistency and scalability. The integration of Continuous Integration/Continuous Deployment (CI/CD) pipelines is explored as a cornerstone of modern deployment workflows, emphasizing their role in accelerating software delivery and maintaining high-quality standards.

The chapter also covers best practices for configuring compute, storage, and networking resources, including the use of APIs, management consoles, and Infrastructure as Code (IaC) tools for efficient and repeatable setups. Techniques for managing deployments across multi-cloud environments are discussed, with practical solutions to interoperability challenges and tools that unify operations. Finally, real-world case studies illustrate successful cloud migrations and lessons learned from deployment failures, offering valuable insights into strategies for optimizing cloud deployments while avoiding common pitfalls.

Cloud Deployment Techniques

Deploying applications in cloud environments requires efficient strategies to ensure reliability, scalability, and ease of management. This section explores two critical aspects of cloud deployment: manual vs. automated deployments and the role of Continuous Integration/Continuous Deployment (CI/CD) pipelines in modern cloud workflows.

Manual vs. Automated Deployments

Manual Deployments

Definition:
Manual deployment involves configuring and deploying resources or applications through direct interaction with the cloud platform, often using a graphical user interface (GUI) or command-line interface (CLI).

Key Features:

- Relies on user intervention for every step of the deployment process.
- Involves tasks like creating virtual machines, configuring networks, and deploying applications manually.

Advantages:

- Simple for small-scale or one-off deployments.
- Provides granular control over the deployment process.

Limitations:

- **Time-Consuming:** Each step must be performed individually, increasing the time required for deployment.
- **Prone to Errors:** Manual processes are more susceptible to misconfigurations or missed steps.
- **Lack of Scalability:** Unsuitable for large-scale or frequent deployments.

Use Cases:

- Initial setup of a proof-of-concept (POC) environment.
- Deployments requiring custom configurations for unique workloads.

Automated Deployments

Definition:
Automated deployment uses scripts, templates, or orchestration tools to configure and deploy resources with minimal user intervention.

Key Features:

- Automates repetitive tasks such as provisioning, configuring, and scaling resources.
- Leverages Infrastructure as Code (IaC) tools like Terraform, AWS CloudFormation, or Azure Resource Manager.

Advantages:

- **Speed and Efficiency:** Reduces deployment time significantly.
- **Consistency:** Ensures uniformity across environments, reducing the risk of misconfigurations.
- **Scalability:** Easily supports large-scale or frequent deployments.
- **Reproducibility:** Enables environments to be recreated on demand for testing, staging, or disaster recovery.

Limitations:

- **Learning Curve:** Requires familiarity with IaC tools and automation platforms.
- **Initial Setup Effort:** Developing automation scripts and pipelines can be time-intensive.

Use Cases:

- Scaling applications dynamically based on demand.
- Deploying environments for development, staging, and production using consistent templates.
- Disaster recovery scenarios requiring rapid environment recreation.

Continuous Integration/Continuous Deployment (CI/CD) Pipelines

Continuous Integration (CI)

Definition:
CI is a development practice where code changes are frequently merged into a shared repository, triggering automated builds and tests.

Key Features:

- Ensures code is integrated and tested regularly, identifying issues early in the development cycle.
- Provides immediate feedback to developers about code quality.

Advantages:

- **Improved Collaboration:** Encourages frequent code commits and integration across teams.

- **Faster Debugging:** Early detection of integration issues reduces development bottlenecks.
- **Higher Code Quality:** Automated tests ensure that code meets predefined standards before deployment.

Use Cases:

- Automated testing of application builds for functional and performance issues.
- Verifying code compatibility with dependencies and configurations.

Continuous Deployment (CD)

Definition:
CD extends CI by automating the release of tested code changes to production environments, ensuring faster delivery of new features and updates.

Key Features:

- Includes automated deployment scripts, configuration management, and monitoring.
- Facilitates rollback mechanisms in case of deployment failures.

Advantages:

- **Faster Time-to-Market:** Reduces the time between development and production.
- **Reliability:** Minimizes human error with automated deployments.
- **Customer Satisfaction:** Enables rapid delivery of updates and fixes.

Use Cases:

- Deploying web applications with frequent updates.
- Managing microservices architectures where independent components are updated regularly.

CI/CD Pipeline Workflow

1. **Source Code Management:**
   - Developers commit code to a version control system (e.g., GitHub, GitLab, Bitbucket).
2. **Build and Test:**
   - The CI system compiles the code and runs automated tests to ensure functionality and performance.
3. **Artifact Creation:**
   - Successful builds generate deployable artifacts, such as containers or packages.
4. **Staging Deployment:**
   - Artifacts are deployed to staging environments for additional testing and quality assurance.

5. **Production Deployment:**
    - After passing all tests, the code is deployed to the production environment automatically or with manual approval (if desired).

Tools for CI/CD Pipelines

1. **Jenkins:**
    - Open-source automation server supporting extensive plugins for CI/CD workflows.
2. **GitLab CI/CD:**
    - Integrated CI/CD features in GitLab for source code management and deployment.
3. **CircleCI:**
    - Cloud-native CI/CD platform with a focus on speed and simplicity.
4. **AWS CodePipeline, Azure DevOps, Google Cloud Build:**
    - Native CI/CD solutions offered by major cloud providers.

Comparing Manual and Automated Deployments with CI/CD Integration

Aspect	Manual Deployment	Automated Deployment	CI/CD Integration
Speed	Slow	Faster	Fastest
Consistency	Varies	Consistent	Highly consistent
Scalability	Limited	Scalable	Fully scalable
Error Tolerance	Prone to human error	Reduced errors	Minimal errors

By adopting automated deployments and integrating CI/CD pipelines, organizations can achieve faster, more reliable cloud deployments while maintaining high code quality and operational efficiency.

Configuring Cloud Services

Configuring cloud services is a fundamental skill for deploying and managing resources effectively in cloud environments. This section covers the setup of compute instances, storage, and networking, as well as managing configurations using APIs and management consoles.

Setting Up Compute Instances, Storage, and Networking

1. **Compute Instances**
    - **Definition:** Compute instances are virtualized servers that provide the processing power for applications and workloads.
    - **Steps to Configure:**
        1. **Select an Instance Type:**
            - Choose from general-purpose, compute-optimized, memory-optimized, or storage-optimized instances.

        - Example: AWS EC2 instance types (t2.micro for general-purpose, c5.large for compute-intensive).
    2. **Specify Configuration:**
        - Configure CPU, memory, and storage requirements.
        - Choose the desired operating system (e.g., Linux, Windows).
    3. **Attach Storage:**
        - Assign block storage volumes (e.g., AWS EBS, Azure Managed Disks) to the instance.
    4. **Security Settings:**
        - Configure security groups and firewalls to control access.
        - Use SSH keys or IAM roles for authentication.
    5. **Launch the Instance:**
        - Deploy the configured instance and connect to it via a management console, SSH, or RDP.
  - **Use Cases:**
    - Hosting web applications, running databases, or providing development environments.

2. **Storage**
   - **Block Storage:**
     - Configure virtual drives for high-performance, low-latency applications like databases.
     - Example: Attach an Amazon EBS volume to an EC2 instance.
   - **Object Storage:**
     - Create storage buckets to store and manage unstructured data.
     - Example: Use AWS S3 or Azure Blob Storage to store backups or media files.
   - **File Storage:**
     - Set up network file systems for shared access.
     - Example: Configure Amazon EFS or Azure Files for distributed teams.
   - **Configuration Tips:**
     - Use lifecycle policies to automate data tiering.
     - Enable encryption for data at rest and in transit.
3. **Networking**
   - **Virtual Networks:**
     - Create isolated networks (e.g., AWS VPC, Azure Virtual Network) to host resources.
     - Define IP ranges, subnets, and routing tables.
   - **Security Groups and Firewalls:**
     - Configure rules to allow or block traffic based on IP, protocol, or port.
   - **Load Balancers:**
     - Deploy load balancers (e.g., AWS Elastic Load Balancer, Azure Load Balancer) to distribute traffic across multiple instances.
   - **DNS Configuration:**
     - Use services like AWS Route 53 or Azure DNS to manage domain name resolution for applications.

Managing Configurations Through APIs and Management Consoles

1. **APIs for Cloud Management**
    - **Definition:** Application Programming Interfaces (APIs) enable programmatic interaction with cloud services, allowing automation of resource provisioning and management.
    - **Common API Tasks:**
        - **Provisioning Resources:** Use APIs to launch compute instances, create storage buckets, or configure networking.
        - **Monitoring and Scaling:** Integrate APIs with monitoring tools to adjust resource allocation dynamically.
        - **Access Control:** Automate the creation of IAM roles, policies, and user access.
    - **Examples:**
        - **AWS CLI & SDKs:** Interact with AWS services programmatically.
        - **Azure REST APIs:** Automate tasks using Azure API interfaces.
        - **Google Cloud SDK:** Manage resources through command-line tools or API calls.
    - **Best Practices:**
        - Secure API keys using secrets management tools.
        - Use rate limiting to avoid exceeding API request quotas.
2. **Management Consoles**
    - **Definition:** Web-based interfaces provided by cloud providers for configuring and managing resources.
    - **Features:**
        - Visual dashboards for monitoring resource usage and performance.
        - Wizards and templates for quick deployment of resources.
        - Easy access to configuration settings, billing, and usage reports.
    - **Examples:**
        - **AWS Management Console:** Manage services like EC2, S3, and CloudFormation through a graphical interface.
        - **Azure Portal:** Provides a unified dashboard for managing Azure resources.
        - **Google Cloud Console:** Simplifies resource creation and monitoring on GCP.
    - **Best Practices:**
        - Enable multi-factor authentication (MFA) for console access.
        - Use role-based access controls (RBAC) to restrict permissions.

Example Configuration Workflow

1. **Provisioning a Compute Instance with Networking and Storage:**
    - **Step 1:** Log in to the management console (e.g., AWS, Azure, or GCP).
    - **Step 2:** Create a virtual network and configure subnets.
    - **Step 3:** Launch a compute instance by selecting an appropriate type and operating system.

   - **Step 4:** Attach a block storage volume for persistent data.
   - **Step 5:** Configure security group rules to allow inbound SSH or HTTP traffic.
   - **Step 6:** Test connectivity and deploy applications.
2. **Automating the Same Workflow Using APIs:**
   - Use IaC tools like Terraform or AWS CloudFormation to define and deploy the same resources programmatically.
   - Example Terraform Script:

```
hcl
Copy code
resource "aws_instance" "example" {
  ami           = "ami-12345678"
  instance_type = "t2.micro"

  network_interface {
    subnet_id = "subnet-12345678"
    security_groups = ["sg-12345678"]
  }
}
```

Efficient configuration and management of cloud services through APIs and management consoles empower organizations to maintain scalability, reliability, and cost efficiency. Combining these methods with automation ensures consistency and minimizes the risk of human error.

Managing Cloud Deployments Across Multi-Cloud Environments

As organizations adopt multi-cloud strategies, managing deployments across multiple cloud providers becomes increasingly complex. This section explores methods for addressing interoperability challenges and highlights tools designed to simplify multi-cloud management.

Addressing Interoperability Challenges

1. Platform-Specific Differences

- **Challenge:** Each cloud provider has unique architectures, APIs, and service offerings, leading to compatibility issues.
- **Solution:**
  - **Adopt Standardized Tools:** Use tools like Kubernetes, Terraform, or Ansible that work across multiple platforms.
  - **Containerization:** Employ containers to package applications consistently, ensuring portability across providers.
  - **APIs and Abstraction Layers:** Use APIs or middleware to abstract provider-specific details.

2. Data Management Across Clouds

- **Challenge:** Ensuring consistent and secure data transfer, replication, and synchronization across providers.
- **Solution:**
  - **Multi-Cloud Data Lakes:** Centralize data storage with solutions like Google BigQuery Omni or AWS S3 Outposts.
  - **Data Integration Tools:** Use tools like Apache Kafka or Snowflake for real-time data syncing.
  - **Latency Management:** Minimize latency by placing data close to the primary workload.

3. Security and Compliance

- **Challenge:** Managing consistent security policies and meeting compliance requirements across different cloud environments.
- **Solution:**
  - **Unified IAM Policies:** Use single sign-on (SSO) and federated identity management solutions to streamline access control.
  - **Compliance Mapping:** Use tools like AWS Artifact, Azure Compliance Manager, or GCP Assured Workloads to ensure adherence to regulations like GDPR, HIPAA, or PCI DSS.
  - **End-to-End Encryption:** Secure data in transit and at rest with encryption and key management solutions like AWS KMS or HashiCorp Vault.

4. Networking Complexities

- **Challenge:** Ensuring seamless connectivity and secure communication between clouds.
- **Solution:**
  - **Hybrid Networking Solutions:** Use VPNs, direct connectivity (e.g., AWS Direct Connect, Azure ExpressRoute), or SD-WAN solutions to interconnect clouds.
  - **Unified DNS and Load Balancing:** Employ global DNS and load balancers like AWS Route 53, Azure Traffic Manager, or Cloudflare to distribute traffic.

Tools for Managing Multi-Cloud Setups

1. Multi-Cloud Management Platforms

- **Features:**
  - Centralized dashboard for monitoring and managing resources across multiple providers.
  - Tools for cost management, workload orchestration, and policy enforcement.
- **Examples:**
  - **HashiCorp Terraform:** Automates infrastructure provisioning with a single configuration language that works across clouds.

  - **Google Anthos:** Manages Kubernetes clusters and services across GCP, AWS, and on-premises environments.
  - **VMware Tanzu:** Simplifies containerized application management in hybrid and multi-cloud environments.
- **Use Case:** An organization manages VMs across AWS, Azure, and GCP using a unified dashboard and automation.

2. Container Orchestration Tools

- **Features:**
  - Deploy and manage containers across multiple cloud platforms.
  - Ensure consistency and scalability for cloud-native applications.
- **Examples:**
  - **Kubernetes:** Open-source container orchestration platform supporting multi-cloud deployments.
  - **OpenShift:** Enterprise-grade Kubernetes solution with built-in multi-cloud capabilities.
- **Use Case:** A microservices application is deployed across AWS and Azure using Kubernetes for consistent orchestration.

3. Cost Management and Optimization Tools

- **Features:**
  - Consolidated billing and cost analytics for multi-cloud environments.
  - Identifies underutilized resources and suggests cost-saving opportunities.
- **Examples:**
  - **CloudHealth by VMware:** Tracks costs, governance, and performance across clouds.
  - **Spot by NetApp:** Optimizes workload placement to minimize costs using reserved and spot instances.
- **Use Case:** An organization reduces costs by optimizing resource allocation across providers using CloudHealth.

4. Security Management Tools

- **Features:**
  - Unified security policy enforcement and monitoring.
  - Real-time threat detection and compliance audits across clouds.
- **Examples:**
  - **Palo Alto Prisma Cloud:** Provides visibility and governance for multi-cloud environments.
  - **Microsoft Defender for Cloud:** Protects workloads across Azure, AWS, and GCP.
- **Use Case:** A healthcare provider ensures HIPAA compliance across all cloud environments with Prisma Cloud.

5. Monitoring and Logging Tools

- **Features:**
  - Aggregates logs and metrics from resources across multiple clouds.
  - Provides real-time monitoring and alerting for performance issues.
- **Examples:**
  - **Datadog:** Monitors infrastructure, applications, and logs in multi-cloud setups.
  - **Elastic Stack (ELK):** Centralized logging and monitoring solution for diverse environments.
- **Use Case:** A retail company monitors latency and uptime of its applications deployed across GCP and Azure using Datadog.

Example Multi-Cloud Workflow

Scenario: A global enterprise uses AWS, Azure, and GCP for different workloads.

1. **Infrastructure Provisioning:**
   - Use Terraform to deploy consistent infrastructure configurations across providers.
   - Example Terraform Code:

```
hcl
Copy code
provider "aws" {
  region = "us-west-1"
}

provider "google" {
  project = "multi-cloud-project"
  region  = "us-central1"
}

resource "aws_instance" "web" {
  ami           = "ami-12345678"
  instance_type = "t2.micro"
}

resource "google_compute_instance" "web" {
  name         = "web-server"
  machine_type = "n1-standard-1"
  zone         = "us-central1-a"
}
```

2. **Application Deployment:**
   - Use Kubernetes to deploy a microservices-based application across all clouds.
   - Manage workloads using Google Anthos or OpenShift for a unified experience.
3. **Monitoring and Security:**
   - Set up Datadog to monitor resource performance and detect anomalies.
   - Use Prisma Cloud to enforce consistent security policies across all environments.

Managing multi-cloud environments requires addressing interoperability challenges and leveraging the right tools. By using standardized frameworks, container orchestration, and multi-cloud management platforms, organizations can achieve seamless operations, optimized costs, and enhanced security across diverse cloud ecosystems.

Infrastructure as Code (IaC)

Infrastructure as Code (IaC) automates cloud resource provisioning, improving consistency and efficiency. It enables teams to define infrastructure using declarative or imperative scripts, reducing manual configuration errors and accelerating deployment.

Key Benefits of IaC

- **Consistency:** Eliminates configuration drift by ensuring environments remain uniform.
- **Scalability:** Automates provisioning for large-scale deployments.
- **Speed & Efficiency:** Reduces time-to-deploy new infrastructure compared to manual configurations.
- **Cost Optimization:** Prevents unnecessary resource allocation and helps track usage with automation.

Key IaC Tools

- **Terraform:** Platform-agnostic IaC tool for provisioning infrastructure across AWS, Azure, and GCP using HashiCorp Configuration Language (HCL).
- **AWS CloudFormation:** Automates AWS resource deployment using JSON/YAML templates, allowing users to define infrastructure as stacks.
- **Azure Resource Manager (ARM):** Defines Azure infrastructure via JSON templates, providing native Azure support.
- **Google Deployment Manager:** Manages Google Cloud infrastructure declaratively using YAML.
- **Pulumi:** A modern IaC tool that supports programming languages like Python, Go, and TypeScript for defining infrastructure.

IaC Implementation Best Practices

- **Use Version Control (Git):** Store IaC scripts in repositories like GitHub or GitLab for tracking changes and collaboration.
- **Implement Modular IaC Templates:** Break infrastructure into reusable components, such as network modules, database modules, and compute modules.
- **Automate Testing:** Use tools like Terratest or Checkov to validate configurations before deployment.
- **Implement CI/CD Pipelines:** Integrate IaC with CI/CD tools like GitHub Actions, Jenkins, or GitLab CI to automate deployment processes.
- **Use Policy-as-Code:** Enforce compliance with tools like AWS Config, Azure Policy, or Open Policy Agent (OPA).

- **Perform Regular Audits:** Continuously evaluate infrastructure security and efficiency using automated scans.

Example IaC Implementations

1. **Terraform Example - AWS S3 and EC2 Deployment:**

```
provider "aws" {
  region = "us-east-1"
}
resource "aws_s3_bucket" "example" {
  bucket = "my-example-bucket"
  acl    = "private"
}
resource "aws_instance" "example" {
  ami           = "ami-12345678"
  instance_type = "t2.micro"
}
```

2. **Azure Resource Manager (ARM) Template - Virtual Machine Deployment:**

```
{
  "$schema": "https://schema.management.azure.com/schemas/2019-04-
01/deploymentTemplate.json#",
  "contentVersion": "1.0.0.0",
  "resources": [
    {
      "type": "Microsoft.Compute/virtualMachines",
      "apiVersion": "2021-03-01",
      "name": "myVM",
      "location": "eastus",
      "properties": {
        "hardwareProfile": {
          "vmSize": "Standard_DS1_v2"
        }
      }
    }
  ]
}
```

3. **CI/CD Pipeline Integration with Terraform in GitHub Actions:**

```
name: Terraform CI/CD Pipeline
on:
  push:
    branches:
      - main
jobs:
  deploy:
    runs-on: ubuntu-latest
    steps:
      - name: Checkout Repository
        uses: actions/checkout@v2
      - name: Setup Terraform
```

```
        uses: hashicorp/setup-terraform@v1
      - name: Terraform Init
        run: terraform init
      - name: Terraform Apply
        run: terraform apply -auto-approve
```

IaC is a critical practice in modern cloud environments, enabling automation, reducing errors, and improving deployment speed. Organizations implementing IaC should follow best practices such as modularization, version control, and automated testing to ensure efficiency and security. As cloud environments continue to evolve, adopting IaC strategies will be crucial for scalable and cost-effective infrastructure management

Cloud-Based CI/CD & DevOps Pipelines

Continuous Integration/Continuous Deployment (CI/CD) is a fundamental practice in modern cloud computing that automates application delivery, reducing errors and improving efficiency. CI/CD pipelines streamline software development by integrating code, running automated tests, and deploying applications to production environments in a reliable and scalable manner. Understanding CI/CD best practices, security considerations, and deployment models is critical for cloud professionals.

CI/CD Pipeline Basics & Best Practices

A CI/CD pipeline automates the build, test, and deployment phases of application development. Below are the key stages:

1. **Code Commit** - Developers push code changes to a repository (e.g., GitHub, GitLab, Bitbucket).
2. **Build Process** - The source code is compiled and packaged for deployment.
3. **Automated Testing** - Various tests, including unit, integration, and security scans, ensure code quality.
4. **Deployment to Staging** - The application is deployed in a pre-production environment for final validation.
5. **Deployment to Production** - If tests pass, the new version is released to end users.
6. **Monitoring & Feedback** - Performance metrics and logs help identify issues in production.

Best Practices for CI/CD Pipelines:

- Use **Infrastructure as Code (IaC)** to automate environment setup.
- Implement **version control** for all pipeline configurations.
- Employ **blue-green deployments** to minimize downtime.
- Enforce **role-based access control (RBAC)** to restrict pipeline access.
- Utilize **automated rollback mechanisms** for failed deployments.

Pipeline Security Considerations

Securing the CI/CD pipeline is crucial to protect sensitive information and prevent supply chain attacks.

Common Security Risks in CI/CD

- **Exposure of Secrets & Credentials** - Hardcoded passwords, API keys, or SSH keys.
- **Untrusted Code Injection** - Malicious commits bypassing security controls.
- **Insufficient Access Controls** - Unauthorized users modifying pipeline configurations.
- **Lack of Compliance & Auditing** - Failure to track pipeline activity for compliance purposes.

Best Practices for CI/CD Security

- **Secrets Management:** Use tools like **AWS Secrets Manager, HashiCorp Vault, or Azure Key Vault**.
- **Code Scanning:** Automate security scanning using **SonarQube, Snyk, or GitHub CodeQL**.
- **Access Control:** Implement **least privilege access** to restrict who can modify pipelines.
- **Immutable Artifacts:** Use cryptographic signing to ensure software integrity.
- **Audit Logging:** Monitor pipeline events with **AWS CloudTrail, Azure Monitor, or Google Cloud Logging**.

Cloud-Based CI/CD Tools

Cloud providers offer native CI/CD tools that integrate with their services for seamless automation.

Cloud Provider	CI/CD Tool	Features
AWS	**AWS CodePipeline**	Fully managed CI/CD service with integration to CodeBuild, Lambda, and ECS.
Azure	**Azure DevOps**	Provides repositories, build pipelines, and release management.
Google Cloud	**Cloud Build**	Serverless CI/CD pipeline with container image automation.
GitHub	**GitHub Actions**	Workflow automation with containerized job execution.
GitLab	**GitLab CI/CD**	Built-in CI/CD pipelines integrated with version control.

Example: A DevOps team automates deployments using **AWS CodePipeline** to trigger **AWS Lambda** updates after a successful code merge.

Containerized Deployments in CI/CD

Containers have revolutionized cloud application deployment by providing consistency across development, testing, and production environments.

Using Docker & Kubernetes in CI/CD

- **Docker:** Packages applications with dependencies for consistency across environments.
- **Kubernetes:** Automates container orchestration for high availability and scaling.
- **Helm Charts:** Define reusable Kubernetes application templates for deployment automation.

Example Workflow:

1. **Developers commit changes** to a GitHub repository.
2. **CI/CD pipeline triggers** an automated Docker image build.
3. **Image is pushed** to a container registry (e.g., **Amazon Elastic Container Registry, Google Artifact Registry**).
4. **Kubernetes deployment script** (e.g., Helm) pulls the new image and updates the running application.

Best Practices:

- Use **multi-stage builds** to reduce container size.
- Implement **Kubernetes-native CI/CD tools** like ArgoCD or Flux.
- Scan containers for vulnerabilities with **Trivy, Clair, or AWS Inspector**.

Serverless DevOps & Event-Driven Deployment Models

Serverless computing eliminates infrastructure management and enables rapid deployment of applications based on event triggers.

Key Serverless CI/CD Components

- **AWS Lambda, Azure Functions, Google Cloud Functions** - Run code in response to events.
- **API Gateway & Event Buses** - Trigger serverless workloads dynamically.
- **Step Functions & Logic Apps** - Automate multi-step CI/CD workflows in a serverless fashion.

Example of Serverless CI/CD Pipeline:

1. **A new code commit** is pushed to a repository.
2. **AWS CodeBuild** compiles the function and runs unit tests.
3. **AWS Lambda is updated** automatically upon successful validation.
4. **CloudWatch Logs** monitor execution and trigger rollback if needed.

Best Practices:

- Minimize cold start latency by **optimizing serverless functions**.
- Implement **event-driven monitoring and alerts** using **AWS CloudWatch, Azure Monitor, or Google Operations Suite**.
- Use **Infrastructure as Code (IaC)** to automate deployments with Terraform or CloudFormation.

API Management in Cloud Computing

APIs (Application Programming Interfaces) are essential for integrating cloud services and automating cloud operations. Effective API management ensures **security, performance, and scalability**, enabling seamless communication between microservices, applications, and external services.

Modern cloud environments rely on APIs for provisioning resources, monitoring applications, and managing cloud-native workloads. Understanding API gateways, authentication mechanisms, and performance optimization techniques is essential for **cloud engineers, developers, and IT professionals**.

REST vs. GraphQL APIs in Cloud Computing

APIs facilitate communication between cloud services and applications. Two of the most widely used API architectures are **REST (Representational State Transfer)** and **GraphQL**.

Feature	REST API	GraphQL API
Data Retrieval	Multiple endpoints for different resources	Single endpoint for all queries
Response Structure	Fixed response format	Clients specify required data fields
Efficiency	Over-fetching or under-fetching of data	Optimized for fetching only necessary data
Use Case	Traditional web services and microservices	Applications requiring flexible queries (e.g., front-end applications)

Example: AWS provides **RESTful APIs** for services like S3 and EC2, while **GraphQL** is used in applications requiring **highly dynamic data retrieval**, such as front-end applications.

API Gateways & Rate Limiting

API Gateways act as intermediaries that **manage, secure, and optimize API traffic**. They provide features like authentication, request validation, logging, and throttling.

Popular Cloud API Gateways:

- **AWS API Gateway:** Manages and secures REST, WebSocket, and GraphQL APIs.
- **Azure API Management:** Enables centralized management of APIs with security, analytics, and caching.
- **Google Cloud Endpoints:** Supports API monitoring and control with IAM-based authentication.

Rate Limiting & Traffic Control

API gateways implement **rate limiting** to prevent abuse and ensure fair resource distribution.

Rate Limiting Strategy	Description	Example
Quota-Based	Limits the number of requests within a time period	1000 requests per hour per user
Throttling	Slows down API requests exceeding a threshold	API returns HTTP 429 Too Many Requests
Token Bucket	Allows bursts of requests while enforcing a steady rate	Each request consumes a token from a predefined bucket

Best Practice: Use **caching mechanisms** in API gateways to reduce redundant API calls and improve performance.

Handling API Authentication & Security

Cloud APIs require robust security measures to protect sensitive data and prevent unauthorized access.

Common API Authentication Mechanisms:

- **OAuth 2.0:** Delegated access using tokens (e.g., used by Google and Microsoft for SSO).
- **JWT (JSON Web Tokens):** Compact and secure way to transmit authentication data.
- **API Keys:** Simple authentication method used for service-to-service communication.
- **Mutual TLS (mTLS):** Ensures encrypted and authenticated communication between services.

Example: Implementing Secure API Authentication in AWS

- Use **AWS Cognito** for OAuth-based authentication.
- Secure API requests with **AWS IAM roles and policies**.
- Enforce HTTPS (TLS 1.2 or higher) for all API interactions.

Best Practice: Rotate API keys regularly and implement **least privilege access** to restrict API usage based on roles.

Common API Performance Issues & Troubleshooting

Inefficient APIs can lead to **latency, high costs, and degraded performance**. Common API-related issues include:

Issue	Cause	Solution
Slow Response Times	Large payloads, inefficient queries	Use **pagination** and **compression (Gzip)**
High Latency	Network congestion, poor region selection	Deploy API endpoints closer to users (AWS Global Accelerator)
Rate-Limited Requests	Exceeding API gateway quotas	Implement **caching** and optimize request batching
Authentication Failures	Expired or invalid tokens	Implement token refresh mechanisms

Example: Use AWS CloudWatch or Azure Monitor to track **API response times, errors, and throughput metrics** for troubleshooting.

Service Mesh & API Orchestration

Service mesh technology is used to **manage API communication between microservices** in cloud-native architectures. It enables traffic control, observability, and security for service-to-service interactions.

Popular Service Mesh Solutions:

- **Istio:** Works with Kubernetes to enforce security policies, traffic management, and telemetry.
- **Envoy:** A high-performance API proxy used for observability and load balancing.
- **Linkerd:** Lightweight service mesh designed for Kubernetes environments.

API Orchestration with Cloud Services

- **AWS Step Functions:** Automates API workflows using state machines.
- **Azure Logic Apps:** Connects cloud services via API triggers and workflows.
- **Google Cloud Workflows:** Manages multi-step processes across different cloud services.

Example: A microservices-based e-commerce platform uses **Istio** to **route API requests dynamically based on traffic load**, ensuring fault tolerance and performance optimization.

Best Practices for API Management & Integration

- **Use API Gateway Security Policies:** Implement **OAuth 2.0, rate limiting, and logging**.

- **Enable API Monitoring & Analytics:** Track usage patterns and detect anomalies with **AWS CloudWatch API Metrics** or **Azure Monitor API Insights**.
- **Adopt Service Mesh for Microservices:** Use **Istio or Envoy** for managing inter-service communication in Kubernetes environments.
- **Implement Efficient API Querying:** Reduce response sizes using **GraphQL for dynamic queries** and **RESTful pagination**.

By mastering API security, service mesh, and performance tuning, cloud professionals can **build resilient, scalable, and efficient cloud-native applications**.

Troubleshooting Deployment Issues

Troubleshooting is a critical skill in cloud environments, as deployment errors can disrupt workflows and affect service availability. This section provides strategies for resolving common deployment errors and debugging cloud-native applications effectively.

Resolving Common Deployment Errors

1. Resource Configuration Errors

- **Symptoms:**
  - Instances fail to launch.
  - Services fail to connect due to misconfigured resources.
- **Common Causes:**
  - Incorrect instance types or regions selected.
  - Resource limits (e.g., quota exceeded for VMs or storage).
  - Misconfigured security groups or firewall rules.
- **Resolution:**
  - Verify resource compatibility with the selected region or availability zone.
  - Check quota limits and request increases if necessary.
  - Review network and security settings to ensure proper access rules.

2. Network Connectivity Issues

- **Symptoms:**
  - Applications cannot communicate with databases or external services.
  - Failed HTTP requests or timeouts.
- **Common Causes:**
  - Incorrect subnet or routing table configurations.
  - Firewall or security group restrictions.
  - Missing or invalid DNS configurations.
- **Resolution:**
  - Use tools like **ping**, **traceroute**, or cloud-specific network diagnostic tools to test connectivity.
  - Validate DNS configurations and ensure the appropriate domain or IP is used.
  - Update firewall or security group rules to allow necessary traffic.

3. Authentication and Authorization Failures

- **Symptoms:**
  - Access denied errors during deployment or resource interaction.
  - Application cannot retrieve secrets or configurations.
- **Common Causes:**
  - Missing or misconfigured IAM roles or policies.
  - Expired or invalid access tokens or API keys.
- **Resolution:**
  - Verify IAM roles and permissions associated with the resources.
  - Rotate expired credentials and securely store new ones using tools like AWS Secrets Manager or Azure Key Vault.
  - Enable detailed logging to identify permission-related errors.

4. Application Dependency Failures

- **Symptoms:**
  - Applications fail to start or crash during execution.
- **Common Causes:**
  - Missing libraries, runtime dependencies, or environment variables.
  - Version mismatches between application dependencies.
- **Resolution:**
  - Use dependency management tools like **pip**, **npm**, or **maven** to verify required packages are installed.
  - Define environment variables in deployment configurations or cloud services like AWS ECS Task Definitions or Kubernetes ConfigMaps.

5. Storage and Data Access Errors

- **Symptoms:**
  - Applications cannot read or write data.
  - Storage volumes are not mounted correctly.
- **Common Causes:**
  - Incorrectly configured storage permissions.
  - Missing or unmounted volumes.
- **Resolution:**
  - Verify storage service configurations, such as S3 bucket policies or Azure Blob Storage permissions.
  - Ensure volumes are attached to the correct instances and mounted properly.

Debugging Cloud-Native Applications

1. Logging and Monitoring

- **Description:** Logs provide detailed records of system and application events, while monitoring tools offer real-time insights into system health.

- **Steps:**
  - Enable logging at the application and platform level (e.g., AWS CloudWatch Logs, Azure Monitor, Google Cloud Logging).
  - Use structured logging formats (e.g., JSON) for easier analysis.
  - Set up log aggregation and visualization tools like ELK Stack or Datadog.
- **Example:**
  - A failed API request is traced to a misconfigured endpoint by analyzing logs.

2. Debugging with Cloud Tools

- **Cloud Provider Tools:**
  - **AWS:** Use CloudTrail to audit API calls, X-Ray for tracing, and CloudWatch for logs and metrics.
  - **Azure:** Utilize Azure Monitor and Application Insights for detailed telemetry.
  - **GCP:** Use Cloud Trace and Error Reporting for debugging distributed systems.
- **Third-Party Debugging Tools:**
  - Debugging platforms like Sentry or Dynatrace help identify and resolve application issues quickly.

3. Tracing Distributed Applications

- **Description:** Distributed tracing follows requests as they traverse through microservices, identifying bottlenecks or failures.
- **Steps:**
  - Implement tracing frameworks such as OpenTelemetry or Jaeger.
  - Visualize traces to identify performance or dependency issues.
- **Example:**
  - A slow API response is traced to a database query, revealing an inefficient SQL statement.

4. Debugging Containers

- **Common Issues:**
  - Container crashes due to incorrect configurations or missing dependencies.
  - Network issues within containerized environments.
- **Steps:**
  - Use `docker logs` or `kubectl logs` to analyze container logs.
  - Debug running containers interactively using `docker exec` or `kubectl exec`.
  - Inspect container images for missing dependencies or configurations.

5. Debugging Deployment Pipelines

- **Symptoms:**
  - CI/CD pipelines fail to build, test, or deploy code.
- **Steps:**
  - Review pipeline logs to identify the failing stage.

- Verify environment variables and secrets used in the pipeline.
- Test pipeline steps locally to replicate issues.

Example Workflow for Resolving Deployment Issues

1. **Identify the Problem:**
    - Review logs, metrics, and monitoring dashboards to isolate the issue.
2. **Analyze the Root Cause:**
    - Check resource configurations, network settings, and application dependencies.
3. **Apply Fixes:**
    - Make configuration changes, update code, or reconfigure services as needed.
4. **Test and Validate:**
    - Redeploy the application and test its functionality to ensure the issue is resolved.
5. **Prevent Future Issues:**
    - Implement automated tests, monitoring alerts, and documentation for recurring problems.

Efficient troubleshooting and debugging in cloud environments require a combination of proactive monitoring, structured logging, and knowledge of cloud-native tools. By systematically addressing issues and using robust debugging workflows, organizations can ensure reliable and resilient deployments.

Case Studies: Real-World Cloud Deployment Scenarios

Examining real-world cloud deployment scenarios provides valuable insights into the strategies, challenges, and solutions organizations face when adopting cloud technologies. This section explores examples of successful cloud migrations and lessons learned from deployment failures.

Examples of Successful Cloud Migrations

1. Netflix: Scaling for Global Streaming

- **Background:** Netflix transitioned from on-premises data centers to a fully cloud-native environment to handle its growing user base and streaming demands.
- **Cloud Provider:** Amazon Web Services (AWS).
- **Key Strategies:**
    - Migrated applications incrementally to minimize risk.
    - Adopted microservices architecture for scalability and resilience.
    - Leveraged AWS Elastic Load Balancing and Auto Scaling to handle fluctuating traffic.
    - Implemented Chaos Engineering with tools like Chaos Monkey to improve system reliability.
- **Outcome:**
    - Achieved global scalability to support millions of simultaneous users.
    - Enhanced availability and reduced downtime.
- **Lessons Learned:**

    - Incremental migration reduces disruption.
    - Building for resilience is critical for high-availability systems.

2. Capital One: Transforming Financial Services

- **Background:** Capital One migrated its IT infrastructure to the cloud to drive innovation and reduce operational costs.
- **Cloud Provider:** AWS.
- **Key Strategies:**
    - Modernized legacy applications using serverless computing and containers.
    - Emphasized security with strict IAM policies and encryption.
    - Utilized DevOps practices and CI/CD pipelines for faster development cycles.
- **Outcome:**
    - Reduced data center footprint significantly.
    - Improved application deployment speed and agility.
- **Lessons Learned:**
    - A well-defined security strategy is essential for sensitive workloads.
    - Automation accelerates cloud adoption and reduces human error.

3. GE Aviation: Optimizing Manufacturing with the Cloud

- **Background:** GE Aviation adopted cloud technologies to enhance analytics and data processing for its manufacturing processes.
- **Cloud Provider:** Microsoft Azure.
- **Key Strategies:**
    - Migrated critical data and analytics workloads to Azure.
    - Leveraged Azure IoT and Machine Learning services for predictive maintenance.
    - Implemented a hybrid cloud approach to retain on-premises control for specific applications.
- **Outcome:**
    - Reduced operational costs by 40%.
    - Enabled real-time data insights for manufacturing optimization.
- **Lessons Learned:**
    - Hybrid cloud models offer flexibility for complex environments.
    - Advanced analytics capabilities unlock new business value.

Lessons Learned from Deployment Failures

1. Target Canada: Overreliance on Technology

- **Background:** Target's Canadian division attempted a rapid rollout of its IT systems, including cloud solutions, to support new stores.
- **Issue:**
    - Misaligned timelines and poor integration of cloud and on-premises systems caused inventory and supply chain failures.
- **Lessons Learned:**

- Proper planning and realistic timelines are critical for large-scale deployments.
- Cloud solutions must be integrated seamlessly with existing systems.

2. Knight Capital: Deployment Script Failure

- **Background:** Knight Capital lost $440 million in 45 minutes due to a faulty deployment script for a trading application.
- **Issue:**
  - A legacy system update failed to propagate to all servers, causing unpredictable trading behavior.
- **Lessons Learned:**
  - Implement thorough testing and validation in deployment pipelines.
  - Use version control and rollback mechanisms to recover from errors.

3. Healthcare.gov: Poor Scalability Planning

- **Background:** The initial launch of Healthcare.gov suffered significant downtime due to overwhelming traffic.
- **Issue:**
  - The infrastructure lacked proper scalability to handle peak demand.
- **Resolution:**
  - Migrated to AWS for auto-scaling and load balancing capabilities.
- **Lessons Learned:**
  - Anticipate peak traffic and implement scalability solutions.
  - Stress testing is vital for high-profile deployments.

Key Takeaways from Case Studies

For Successful Deployments:

- **Incremental Migration:** Reduces risk and allows time for testing and validation.
- **Security Focus:** Implement robust IAM, encryption, and compliance frameworks.
- **Automation:** Use CI/CD pipelines and Infrastructure as Code (IaC) to streamline deployments.
- **Cloud-Native Design:** Adopt microservices, serverless, and containerization for scalability and resilience.

For Avoiding Failures:

- **Plan Thoroughly:** Align cloud strategies with business goals and set realistic timelines.
- **Test Extensively:** Perform rigorous testing, including load and stress tests, before going live.
- **Monitor Continuously:** Use monitoring and alerting tools to detect issues early.
- **Prepare for Recovery:** Implement disaster recovery plans and rollback mechanisms to handle failures effectively.

By analyzing these real-world scenarios, organizations can learn from both successes and failures, guiding their cloud deployments toward better outcomes with reduced risk.

Chapter 7: Cloud Maintenance and Operations

Chapter 7 explores the essential practices and tools for maintaining and operating cloud environments efficiently. It begins with an in-depth discussion on patching and updating cloud resources, emphasizing the importance of automated solutions for ensuring security, performance, and compliance. Strategies for minimizing downtime and addressing compatibility challenges are highlighted to maintain operational continuity.

The chapter delves into monitoring and logging, showcasing tools and best practices for real-time performance and security insights. Readers will learn to set up effective alerts and leverage centralized logging for proactive issue resolution. Disaster recovery and business continuity planning are addressed next, with guidance on defining Recovery Time Objectives (RTO) and Recovery Point Objectives (RPO), and leveraging cloud-based disaster recovery solutions to ensure resilience.

Cost management strategies are presented, focusing on identifying cost drivers and optimizing expenses through right-sizing, lifecycle policies, and multi-cloud approaches. Finally, the chapter covers cloud vendor management and Service Level Agreements (SLAs), offering actionable insights into evaluating performance guarantees, ensuring accountability, and mitigating risks like vendor lock-in. Real-world scenarios and lessons learned provide practical context for mastering cloud maintenance and operations.

Patching and Updating Cloud Resources

Regular patching and updating of cloud resources is essential to maintain security, performance, and compliance in dynamic cloud environments. This section covers automated patch management solutions and strategies for addressing compatibility and downtime concerns.

Automated Patch Management Solutions

Automated patch management minimizes manual intervention by scheduling, testing, and applying updates across cloud resources. These solutions are critical for managing large-scale environments and ensuring consistent security.

Key Features of Automated Patch Management:

1. **Scheduling:**
   - Enables updates to be applied during predefined maintenance windows to minimize disruption.
   - Allows recurring schedules for critical updates and routine maintenance.
2. **Compliance Reporting:**
   - Tracks patch status across resources and provides detailed reports to ensure compliance with regulatory requirements (e.g., HIPAA, PCI DSS).
3. **Integration with Monitoring Tools:**
   - Works with monitoring platforms to identify outdated or vulnerable systems.
4. **Rollback Capabilities:**
   - Provides mechanisms to revert patches in case of failures or compatibility issues.

Examples of Automated Patch Management Solutions:

1. **AWS Systems Manager Patch Manager:**
   - Automates the process of patching operating systems and applications on EC2 instances.
   - Features predefined patch baselines and compliance reporting.
2. **Azure Update Management:**
   - Manages updates for both Windows and Linux virtual machines in Azure and on-premises environments.
   - Integrates with Azure Automation to provide scheduling and monitoring.
3. **Google Cloud OS Patch Management:**
   - Automates patching for VMs on Google Cloud.
   - Allows patching by group, schedule, or based on compliance status.
4. **Third-Party Tools:**
   - **Chef Automate:** Offers patching capabilities alongside configuration management.
   - **Ansible:** Provides modules for automating updates across diverse environments.
   - **Ivanti:** Specializes in patch management for both cloud and on-premises resources.

Addressing Compatibility and Downtime Concerns

1. Compatibility Challenges

- **Issues:**
  - Updates may introduce conflicts with existing applications or dependencies.
  - Operating system patches could break compatibility with legacy software.
- **Mitigation Strategies:**
  - **Test Updates in Staging:** Use staging environments to validate patches before applying them to production.
  - **Dependency Management:** Track application dependencies and verify compatibility with patch updates.
  - **Version Locking:** Lock critical components to stable versions while testing new patches.

2. Downtime Minimization

- **Issues:**
  - Patching requires system restarts or service interruptions, affecting availability.
- **Mitigation Strategies:**
  - **Rolling Updates:** Apply updates incrementally across multiple instances or nodes to avoid full downtime.
  - **Blue-Green Deployments:**
    - Use parallel environments (e.g., "Blue" for current and "Green" for updated) to ensure seamless transitions.
  - **Load Balancers:** Route traffic to healthy instances while updating others.

3. Security Considerations

- **Issues:**
  - Delayed patches can expose systems to vulnerabilities.
- **Mitigation Strategies:**
  - **Prioritize Critical Updates:** Apply security patches promptly using automated tools.
  - **Enable Automatic Updates:** For non-critical systems, configure automatic updates to reduce exposure time.

4. Managing Cloud-Native Applications

- **Challenges:**
  - Containerized applications require patching at both the container image and underlying infrastructure levels.
- **Mitigation Strategies:**
  - Regularly rebuild container images with updated base layers.
  - Use tools like Docker Hub or Amazon Elastic Container Registry (ECR) for version control and updates.

Best Practices for Patching Cloud Resources

1. **Develop a Patch Management Policy:**
   - Define processes for identifying, testing, and deploying patches.
   - Include escalation procedures for critical vulnerabilities.
2. **Leverage Monitoring and Alerts:**
   - Set up alerts to notify administrators of available patches or outdated resources.
   - Use monitoring tools to track the status of patches across environments.
3. **Use Maintenance Windows:**
   - Schedule patches during off-peak hours to minimize user impact.
   - Inform stakeholders about maintenance windows in advance.
4. **Automate Where Possible:**
   - Use automated patch management tools to reduce manual effort and ensure timely updates.
   - Integrate patching workflows with CI/CD pipelines for cloud-native applications.
5. **Document and Track Changes:**
   - Maintain a change log for all updates to simplify troubleshooting and rollback if needed.

Example Workflow: Automated Patch Deployment

1. **Identify Resources:**
   - Use a patch management tool (e.g., AWS Systems Manager) to scan for outdated instances or applications.
2. **Apply Updates in Staging:**
   - Test patches in a staging environment to validate compatibility.
3. **Schedule Updates:**
   - Schedule patch deployments during a predefined maintenance window.
4. **Monitor and Verify:**
   - Use logs and dashboards to monitor the patching process and verify completion.
5. **Rollback if Needed:**
   - Use automated rollback mechanisms for any failed updates.

Automated patch management and thoughtful strategies for compatibility and downtime ensure secure and efficient cloud resource management. By integrating these practices, organizations can maintain robust, compliant, and high-performing cloud environments.

Monitoring and Logging in Cloud Environments

Monitoring and logging are critical components of managing cloud environments, ensuring performance, reliability, and security. This section explores tools for collecting and analyzing logs and provides guidance on setting up alerts for system performance and security.

Tools for Collecting and Analyzing Logs

Cloud platforms and third-party tools provide powerful capabilities for log collection, analysis, and visualization. These tools help administrators track resource utilization, detect anomalies, and troubleshoot issues.

1. Native Cloud Monitoring and Logging Tools

- **AWS CloudWatch:**
  - **Capabilities:** Collects and monitors logs and metrics from AWS resources like EC2, RDS, and Lambda.
  - **Features:**
    - Log aggregation and filtering.
    - Real-time metrics and dashboards.
    - Configurable alarms for performance and security thresholds.
  - **Use Case:** Monitoring the performance of an EC2 instance and setting alerts for high CPU utilization.
- **Azure Monitor:**
  - **Capabilities:** Tracks metrics and logs across Azure services.
  - **Features:**
    - Integration with Azure Log Analytics for advanced querying.
    - Built-in support for creating custom alerts.
  - **Use Case:** Analyzing application insights to optimize database queries.
- **Google Cloud Operations Suite (formerly Stackdriver):**
  - **Capabilities:** Provides logging, monitoring, and traceability for GCP resources.
  - **Features:**
    - Centralized logging for GCP and hybrid environments.
    - Real-time alerts and tracing for distributed applications.
  - **Use Case:** Tracking API latency and identifying bottlenecks.

2. Third-Party Monitoring and Logging Tools

- **Splunk:**
  - **Capabilities:** Offers enterprise-grade log management and analytics.
  - **Features:**
    - Advanced search and data visualization.
    - Real-time correlation for security events.
  - **Use Case:** Aggregating and analyzing logs from multi-cloud environments.
- **Datadog:**
  - **Capabilities:** Combines infrastructure monitoring, application performance management (APM), and log analysis.
  - **Features:**
    - Unified dashboards for logs, metrics, and traces.
    - AI-driven anomaly detection.
  - **Use Case:** Monitoring containerized applications deployed across AWS and Azure.

- **Elastic Stack (ELK):**
    - **Components:**
        - **Elasticsearch:** Search and analyze log data.
        - **Logstash:** Collects, processes, and enriches logs.
        - **Kibana:** Visualizes log data through interactive dashboards.
    - **Use Case:** Centralizing logs from on-premises and cloud resources for in-depth analysis.
- **Prometheus and Grafana:**
    - **Prometheus:** Collects and stores metrics data for cloud environments.
    - **Grafana:** Visualizes metrics with customizable dashboards.
    - **Use Case:** Monitoring microservices and containerized applications.

Setting Up Alerts for System Performance and Security

1. Configuring Performance Alerts

Performance alerts notify administrators of issues like high resource utilization, application latency, or degraded services.

- **Key Metrics to Monitor:**
    - **Compute:** CPU and memory usage, disk I/O, and instance uptime.
    - **Storage:** Disk utilization, read/write latency, and throughput.
    - **Network:** Bandwidth usage, packet loss, and latency.
- **Steps to Configure Performance Alerts:**

1. **Define Thresholds:**
    - Set thresholds for metrics, such as CPU utilization > 80% for sustained periods.
2. **Create Alert Rules:**
    - Use native tools like CloudWatch Alarms, Azure Alerts, or Google Cloud Monitoring.
3. **Set Notification Channels:**
    - Send alerts to email, SMS, or collaboration tools like Slack or Microsoft Teams.
4. **Integrate with Incident Management:**
    - Route alerts to incident management platforms like PagerDuty for escalation.

2. Configuring Security Alerts

Security alerts detect and notify administrators of potential threats, such as unauthorized access or suspicious activity.

- **Key Security Events to Monitor:**
    - Failed login attempts or unusual authentication activity.
    - Changes to security configurations (e.g., IAM policies, firewall rules).
    - Access to sensitive data or resources.

- **Steps to Configure Security Alerts:**

1. **Enable Audit Logs:**
    - Collect logs for API calls, user activities, and configuration changes using tools like AWS CloudTrail or Azure Activity Logs.
2. **Define Security Policies:**
    - Use security monitoring tools to identify deviations from expected behavior.
    - Example: AWS Config or Azure Security Center.
3. **Set Up Alerts:**
    - Create alerts for critical events, such as failed IAM authentication or unauthorized S3 bucket access.
4. **Automate Responses:**
    - Integrate alerts with automation tools to trigger predefined responses, such as isolating compromised resources.

Best Practices for Monitoring and Logging

1. **Centralize Logs:**
    - Use log aggregation tools to consolidate logs from diverse resources into a single system for analysis.
2. **Implement Log Retention Policies:**
    - Define retention periods to balance compliance requirements with storage costs.
3. **Enable Real-Time Monitoring:**
    - Use dashboards and real-time alerts to stay ahead of performance or security issues.
4. **Automate Responses:**
    - Leverage tools like AWS Lambda or Azure Logic Apps to automate corrective actions.
5. **Perform Regular Audits:**
    - Periodically review monitoring configurations and refine thresholds to align with evolving workloads.

Example Workflow for Setting Up Alerts

Scenario: A web application running on AWS needs monitoring for performance and security.

1. **Performance Monitoring:**
    - Use **CloudWatch Metrics** to monitor EC2 instance CPU utilization.
    - Create a **CloudWatch Alarm** to notify when CPU usage exceeds 85% for 5 minutes.
    - Send notifications to an **SNS Topic** for email alerts.
2. **Security Monitoring:**
    - Enable **CloudTrail** to log all API activity.
    - Use **AWS Config** to monitor changes to S3 bucket policies.
    - Set an alert for any public access settings applied to sensitive S3 buckets.

By leveraging powerful logging and monitoring tools and configuring alerts effectively, organizations can maintain optimal performance, ensure security, and respond proactively to potential issues in cloud environments.

Disaster Recovery and Business Continuity Planning

Disaster Recovery (DR) and Business Continuity Planning (BCP) are essential for ensuring operational resilience in the face of disruptions. Cloud-based solutions provide scalable, cost-effective tools to support these objectives. This section covers developing recovery time objectives (RTO) and recovery point objectives (RPO) and highlights cloud-based disaster recovery solutions.

Developing Recovery Time Objectives (RTO) and Recovery Point Objectives (RPO)

1. Recovery Time Objective (RTO)

- **Definition:**
  RTO is the maximum acceptable time an application or system can be offline after a disruption before it significantly impacts business operations.
- **Considerations:**
  - **Criticality of Services:** Identify services that must be restored immediately (e.g., customer-facing applications) and those that can tolerate longer downtimes.
  - **Dependencies:** Assess interdependencies among systems to determine restoration priorities.
- **Example:**
  - An e-commerce platform may set an RTO of 30 minutes for its website but allow 24 hours for internal reporting systems.

2. Recovery Point Objective (RPO)

- **Definition:**
  RPO is the maximum acceptable amount of data loss, measured in time, that a business can tolerate after an incident.
- **Considerations:**
  - **Frequency of Backups:** Determine how often backups are performed to meet RPO targets.
  - **Cost vs. Risk:** Balancing the cost of frequent backups with the risk of losing critical data.
- **Example:**
  - A financial institution might set an RPO of 5 minutes for transaction databases, requiring frequent data replication.

3. Developing RTO and RPO for Business Continuity

- **Steps:**
  1. **Conduct a Business Impact Analysis (BIA):**

- Identify critical systems and evaluate the potential impact of their downtime or data loss.

2. **Define Service Tiers:**
   - Categorize systems based on their criticality (e.g., Tier 1 for mission-critical, Tier 2 for important, Tier 3 for non-critical).
3. **Set Realistic Objectives:**
   - Establish RTO and RPO targets based on the business's risk tolerance and operational needs.
4. **Review and Update Regularly:**
   - Adjust RTO and RPO as business requirements and technologies evolve.

Using Cloud-Based Disaster Recovery Solutions

Cloud-based DR solutions offer flexibility, scalability, and cost-effectiveness compared to traditional on-premises methods. These solutions enable organizations to replicate, back up, and restore data and systems quickly in the event of a disaster.

1. Disaster Recovery-as-a-Service (DRaaS)

- **Definition:**
  DRaaS enables businesses to replicate critical systems and data to the cloud, ensuring rapid failover and recovery.
- **Features:**
  - Automated failover and failback processes.
  - Support for multiple recovery scenarios (e.g., application-level, site-level).
  - Integration with backup and storage services.
- **Examples:**
  - **AWS Elastic Disaster Recovery (AWS DRS):** Automates failover for applications running on AWS or on-premises.
  - **Azure Site Recovery (ASR):** Orchestrates disaster recovery for Azure VMs and on-premises servers.
  - **Google Cloud Disaster Recovery:** Offers managed solutions using Velostrata for hybrid cloud scenarios.

2. Cloud Backup Solutions

- **Definition:**
  Cloud backup involves storing copies of data in the cloud, ensuring it is accessible in case of hardware failures or cyberattacks.
- **Features:**
  - Incremental and scheduled backups.
  - Encryption for data security.
  - Long-term archival options.
- **Examples:**
  - **AWS Backup:** Centralized management for backing up AWS resources and on-premises servers.

   - **Azure Backup:** Provides backup for VMs, databases, and file shares.
   - **Google Cloud Storage:** Supports backup for unstructured data with multiple storage classes (e.g., Nearline, Coldline).

3. Hybrid Cloud Disaster Recovery

- **Definition:**
  Combines on-premises and cloud resources for a more tailored approach to DR.
- **Features:**
   - Data replication between on-premises systems and the cloud.
   - Workload portability between environments.
- **Example Use Case:**
   - A healthcare provider replicates critical patient data to the cloud while maintaining on-premises systems for real-time access.

4. Automated Testing and Validation

- **Importance:**
  Regularly testing DR plans ensures they will work as expected during an actual disaster.
- **Cloud Features:**
   - Automated testing workflows to simulate failovers.
   - Reports for compliance and improvement.
- **Examples:**
   - AWS Elastic Disaster Recovery allows non-disruptive DR testing.
   - Azure Site Recovery includes recovery drill simulations.

Strategies for Effective Disaster Recovery

1. **Implement a Multi-Region Strategy:**
   - Distribute workloads and backups across multiple geographic regions to ensure resilience against regional outages.
2. **Leverage Snapshots and Replication:**
   - Use snapshot-based backups for rapid restoration.
   - Employ continuous replication for near-zero RPO in critical systems.
3. **Adopt Tiered Storage:**
   - Store frequently accessed backups in "hot" storage and archival backups in "cold" or "glacier" storage tiers to balance cost and accessibility.
4. **Monitor and Audit Continuously:**
   - Use cloud monitoring tools to track the health of DR systems and identify potential issues.
5. **Design for Scalability:**
   - Ensure DR solutions can scale to accommodate growing workloads and data volumes.

Example Disaster Recovery Workflow

Scenario: A retail company needs to ensure business continuity for its e-commerce platform.

1. **Set Objectives:**
    - RTO: 1 hour for the website; 4 hours for analytics systems.
    - RPO: 5 minutes for customer transactions; 1 hour for reporting data.
2. **Implement Cloud-Based DR:**
    - Use AWS Elastic Disaster Recovery for failover and failback.
    - Configure continuous replication of databases to a secondary AWS region.
3. **Test the Plan:**
    - Conduct quarterly failover tests to validate recovery processes.
    - Review logs and performance metrics to refine the DR strategy.
4. **Monitor and Update:**
    - Use AWS CloudWatch and AWS Config to monitor DR resources and ensure compliance with SLAs.

By defining clear RTO and RPO, leveraging cloud-based disaster recovery solutions, and implementing robust testing procedures, organizations can build resilient systems capable of withstanding disruptions and ensuring business continuity.

Cost Management and Optimization

Effectively managing cloud costs is critical for maintaining operational efficiency and staying within budget. This section explores how to identify and manage key cloud cost drivers and outlines strategies for reducing expenses while maintaining performance and scalability.

Identifying and Managing Cloud Cost Drivers

Cloud costs can quickly escalate without proper oversight. Understanding the primary cost drivers is the first step toward effective cost management.

1. Compute Costs

- **Description:** Charges for running virtual machines (VMs), containers, and serverless compute resources.
- **Drivers:**
    - Instance type and size.
    - Uptime of resources (e.g., VMs running 24/7).
    - Idle or underutilized instances.
- **Management:**
    - Right-size instances based on workload requirements.
    - Use autoscaling to adjust resources dynamically.
    - Leverage reserved or spot instances for predictable workloads.

2. Storage Costs

- **Description:** Charges for storing data in block, object, or file storage solutions.

- **Drivers:**
    - Volume of data stored.
    - Type of storage tier (e.g., standard, archival, or high-performance).
    - Data egress charges for transferring data out of the cloud.
- **Management:**
    - Implement data lifecycle policies to move infrequently accessed data to lower-cost tiers.
    - Delete unused snapshots, backups, and redundant data.
    - Optimize data transfer strategies to minimize egress fees.

3. Networking Costs

- **Description:** Costs associated with data transfer between regions, zones, or external networks.
- **Drivers:**
    - Inter-region and inter-zone traffic.
    - Inbound and outbound data transfer volumes.
- **Management:**
    - Use content delivery networks (CDNs) to cache data closer to users.
    - Optimize data replication strategies to minimize cross-region traffic.
    - Consolidate workloads within a single region or zone when possible.

4. Licensing and Marketplace Costs

- **Description:** Costs for using licensed software or services purchased through cloud marketplaces.
- **Drivers:**
    - Software subscriptions and licensing models.
    - Overprovisioning of licensed resources.
- **Management:**
    - Audit licenses to ensure usage aligns with requirements.
    - Opt for open-source alternatives when appropriate.

5. Monitoring and Logging Costs

- **Description:** Charges for log storage, monitoring tools, and alerting services.
- **Drivers:**
    - Volume of logs collected and retained.
    - Frequency and granularity of monitoring metrics.
- **Management:**
    - Aggregate and filter logs to capture only relevant data.
    - Set retention policies to archive or delete old logs.

Strategies for Reducing Cloud Expenses

Once cost drivers are identified, organizations can implement targeted strategies to optimize expenses without compromising performance.

1. Use Cost Management Tools

- **Examples:**
  - **AWS Cost Explorer:** Analyzes usage trends and forecasts future costs.
  - **Azure Cost Management and Billing:** Tracks spending and provides recommendations for optimization.
  - **Google Cloud Billing Reports:** Offers detailed insights into billing and cost trends.
- **Benefits:**
  - Identifies overprovisioned resources and unused assets.
  - Helps set budgets and alerts to avoid unexpected charges.

2. Rightsizing Resources

- **Description:** Adjust resource configurations (e.g., instance type, size, and region) to align with workload requirements.
- **Example:**
  - Replace underutilized large instances with smaller or burstable instances (e.g., AWS T3, Azure B-series).
- **Tools:**
  - **AWS Compute Optimizer:** Recommends optimal instance types.
  - **Azure Advisor:** Suggests resizing options for VMs and databases.

3. Adopt Reserved and Spot Instances

- **Reserved Instances:**
  - Commit to long-term usage (e.g., 1-year or 3-year terms) for significant cost savings.
  - Example: AWS Reserved Instances, Azure Reserved VM Instances.
- **Spot Instances:**
  - Leverage excess cloud capacity at discounted rates for non-critical or flexible workloads.
  - Example: AWS Spot Instances, Google Preemptible VMs.

4. Implement Data Lifecycle Policies

- **Description:** Automate the movement of data between storage tiers based on access frequency.
- **Example:**
  - Move cold data to archival storage like AWS S3 Glacier or Azure Cool Blob Storage.

- **Tools:**
  - **AWS S3 Lifecycle Policies:** Automates data transitions and expiration.
  - **Azure Blob Storage Tiering:** Offers seamless integration with archival tiers.

5. Optimize Networking Costs

- **Description:** Minimize data transfer costs by optimizing traffic routing and caching.
- **Example:**
  - Use CDNs like AWS CloudFront or Azure Front Door to reduce outbound data transfer charges.
- **Additional Tips:**
  - Consolidate data processing within a single region.
  - Minimize inter-region replication unless required for compliance or redundancy.

6. Automate Resource Management

- **Description:** Automate the detection and management of idle or unused resources.
- **Examples:**
  - Use AWS Lambda or Azure Logic Apps to shut down idle VMs after business hours.
  - Automate deletion of unattached volumes and snapshots.

7. Use Multi-Cloud or Hybrid Cloud Strategies

- **Description:** Distribute workloads across providers to leverage the best pricing and features.
- **Example:**
  - Use Google Cloud for AI/ML workloads and AWS for compute-intensive tasks.

8. Leverage Free and Discounted Services

- **Free Tiers:** Take advantage of free-tier offerings for lightweight workloads.
- **Savings Plans:** Commit to predictable usage patterns for additional discounts (e.g., AWS Savings Plans).

Example Cost Optimization Workflow

Scenario: An organization is experiencing high costs due to overprovisioned resources and inefficient data management.

1. **Analyze Costs:**
   - Use AWS Cost Explorer to identify high-cost services and unused resources.
2. **Right-Size Resources:**
   - Apply recommendations from AWS Compute Optimizer to reduce instance sizes.
3. **Implement Lifecycle Policies:**

   - Configure AWS S3 Lifecycle Rules to move infrequently accessed data to Glacier storage.
4. **Monitor and Automate:**
   - Set up AWS Budgets to receive alerts when costs exceed predefined thresholds.
   - Use AWS Lambda to automatically shut down idle development environments.

By identifying cost drivers and implementing targeted optimization strategies, organizations can effectively manage cloud expenses while maintaining operational efficiency and scalability.

Cloud Licensing & Software Usage Policies

Understanding cloud licensing models is essential for optimizing costs and ensuring compliance when using vendor software in cloud environments. Cloud customers must navigate different licensing structures depending on workload requirements, multi-cloud strategies, and vendor-specific policies.

BYOL (Bring Your Own License) vs. SaaS Licensing

Organizations can acquire cloud software through two main licensing models:

Licensing Model	Description	Best Use Case
BYOL (Bring Your Own License)	Customers use existing software licenses in the cloud. Typically used for enterprise software requiring customization.	Companies with existing enterprise agreements looking to extend software to the cloud.
SaaS Licensing	Software is provided as a subscription service, including maintenance, updates, and cloud infrastructure.	Businesses needing a fully managed solution without infrastructure management.

Example: A company using Microsoft SQL Server can either **BYOL with an Azure Hybrid Benefit** or subscribe to **SaaS-based SQL Server on AWS RDS**.

Software Subscription Models

Cloud software is typically licensed using one of the following pricing models:

Subscription Model	Description	Examples
Per-User Licensing	Software access is billed per user per month or year.	Microsoft 365, Google Workspace
Per-Instance Licensing	Pricing is based on the number of virtual machines or compute instances running the software.	Windows Server on AWS, Red Hat Enterprise Linux (RHEL) on Azure

Subscription Model	Description	Examples
Consumption-Based Licensing	Users pay based on actual resource consumption (e.g., per vCPU/hour, per GB of data).	AWS Lambda, Azure SQL Database
Enterprise Agreements (EA)	Bulk licensing with volume discounts for large enterprises.	Microsoft Enterprise Agreement, Oracle ULA (Unlimited License Agreement)

Best Practice: Businesses should evaluate **total cost of ownership (TCO)** when selecting a licensing model, considering **scalability, compliance, and renewal flexibility**.

Multi-Cloud Licensing Challenges

Using licensed software across multiple cloud providers presents unique challenges:

- **Vendor Restrictions:** Some vendors, like Microsoft, impose restrictions on running their software on competing clouds (e.g., Microsoft Windows Server licensing on AWS vs. Azure).
- **Cost Considerations:** Licensing prices vary across cloud providers, sometimes favoring the vendor's native platform (e.g., Oracle databases on Oracle Cloud vs. AWS RDS).
- **Compliance & Audits:** Multi-cloud environments require strict tracking of license usage to avoid non-compliance penalties.
- **Hybrid Cloud Licensing:** Licensing policies may differ between on-premises and cloud environments.

Example: Microsoft's **Service Provider License Agreement (SPLA)** restricts Windows and SQL Server usage on AWS, making Azure a more cost-effective choice for Microsoft workloads.

Vendor-Specific Licensing Considerations

Each cloud provider and software vendor has distinct licensing benefits and challenges. Understanding these policies helps businesses optimize costs and avoid compliance pitfalls.

Microsoft Licensing Considerations

- **Azure Hybrid Benefit:** Allows enterprises to use existing Windows Server and SQL Server licenses in Azure at a reduced cost.
- **License Mobility through Software Assurance:** Permits software transfers between on-prem and cloud environments.
- **Restrictions on AWS & Google Cloud:** Microsoft restricts licensing flexibility on competing cloud platforms, requiring additional fees for running Windows workloads outside Azure.

Oracle Licensing Considerations

- **Oracle Cloud vs. AWS Licensing:** Oracle software is often licensed per-core, but Oracle Cloud provides **licensing advantages** that make running Oracle databases more cost-effective.
- **Bring Your Own License (BYOL):** Oracle allows customers to transfer on-prem licenses to the cloud, but restrictions apply depending on **CPU architecture and hypervisor use**.

Red Hat & Linux Distributions

- **Subscription-based Licensing:** RHEL and SUSE Linux are billed **per-instance or per-core**, with pricing differences based on **support levels and SLA requirements**.
- **Cloud Marketplace Considerations:** Licensing terms may differ when purchasing from **AWS Marketplace vs. Azure Marketplace**.

VMware Licensing in the Cloud

- **VMware Cloud on AWS & Azure VMware Solutions:** Special licensing agreements exist for running VMware workloads natively on AWS or Azure.
- **vSphere & vSAN Licensing:** VMware environments require proper license tracking to ensure compliance with **cloud provider-specific agreements**.

Best Practices for Cloud Licensing & Cost Optimization

- **Assess Licensing Costs Across Cloud Providers:** Compare **Microsoft SQL Server on Azure vs. AWS RDS** or **Oracle Cloud vs. AWS EC2 for Oracle databases**.
- **Track License Usage Proactively:** Use **cloud-native tools** like AWS License Manager or Azure Cost Management.
- **Negotiate Enterprise Agreements (EAs):** Large enterprises can often **reduce costs with bulk licensing agreements**.
- **Consider Open-Source Alternatives:** In some cases, **switching to PostgreSQL or MariaDB instead of SQL Server** can provide significant cost savings.
- **Leverage Multi-Cloud Licensing Strategies:** Ensure that licensing policies allow **flexibility for hybrid and multi-cloud deployments**.

Cloud Cost Optimization Strategies

Managing cloud costs efficiently is a critical skill for IT professionals. The dynamic and on-demand nature of cloud computing makes cost management challenging but essential. Without proper planning, organizations can quickly exceed their budget due to inefficient resource allocation, over-provisioning, or underutilization.

1. Understanding Cloud Pricing Models

Cloud providers offer different pricing models that organizations can leverage to optimize costs:

- **Pay-as-You-Go (On-Demand):** Best for short-term, unpredictable workloads but can be expensive for long-term use.
- **Reserved Instances (RIs) & Savings Plans:** Provide significant discounts for long-term commitment (1-3 years).
- **Spot & Preemptible Instances:** Allow organizations to purchase unused capacity at a lower price, suitable for non-critical workloads.
- **Free Tier & Trial Services:** Providers like AWS, Azure, and Google Cloud offer free-tier services that can help with development and testing.

Optimization Tip: Assess workload patterns and select the most cost-effective pricing model.

2. Implementing Cost Allocation Tags

Using cost allocation tags enables organizations to track expenses more efficiently. Tags help categorize cloud costs by:

- **Departments (e.g., Finance, HR, IT)**
- **Projects (e.g., Development, Production, Staging)**
- **Environments (e.g., Test, Dev, Prod)**
- **Business Units or Clients**

Most cloud providers support **resource tagging**, and cost analysis tools (e.g., AWS Cost Explorer, Azure Cost Management) allow organizations to filter spending by tags.

Optimization Tip: Enforce a **tagging policy** to ensure all cloud resources are properly labeled.

3. Rightsizing Compute & Storage Resources

Many organizations over-provision cloud resources, leading to unnecessary expenses. Rightsizing ensures that workloads use appropriately sized compute, memory, and storage resources.

Compute Rightsizing:

- **Analyze CPU & Memory Usage** to identify underutilized instances.
- **Scale down** over-provisioned VMs or containers to smaller sizes.
- **Use auto-scaling** to adjust resources based on real-time demand.

Storage Optimization:

- **Enable tiered storage** (Hot, Cool, Archive) to reduce costs for less frequently accessed data.
- **Schedule lifecycle policies** to automatically delete or move old data to cheaper storage.
- **Deduplicate & compress data** to save space.

Optimization Tip: Review resource utilization reports and downsize instances where necessary.

4. Leveraging Spot & Preemptible Instances

Spot instances (AWS), Preemptible VMs (Google Cloud), and Low-Priority VMs (Azure) allow organizations to access unused cloud capacity at a fraction of the cost.

Best Use Cases for Spot Instances:

- Batch processing
- Rendering workloads
- Big data analytics
- Machine learning training
- CI/CD pipeline builds

Spot instances may be **terminated at any time** if capacity is needed elsewhere, so they should only be used for **fault-tolerant applications**.

Optimization Tip: Use **auto-scaling groups** and **checkpointing** to handle interruptions gracefully.

5. Implementing Auto-Scaling & Load Balancing

Auto-scaling helps adjust resource allocation dynamically, ensuring cost efficiency while maintaining performance.

Key Strategies:

- **Horizontal Scaling:** Automatically add/remove instances based on traffic demand.
- **Vertical Scaling:** Dynamically increase or decrease CPU, RAM, or disk allocation for individual instances.
- **Scheduled Scaling:** Scale up during peak hours and down during off-hours.

Load balancing optimizes resource distribution across multiple instances, reducing over-reliance on expensive, high-performance resources.

Optimization Tip: Set up **auto-scaling rules** to avoid unnecessary spending during low-traffic periods.

6. Monitoring & Cost Management Tools

Most cloud providers offer built-in cost monitoring tools:

- **AWS Cost Explorer** – Visualize spending trends and forecast costs.
- **Azure Cost Management & Billing** – Provides detailed breakdowns of usage and costs.

- **Google Cloud Billing Reports** – Helps track and analyze resource consumption.

Third-party tools such as **CloudHealth by VMware**, **Spot.io**, and **Cloudability** provide cross-cloud cost management and optimization recommendations.

Optimization Tip: Set budget alerts to track spending and avoid unexpected charges.

7. Implementing Serverless & Managed Services

Using **serverless computing** and **managed cloud services** can help optimize costs:

- **Serverless Functions (e.g., AWS Lambda, Azure Functions, Google Cloud Functions)**: Pay only for execution time.
- **Managed Databases (e.g., AWS RDS, Azure SQL, Google Cloud Spanner)**: Reduce overhead costs by outsourcing database maintenance.
- **CDN Services (e.g., CloudFront, Azure CDN, Google Cloud CDN)**: Minimize bandwidth costs by caching content closer to users.

Optimization Tip: Adopt a serverless-first approach for applications with variable workloads.

8. Implementing FinOps (Cloud Financial Operations)

FinOps is the practice of **bringing financial accountability to cloud spending** and aligning cloud costs with business objectives.

Key FinOps Practices:

- Regular **cloud cost reviews** and governance policies.
- Engaging **cross-functional teams** (Finance, IT, DevOps) in cost decisions.
- Setting **spending limits & budgets** for projects.
- Using **Reserved Instances and Savings Plans** strategically.

Optimization Tip: Assign a **FinOps team** to monitor cloud spending and enforce cost-control best practices.

To effectively manage cloud costs, organizations should:

- Use **cost allocation tags** and track spending by department or project.
- **Right-size compute & storage** resources to prevent over-provisioning.
- **Leverage spot instances** for cost-effective, non-critical workloads.
- **Implement auto-scaling** and optimize workloads dynamically.
- **Monitor expenses** using built-in or third-party cost management tools.
- **Adopt serverless computing** for cost-efficient execution.
- **Apply FinOps practices** to improve financial accountability.

Cloud Vendor Management and SLAs

Cloud vendor management and service-level agreements (SLAs) are at the heart of successful cloud adoption and operation. They define the relationship between the organization and the cloud provider, outlining expectations, performance guarantees, and remedies in case of failures. This chapter delves into the intricacies of evaluating SLAs and ensuring accountability while providing a narrative perspective on their real-world importance.

Understanding SLAs: The Foundation of Vendor Relationships

Imagine a growing e-commerce business deciding to migrate its operations to the cloud. The company must ensure that its website remains available to customers 24/7, especially during high-traffic events like Black Friday. The team evaluates cloud providers, focusing on one critical document: the SLA.

An SLA is more than a technical agreement; it's a promise from the vendor about how their service will perform. For the e-commerce team, the uptime guarantee is paramount. A 99.99% uptime promise sounds excellent—it equates to less than an hour of downtime per year. But what happens if the vendor doesn't meet this promise? That's where the SLA's compensation clauses come into play.

Evaluating Vendor SLAs

Availability and Uptime Guarantees

For the e-commerce business, the vendor's SLA specifies a 99.99% uptime for web hosting. On the surface, this guarantee seems sufficient. However, the business team digs deeper:

- **What services are included?** Is the uptime guarantee only for the virtual machines, or does it also cover the database and content delivery network (CDN)?
- **How is downtime calculated?** Does it include scheduled maintenance?
- **What happens if the promise isn't met?** The SLA offers service credits—but will these credits adequately compensate for lost revenue and customer trust?

Performance Metrics

Performance metrics are equally critical. Latency, throughput, and response times are often part of the SLA. For a business relying on real-time transactions, even a few milliseconds of delay can impact customer satisfaction. The e-commerce team evaluates vendors that promise sub-50ms latency for database queries and compares this metric with their application needs.

Ensuring Accountability and Performance

Scenario: A Minor Breach Escalates

Three months into the partnership, the e-commerce business experiences a two-hour outage during a high-traffic period. The vendor's SLA promises credits for downtime, but the business's losses in customer trust and sales far exceed the compensation. The company realizes that having an SLA is not enough—it must proactively monitor and enforce it.

1. Monitoring Vendor Performance

The IT team implements **AWS CloudWatch** to track uptime and resource utilization. Dashboards show real-time metrics, and alerts notify the team of any anomalies. For added security, they integrate a third-party tool, **Datadog**, which provides a holistic view of performance across their multi-cloud environment.

2. Regular Vendor Audits

To ensure ongoing compliance, the team schedules quarterly reviews with their cloud provider. During these reviews, they compare SLA promises with actual performance data. When discrepancies arise, they document the issues and push for accountability, using the SLA as leverage.

3. Managing the Unexpected

When another outage occurs six months later, the company is prepared. Escalation protocols defined in the SLA ensure immediate vendor response. Within minutes, the vendor's support team is engaged, and the issue is resolved quickly. This incident highlights the value of clear escalation paths and robust monitoring.

Avoiding Vendor Lock-In: A Strategic Narrative

The e-commerce company initially relied on a single vendor. However, as the business grew, it became apparent that dependency on one provider posed risks. To mitigate these, the company adopted a multi-cloud strategy.

They started using **Google Cloud Platform** (GCP) for AI-driven product recommendations while retaining AWS for hosting. This diversification allowed the company to negotiate better terms with both vendors and ensured resilience. A failure in one provider's services would no longer cripple operations.

Real-World Example: Lessons in SLA Management

The Healthcare Provider's Wake-Up Call

A healthcare provider signed with a cloud vendor promising 99.9% uptime for critical patient records. For months, operations were smooth, until a regional outage left doctors unable to access medical histories during emergencies.

The SLA promised credits, but the damage to patient trust was incalculable. Post-incident analysis revealed gaps in the provider's vendor management:

1. They hadn't monitored uptime independently, relying solely on vendor reports.
2. Escalation procedures weren't defined clearly in the SLA, causing delays in resolution.

The organization learned from its mistakes, implementing these measures:

- **Independent Monitoring:** They used **Azure Monitor** to track uptime in real time.
- **Clear SLAs:** New contracts included detailed escalation paths and penalties beyond service credits.
- **Multi-Region Deployments:** Patient data was replicated across multiple regions to prevent future disruptions.

Best Practices for SLA and Vendor Management

1. **Start with the SLA:**
    - Don't just look for high availability guarantees; analyze the fine print. Understand what's covered and what isn't, and ensure the SLA aligns with your business-critical needs.
2. **Monitor, Don't Assume:**
    - Use tools like CloudWatch, Azure Monitor, or Splunk to track vendor performance. Proactive monitoring allows you to identify and address issues before they escalate.
3. **Maintain Transparency:**
    - Schedule regular vendor meetings to review performance data and address concerns.
4. **Prepare for the Worst:**
    - Include robust escalation paths and termination clauses in your SLA.
    - Ensure disaster recovery and failover plans are in place, even for cloud-hosted services.

Final Thought:

An SLA is a vital safety net, but its effectiveness depends on how well it's understood, monitored, and enforced. Organizations that treat vendor management as an ongoing partnership—not a one-time contract—set themselves up for greater reliability, resilience, and success in the cloud.

Chapter 8: Troubleshooting Cloud Issues

Chapter 8 serves as a practical guide for addressing and resolving common challenges in cloud environments, including network latency, storage performance issues, and misconfigurations. It offers a structured approach to diagnosing connectivity and bandwidth problems, optimizing resource utilization, and enhancing performance. Tools and techniques for monitoring, logging, and analyzing metrics are presented to facilitate efficient problem identification and resolution.

Detailed strategies for handling security incidents, such as breaches, malware, and unauthorized access, are explored alongside workflows for restoring systems to a secure state. Practical troubleshooting exercises are integrated into the narrative, showcasing real-world scenarios and step-by-step solutions for addressing bottlenecks in compute, storage, and networking, resolving pipeline failures, and managing high-latency issues in multi-region applications.

The chapter emphasizes the importance of monitoring baselines, incident documentation, and cross-team collaboration, equipping readers with the skills to proactively address cloud challenges, maintain operational stability, and deliver a seamless user experience. Through case studies and actionable insights, it provides the knowledge and tools necessary to troubleshoot effectively and optimize cloud operations.

Common Cloud Issues and Solutions

Cloud environments, while highly flexible and scalable, can face a variety of challenges that impact performance, security, and cost efficiency. This section focuses on addressing network latency, storage performance issues, and misconfigurations while outlining best practices for identifying root causes.

Network Latency

Symptoms:

- Slow application response times.
- Delays in data transfer between regions or services.
- Reduced performance for real-time applications like video streaming or gaming.

Common Causes:

1. **Geographic Distance:**
    - Data traveling between regions or continents experiences higher latency.
2. **Suboptimal Routing:**
    - Inefficient routing paths can lead to increased travel times for data packets.
3. **Congested Networks:**
    - High traffic in shared networks leads to bottlenecks.

Solutions:

1. **Use Content Delivery Networks (CDNs):**
    - Distribute content to servers closer to end users.
    - Example: AWS CloudFront, Azure Front Door, Google Cloud CDN.
2. **Implement Direct Connectivity:**
    - Use dedicated links like AWS Direct Connect or Azure ExpressRoute to reduce latency for critical workloads.
3. **Optimize Network Topology:**
    - Deploy workloads in regions closest to users to minimize geographic latency.
4. **Monitor and Diagnose:**
    - Use tools like traceroute or cloud-native network monitoring to identify latency sources.

Best Practice:

- Regularly test application performance across regions to ensure acceptable latency levels.

Storage Performance Issues

Symptoms:

- Slow read/write speeds.
- High I/O wait times impacting application performance.
- Increased latency in accessing storage.

Common Causes:

1. **Incorrect Storage Tier:**
   - Using low-cost storage designed for archival purposes instead of high-performance tiers.
2. **Overloaded Disks:**
   - Insufficient disk IOPS for applications requiring high throughput.
3. **Suboptimal Configuration:**
   - Improper settings for storage caching or striping.

Solutions:

1. **Match Storage Tier to Workload:**
   - Use SSD-backed volumes for high-performance needs (e.g., AWS EBS gp3, Azure Premium Disks).
   - Archive infrequently accessed data in cold storage tiers (e.g., AWS S3 Glacier, Azure Cool Blob Storage).
2. **Increase IOPS or Throughput:**
   - Provision additional resources to meet demand.
   - Use RAID configurations or striped volumes to improve performance.
3. **Optimize Data Placement:**
   - Deploy data closer to compute resources to reduce latency.
4. **Monitor Storage Metrics:**
   - Use native tools like AWS CloudWatch or Azure Monitor to track throughput, latency, and IOPS.

Best Practice:

- Perform regular performance assessments to ensure storage configurations align with application needs.

Misconfigurations

Symptoms:

- Unexpected downtime or service disruptions.
- Security vulnerabilities, such as open ports or overly permissive IAM policies.
- Increased costs due to misallocated resources.

Common Causes:

1. **Human Error:**
    - Incorrect manual configurations during setup.
2. **Lack of Configuration Management:**
    - No centralized system to track or enforce configurations.
3. **Poor Security Practices:**
    - Weak IAM policies, unencrypted data, or exposed endpoints.

Solutions:

1. **Implement Infrastructure as Code (IaC):**
    - Use tools like Terraform, CloudFormation, or Ansible to standardize configurations.
2. **Automate Configuration Checks:**
    - Use tools like AWS Config, Azure Policy, or GCP Config Validator to enforce compliance.
3. **Enable Logging and Auditing:**
    - Turn on CloudTrail (AWS) or Activity Logs (Azure) to track changes and detect anomalies.
4. **Perform Regular Security Scans:**
    - Use security tools like AWS Inspector, Azure Security Center, or third-party solutions to identify vulnerabilities.

Best Practice:

- Use a CI/CD pipeline with automated validation to catch configuration errors before deployment.

Best Practices for Identifying Root Causes

1. **Establish Monitoring Baselines:**
    - Track normal performance metrics to identify deviations during issues.
    - Example tools: Datadog, Splunk, Prometheus, or native cloud monitoring tools.
2. **Centralize Logs and Metrics:**
    - Use log aggregation platforms like ELK Stack or Cloud-native logging tools to correlate events.
3. **Conduct Incident Postmortems:**
    - Review the root cause and mitigation steps after resolving an issue to prevent recurrence.
4. **Use Distributed Tracing:**
    - Implement tracing tools (e.g., OpenTelemetry, AWS X-Ray) to analyze issues in distributed systems.
5. **Document Known Issues:**
    - Maintain a repository of previous incidents and resolutions to accelerate troubleshooting.

Example Troubleshooting Workflow

Scenario: A retail application experiences slow response times during peak traffic.

1. **Monitor Metrics:**
    - Use AWS CloudWatch to check CPU, memory, and network utilization.
2. **Diagnose Latency:**
    - Run a traceroute to identify network bottlenecks.
    - Use CloudFront to cache static assets closer to users.
3. **Optimize Storage:**
    - Upgrade storage from AWS EBS gp2 to gp3 for higher IOPS.
4. **Audit Configurations:**
    - Review IAM policies and firewall settings for potential misconfigurations.
5. **Implement Fixes:**
    - Apply changes incrementally and monitor results to confirm resolution.

By addressing network latency, storage performance, and misconfigurations with proactive monitoring and well-defined workflows, organizations can maintain smooth operations and ensure the reliability of their cloud environments.

Networking Troubleshooting in the Cloud

Networking is the backbone of cloud environments, enabling communication between services, resources, and users. When network issues arise, they can significantly impact application performance and availability. This section focuses on diagnosing connectivity and bandwidth issues and highlights tools for monitoring and resolving network problems.

Diagnosing Connectivity and Bandwidth Issues

Connectivity and bandwidth issues can manifest as slow application responses, failed API calls, or complete communication breakdowns. Identifying the root cause requires a structured approach.

1. Common Symptoms and Causes

- **Symptoms:**
    - Intermittent or complete loss of connectivity.
    - Slow data transfer rates.
    - Packet drops or high latency.
- **Common Causes:**
    - Misconfigured network settings (e.g., subnets, routing tables, or security groups).
    - Bandwidth bottlenecks due to high traffic volumes.
    - Geographic distance between resources.
    - Firewall or access control restrictions.

2. Troubleshooting Steps

Step 1: Verify Resource Configuration

- **Action:** Check the configuration of virtual networks, subnets, and routing tables.
- **Common Issues:**
  - Incorrect CIDR ranges in subnets.
  - Misconfigured NAT gateways or VPNs.
  - Missing or conflicting routes in routing tables.
- **Example:**
  - A web server in AWS cannot access the internet because an internet gateway is not attached to the VPC.

Step 2: Test Connectivity

- **Action:** Use diagnostic tools to test network paths and connectivity.
- **Common Tools:**
  - **ping:** Tests reachability between resources.
  - **traceroute (or tracert):** Identifies routing paths and potential bottlenecks.
  - **telnet or nc:** Checks if specific ports are open and reachable.
- **Example:**
  - Run `ping <destination IP>` to test connectivity between a virtual machine and a database.

Step 3: Analyze Security Settings

- **Action:** Review firewall rules, security groups, and access control lists (ACLs).
- **Common Issues:**
  - Overly restrictive rules blocking required traffic.
  - Inconsistent rules across subnets or resources.
- **Example:**
  - A Lambda function fails to connect to a database due to missing inbound rules for the database port in the security group.

Step 4: Evaluate Bandwidth and Latency

- **Action:** Measure bandwidth utilization and latency.
- **Common Issues:**
  - Bandwidth limitations on virtual machines or network interfaces.
  - Latency caused by geographic distance or overloaded links.
- **Example:**
  - A multi-region application experiences high latency due to inter-region data transfers.

Step 5: Check Provider-Specific Issues

- **Action:** Investigate cloud provider status pages or incident reports.
- **Example:**
  - A regional outage in AWS affects connectivity to resources.

Tools for Monitoring and Fixing Network Problems

Cloud-native and third-party tools provide powerful capabilities for monitoring and resolving network issues.

1. Native Cloud Monitoring Tools

- **AWS:**
  - **VPC Flow Logs:** Captures IP traffic data for troubleshooting connectivity.
  - **CloudWatch:** Monitors metrics like network traffic, packet loss, and latency.
  - **AWS Reachability Analyzer:** Identifies connectivity issues between VPC resources.
- **Azure:**
  - **Network Watcher:** Offers tools like connection monitors, packet captures, and topology diagrams.
  - **Traffic Analytics:** Provides insights into network traffic patterns.
  - **Azure Monitor:** Tracks network performance and generates alerts for anomalies.
- **Google Cloud:**
  - **Network Intelligence Center:** Includes tools for connectivity tests, performance monitoring, and topology visualization.
  - **Cloud Logging:** Aggregates logs for VPC and firewall activity.

2. Third-Party Tools

- **Wireshark:**
  - A network protocol analyzer for in-depth packet inspection.
  - Useful for identifying specific network protocol issues.
- **NetFlow Tools:**
  - Tools like SolarWinds NetFlow Analyzer monitor traffic flows and identify bottlenecks.
- **Datadog:**
  - Provides comprehensive network performance monitoring with visual dashboards and alerts.
- **Zabbix:**
  - An open-source tool for monitoring network devices and cloud resources.

3. Automated Remediation Tools

- **Cloud Automation Platforms:**
  - Use automation tools like AWS Lambda, Azure Automation, or Google Cloud Functions to resolve recurring issues.
  - Example: Automatically adjusting security group rules when traffic anomalies are detected.
- **AI-Based Solutions:**
  - Tools like Dynatrace and AppDynamics use AI to detect and resolve network issues proactively.

Best Practices for Network Troubleshooting

1. **Establish a Baseline:**
   - Use monitoring tools to define normal network behavior, including average latency, bandwidth utilization, and packet loss rates.
2. **Enable Logging and Alerts:**
   - Configure alerts for anomalies like high latency, dropped packets, or unauthorized access attempts.
3. **Segment the Problem:**
   - Isolate the issue by testing connectivity between specific components, such as VMs, databases, or external endpoints.
4. **Document Known Issues:**
   - Maintain a repository of past network issues and their resolutions to expedite future troubleshooting.
5. **Simulate Failures:**
   - Regularly test network resilience using tools like Chaos Monkey or Traffic Manager to identify potential weaknesses.

Example Scenario: Troubleshooting a Cloud Network Issue

Scenario: A multi-region application hosted on AWS is experiencing intermittent connectivity issues between the web server and the database.

1. **Verify Resource Configuration:**
   - Check VPC routing tables and subnets.
   - Confirm that NAT gateways are configured for outbound traffic.
2. **Test Connectivity:**
   - Use `traceroute` to identify where packets are dropping.
   - Run `ping` from the web server to the database to test reachability.
3. **Review Security Settings:**
   - Check the security groups for inbound and outbound rules.
   - Verify that the database is accessible on the correct port (e.g., 3306 for MySQL).
4. **Monitor Bandwidth:**
   - Use AWS CloudWatch to track network traffic and identify bottlenecks.
5. **Resolve the Issue:**

- Update routing tables and security group rules to allow traffic.
- Adjust the database configuration to accept connections from the web server's subnet.

By following a structured approach and leveraging cloud-native and third-party tools, organizations can quickly diagnose and resolve networking issues, ensuring reliable cloud operations and optimal application performance.

Diagnosing Performance Bottlenecks

Performance bottlenecks in cloud environments can significantly impact application responsiveness, user experience, and overall efficiency. This section explores methods to identify bottlenecks in compute, storage, and networking and provides strategies for optimizing resource utilization to maintain high performance.

Identifying Issues in Compute, Storage, and Networking

1. Compute Bottlenecks

Symptoms:

- High CPU or memory utilization.
- Application latency or crashes during peak loads.
- Long task completion times.

Causes:

- Underprovisioned resources (e.g., insufficient CPU or memory).
- Inefficient application code or algorithms.
- Concurrent workloads exceeding resource limits.

Diagnosis:

1. **Monitor Compute Metrics:**
    - Use tools like AWS CloudWatch, Azure Monitor, or Google Cloud Operations Suite.
    - Track CPU utilization, memory usage, and thread counts.
2. **Analyze Resource Allocation:**
    - Check instance type and size to ensure they align with workload requirements.
    - Look for underutilized resources contributing to inefficiency.
3. **Identify Application Bottlenecks:**
    - Use APM (Application Performance Management) tools like New Relic or Datadog to profile code execution and pinpoint inefficiencies.

Solution:

- **Right-Size Instances:** Adjust instance types and sizes based on workload needs.
- **Autoscaling:** Enable dynamic scaling to handle fluctuating workloads.
- **Optimize Code:** Refactor inefficient code and optimize database queries.
- **Containerization:** Use lightweight containers to allocate resources more effectively.

2. Storage Bottlenecks

Symptoms:

- Slow read/write operations.
- High disk latency impacting application performance.
- Errors during data-intensive operations.

Causes:

- Mismatch between storage tier and workload (e.g., using cold storage for frequent access).
- Overloaded storage volumes.
- Inefficient data retrieval or excessive IOPS demand.

Diagnosis:

1. **Monitor Storage Metrics:**
    - Track IOPS, throughput, and latency using native tools like AWS CloudWatch or Azure Monitor.
2. **Analyze Workload Patterns:**
    - Review access patterns to determine if data retrieval aligns with the storage type.
3. **Inspect Configuration:**
    - Ensure that volumes are properly attached and configured for performance.

Solution:

- **Upgrade Storage Tiers:** Use high-performance storage like SSDs for latency-sensitive workloads (e.g., AWS EBS gp3, Azure Premium Disks).
- **Implement Caching:** Deploy caching layers (e.g., AWS ElastiCache, Azure Cache for Redis) to reduce storage overhead.
- **Optimize Data Placement:** Distribute data across multiple volumes or regions to reduce contention.
- **Enable Compression and Deduplication:** Reduce the size of stored data to optimize IOPS usage.

3. Networking Bottlenecks

Symptoms:

- High latency in application responses.
- Packet loss or timeouts during data transfer.
- Degraded performance in multi-region applications.

Causes:

- Congested network paths.
- Suboptimal routing between resources.
- Insufficient bandwidth for high-traffic applications.

Diagnosis:

1. **Monitor Network Metrics:**
   - Use tools like AWS VPC Flow Logs, Azure Network Watcher, or Google Network Intelligence Center.
   - Analyze metrics such as latency, bandwidth usage, and packet loss.
2. **Test Connectivity:**
   - Run tools like `ping`, `traceroute`, or cloud-specific network tests to identify problematic links.
3. **Inspect Traffic Patterns:**
   - Use network analyzers to identify heavy traffic sources or hotspots.

Solution:

- **Optimize Routing:** Adjust routing tables or use direct connectivity solutions like AWS Direct Connect or Azure ExpressRoute.
- **Implement Load Balancing:** Distribute traffic across multiple resources using tools like AWS Elastic Load Balancer or Azure Traffic Manager.
- **Scale Network Resources:** Increase bandwidth or provision additional endpoints for high-demand services.
- **Leverage CDNs:** Use content delivery networks (e.g., AWS CloudFront, Azure Front Door) to cache content closer to end users.

Optimizing Resource Utilization

Once bottlenecks are identified, the next step is to optimize resource utilization to prevent recurrence and enhance efficiency.

1. Implement Autoscaling

- **Definition:** Dynamically adjust compute resources based on workload demand.
- **Example:**

  - Use AWS Auto Scaling to increase instance capacity during traffic spikes and scale down during off-peak hours.

2. Use Resource Monitoring and Alerts

- **Tools:**
  - AWS CloudWatch, Azure Monitor, Google Cloud Operations Suite.
- **Benefits:**
  - Set thresholds and alerts for metrics like CPU, memory, and network traffic.
  - Proactively address issues before they escalate.

3. Adopt Infrastructure as Code (IaC)

- **Definition:** Manage and provision infrastructure through code using tools like Terraform, AWS CloudFormation, or Ansible.
- **Benefits:**
  - Standardized configurations reduce the risk of misconfigurations.
  - Enable quick re-provisioning and scalability.

4. Optimize Application Design

- **Techniques:**
  - Use microservices architecture to isolate workloads.
  - Implement serverless functions (e.g., AWS Lambda, Azure Functions) for event-driven tasks.
  - Use efficient data structures and algorithms.

5. Right-Size Resources

- **Description:** Continuously analyze workloads and adjust instance types, sizes, and tiers accordingly.
- **Example:**
  - Replace overprovisioned instances with burstable instance types like AWS T3 or Azure B-series.

Example Scenario: Diagnosing and Resolving Bottlenecks

Scenario: A video streaming platform experiences slow playback and buffering during peak usage.

Diagnosis:

1. **Compute:**
   - High CPU utilization detected on web servers.
   - Solution: Add more web server instances using autoscaling.
2. **Storage:**

- Increased latency on storage volumes due to high IOPS demand.
- Solution: Upgrade to SSD-backed volumes and implement a caching layer.

3. **Networking:**
   - Latency spikes in multi-region traffic.
   - Solution: Implement a CDN (e.g., AWS CloudFront) to cache content closer to users.

Result:

- Playback latency reduced by 50%.
- Resources dynamically scaled to handle peak demand.

By systematically identifying performance bottlenecks in compute, storage, and networking and applying optimization strategies, organizations can ensure their cloud environments remain efficient, scalable, and high-performing.

Resolving Security Incidents in Cloud Environments

Security incidents in cloud environments, such as breaches, malware infections, and unauthorized access, pose significant threats to an organization's operations and reputation. Effective incident response involves quickly identifying, containing, and remediating threats while restoring systems to a secure state. This section outlines strategies for handling common security incidents and ensuring rapid recovery.

Handling Breaches, Malware, and Unauthorized Access

1. Breaches: Data Exfiltration or Exposure

Definition:
A breach occurs when sensitive data is accessed or exposed without authorization, often through vulnerabilities or misconfigurations.

Steps to Address a Breach:

1. **Detect and Assess:**
   - Monitor logs for suspicious activity, such as unusual API calls, large data transfers, or access from unknown IPs.
   - Tools: AWS CloudTrail, Azure Monitor, Google Cloud Logging.
2. **Contain the Breach:**
   - Restrict access by modifying IAM policies or revoking compromised credentials.
   - Isolate affected resources, such as S3 buckets or databases, to prevent further data leakage.
3. **Investigate the Cause:**
   - Identify vulnerabilities or misconfigurations that enabled the breach.
   - Tools: Vulnerability scanners (e.g., Nessus, Qualys).
4. **Remediate:**

- Apply patches or updates to fix the vulnerability.
- Enhance access controls and enable encryption for sensitive data.

5. **Notify Stakeholders:**
   - Inform affected parties, including customers, regulators, and internal teams, as required by compliance laws.

2. Malware Infections

Definition:
Malware in cloud environments can compromise systems, exfiltrate data, or disrupt services.

Steps to Address Malware:

1. **Identify Symptoms:**
   - Look for unusual resource usage, such as CPU spikes or outbound traffic to unknown destinations.
   - Use threat detection tools like AWS GuardDuty or Azure Defender.
2. **Isolate Affected Resources:**
   - Quarantine infected instances or containers to prevent spread.
   - Disable compromised accounts or services.
3. **Scan and Remove Malware:**
   - Perform malware scans using tools like CrowdStrike or Microsoft Defender for Endpoint.
   - Terminate infected resources if necessary and redeploy clean instances from a trusted image.
4. **Restore Services:**
   - Replace infected components with patched or updated versions.
   - Update firewalls and endpoint protection systems to block similar threats.
5. **Perform a Root Cause Analysis:**
   - Determine how the malware entered (e.g., phishing, outdated software) and address underlying weaknesses.

3. Unauthorized Access

Definition:
Unauthorized access occurs when an attacker gains entry to systems, applications, or data without proper permissions.

Steps to Address Unauthorized Access:

1. **Detect Unauthorized Activity:**
   - Use log analysis and anomaly detection to identify access from unusual IPs or times.
   - Tools: AWS CloudWatch, Azure Sentinel, Google Cloud Security Command Center.
2. **Revoke Access:**

    - Disable compromised accounts or API keys immediately.
    - Change passwords and rotate access credentials.
3. **Investigate the Method:**
    - Check for compromised credentials, misconfigured IAM policies, or brute-force attempts.
    - Identify which systems or data the attacker accessed.
4. **Harden Security:**
    - Enable multi-factor authentication (MFA) for all accounts.
    - Apply the principle of least privilege to IAM roles and access controls.
5. **Monitor for Recurrence:**
    - Set up alerts for failed login attempts, privilege escalations, or other suspicious actions.

Restoring Systems to a Secure State

After containing the threat, restoring systems to normal operations while ensuring they are secure is critical.

1. Eradicate the Threat:

- Remove malware, backdoors, or unauthorized configurations.
- Reimage or rebuild compromised systems from clean backups.

2. Validate System Integrity:

- Run integrity checks on system files, configurations, and binaries.
- Use tools like Tripwire or AWS Inspector to detect anomalies.

3. Apply Patches and Updates:

- Patch vulnerabilities exploited in the incident.
- Regularly update operating systems, applications, and firmware.

4. Review and Harden Security Policies:

- Conduct a comprehensive review of IAM roles, security group rules, and encryption settings.
- Enforce policies such as MFA, least privilege, and network segmentation.

5. Test Recovery and Readiness:

- Perform disaster recovery tests to ensure backups are reliable.
- Use simulation tools like Chaos Monkey or Azure Resilience to validate system resilience.

6. Monitor Post-Recovery Activity:

- Increase monitoring of affected resources for unusual activity.
- Tools: SIEM platforms like Splunk, Datadog, or Sentinel.

Example Incident Response Workflow

Scenario: A company discovers that an unauthorized user accessed an S3 bucket containing sensitive customer data.

1. **Detection:**
    - AWS CloudTrail logs show unauthorized API calls to list and download bucket contents.
2. **Containment:**
    - Update the bucket policy to block public access.
    - Revoke the IAM user's credentials and disable the associated access key.
3. **Investigation:**
    - Use AWS Config to review changes to the bucket policy and identify misconfigurations.
    - Determine the scope of the data accessed or downloaded.
4. **Remediation:**
    - Apply encryption to the bucket and implement bucket-level logging.
    - Enforce IAM policies that restrict access to authorized IP ranges.
5. **Recovery:**
    - Notify affected customers and comply with regulatory reporting requirements.
    - Conduct a post-incident review to refine security practices.

Best Practices for Incident Response in Cloud Environments

1. **Prepare an Incident Response Plan:**
    - Define roles, responsibilities, and escalation paths for handling incidents.
2. **Enable Comprehensive Logging:**
    - Turn on audit logs for all critical services (e.g., AWS CloudTrail, Azure Activity Logs).
3. **Implement Proactive Monitoring:**
    - Use anomaly detection and behavioral analytics to identify threats early.
4. **Perform Regular Security Assessments:**
    - Conduct penetration testing and vulnerability scans to find and fix weaknesses.
5. **Train Response Teams:**
    - Conduct tabletop exercises and simulations to prepare teams for real-world incidents.
6. **Leverage Automation:**
    - Automate incident response workflows using tools like AWS Lambda or Azure Logic Apps.

By following a structured approach to handling security incidents and restoring systems to a secure state, organizations can mitigate risks, minimize downtime, and maintain customer trust in cloud environments.

Practical Troubleshooting Scenarios and Exercises

Hands-on troubleshooting not only develops technical expertise but also instills a mindset of logical problem-solving. This section narratively walks through real-world cloud challenges, weaving exercises into stories that mimic the dynamic, high-stakes nature of cloud operations. These scenarios provide both technical insight and practical solutions.

Exercise 1: Diagnosing Compute Bottlenecks

Scenario:
It's Cyber Monday, and an online retailer is basking in the glory of record-breaking traffic—until customers start complaining about slow checkout processes. The development team scrambles to identify the problem.

Step-by-Step:

- The **CloudWatch dashboard** reveals CPU utilization on the application server hovering near 100%. With sweat on their brows, the engineers realize the compute resources are inadequate for the traffic spike.
- To buy time, they restart the application, temporarily alleviating the issue.
- After analyzing workload demands, they decide to upgrade the EC2 instance type to a **compute-optimized option**. They also implement **autoscaling** so the system can handle future surges without intervention.
- With the application back on track, the checkout process speeds up, and sales flow smoothly again. The lesson? Always plan for scale during peak events.

Exercise 2: Resolving a Network Connectivity Issue

Scenario:
A fintech company launches a new feature that requires the web server to interact with a database. On day one, users encounter error messages, and the operations team realizes the web server cannot connect to the database.

Step-by-Step:

- The team first reviews **VPC configurations** and finds the database and web server on different subnets within the same VPC, confirming they should theoretically connect.
- The investigation shifts to **security groups**, where they discover a missing inbound rule on the database's group that should allow traffic from the web server on port 3306.
- After adding the rule, they test connectivity using **telnet** and confirm success.
- They take a deep breath of relief, document the fix, and implement stricter **change control processes** to avoid similar mishaps.

Exercise 3: Optimizing Storage Performance

Scenario:
A machine learning (ML) team complains that their training jobs take hours longer than expected. Frustrated, they approach the cloud infrastructure team for help.

Step-by-Step:

- The ML workloads are analyzed, revealing that the EBS volume in use is a **gp2 general-purpose SSD**, which isn't delivering the IOPS required for high-intensity data processing.
- The team upgrades the storage to a **gp3 SSD**, which provides better performance at a similar cost. They also adjust the training pipeline to cache frequently used data in **ElastiCache**.
- As the training speeds up, the ML team can focus on building better models, and the infrastructure team earns accolades for their quick thinking.

Exercise 4: Resolving a Security Breach

Scenario:
A healthcare organization detects unauthorized access to an S3 bucket containing sensitive patient records. The CEO demands immediate answers.

Step-by-Step:

- The security team immediately restricts public access to the bucket and disables the compromised IAM credentials identified in the **CloudTrail logs**.
- Using the logs, they trace the breach to a developer who unintentionally uploaded access keys to a public repository.
- After containing the threat, they enhance the bucket's security by enabling **encryption** and restricting permissions to specific roles.
- Post-incident, the team rolls out organization-wide **training on secure coding practices**, ensuring this oversight doesn't recur. Transparency with regulators and swift action help maintain public trust.

Exercise 5: Debugging Application Errors in a CI/CD Pipeline

Scenario:
A startup deploys an exciting new feature, only to see their CI/CD pipeline break. A cryptic error about a missing dependency halts progress.

Step-by-Step:

- The developer team gathers to debug. The error logs pinpoint a missing library in the application's environment.

- One developer replicates the pipeline locally and confirms the issue is due to a version mismatch in the **package.json** file.
- After updating the dependency version, they push the fix to the repository and rerun the pipeline. This time, the build passes, and deployment proceeds smoothly.
- The team adds a **pre-build dependency validation step** to their pipeline to catch such issues earlier in the future.

Exercise 6: Handling High Latency in a Multi-Region Application

Scenario:
A gaming company hosting its multiplayer platform in a US-based region receives complaints from players in Asia about unbearable lag. Frustrated users start leaving negative reviews.

Step-by-Step:

- Engineers run **latency tests** using tools like **Pingdom** and confirm high response times for players accessing resources from Asia.
- To resolve the issue, the team deploys instances of the gaming platform in an **Asia-Pacific region** and uses a **DNS-based traffic manager** to route players to the closest server.
- To further reduce latency, they integrate **AWS CloudFront** to cache static assets and deliver them locally.
- Latency complaints drop, and the platform's ratings recover. The team celebrates with a round of their own game—played lag-free, of course.

Takeaways from Practical Troubleshooting

1. **Expect the Unexpected:**
    - Real-world problems often arise from a combination of factors. Adopt a systematic approach to uncover root causes.
2. **Prioritize Monitoring:**
    - Use tools like CloudWatch, Azure Monitor, or Splunk to track metrics and set alerts that highlight anomalies before they escalate.
3. **Document Solutions:**
    - Maintain a knowledge base of resolved incidents to improve response times for similar issues.
4. **Collaborate and Communicate:**
    - Troubleshooting often involves multiple teams. Clear communication is key to resolving issues quickly.

Through these scenarios and exercises, cloud professionals can develop a deeper understanding of how to diagnose and resolve the most common challenges in cloud environments while fostering a proactive and resilient approach to cloud operations.

Chapter 9: Governance, Risk, and Compliance

Chapter 9 introduces the concept of cloud governance frameworks as essential tools for managing cloud environments effectively. These frameworks provide structured guidelines, policies, and controls to ensure consistency, security, and compliance in resource provisioning, cost management, and operations. By establishing clear policies, such as naming conventions, tagging standards, and resource quotas, organizations can prevent misconfigurations, security vulnerabilities, and financial inefficiencies. This chapter emphasizes the importance of governance in enabling teams to innovate within defined guardrails while maintaining alignment with organizational goals.

The chapter explores practical approaches to implementing governance frameworks, including the use of automation tools like Terraform, AWS Config, and Azure Policy to standardize configurations and enforce compliance. It highlights the role of centralized governance teams, such as Cloud Centers of Excellence, in defining and maintaining policies. Real-world examples demonstrate the impact of governance, such as reducing costs, enhancing security, and ensuring operational consistency across teams and regions. Readers are equipped with best practices to build robust governance frameworks that balance agility with control, enabling secure, scalable, and cost-effective cloud operations.

Defining Cloud Governance Frameworks

A cloud governance framework provides a structured approach to managing cloud resources, ensuring consistency, security, and compliance across teams and environments. This chapter explores the key components of cloud governance, strategies for developing effective policies, and techniques for maintaining alignment in diverse operational contexts.

What is a Cloud Governance Framework?

Imagine a rapidly growing organization adopting the cloud to scale its operations. Without clear policies, teams provision resources without oversight, leading to inconsistent configurations, security vulnerabilities, and unexpected costs. A cloud governance framework solves these problems by establishing rules and practices for managing cloud operations effectively.

A governance framework typically includes:

- **Policies:** Guidelines for resource provisioning, cost management, security, and compliance.
- **Controls:** Mechanisms to enforce policies and ensure adherence.
- **Tools:** Technologies that enable monitoring, automation, and reporting.

Policies for Managing Cloud Resources and Operations

1. Resource Provisioning and Configuration

- **Objective:** Prevent over-provisioning, underutilization, and misconfigurations.
- **Policy Components:**
    - Define naming conventions for resources (e.g., `<Team>-<Environment>-<ResourceType>`).
    - Establish quotas and limits to control resource sprawl.
    - Use tagging standards to categorize resources by department, project, or environment.
- **Example:**
    - Require all resources to be tagged with `ProjectName` and `Owner` to track accountability.

2. Cost Management

- **Objective:** Maintain financial transparency and control over cloud spending.
- **Policy Components:**
    - Set budgets for teams or projects and enforce cost alerts.
    - Require approval workflows for provisioning high-cost resources.
    - Implement lifecycle management policies to delete unused resources.
- **Example:**
    - Use AWS Budgets or Azure Cost Management to notify teams when they exceed 80% of their monthly budget.

3. Security and Compliance

- **Objective:** Protect data, systems, and applications from threats while meeting regulatory requirements.
- **Policy Components:**
  - Enforce encryption for data at rest and in transit.
  - Mandate the use of multi-factor authentication (MFA) for all accounts.
  - Use IAM roles to implement the principle of least privilege.
- **Example:**
  - Automatically disable public access to S3 buckets using AWS Config rules.

4. Operational Policies

- **Objective:** Ensure consistency and reliability in daily operations.
- **Policy Components:**
  - Define standardized CI/CD pipelines for deploying applications.
  - Mandate regular backups and disaster recovery drills.
  - Require periodic patching and vulnerability scans.
- **Example:**
  - Use Azure Policy to enforce a rule that all VMs have daily backups enabled.

Ensuring Consistency Across Teams and Environments

1. Establish Centralized Governance

- **Cloud Center of Excellence (CCoE):**
  - Form a team of cloud architects, security experts, and business stakeholders to define governance standards.
- **Responsibilities:**
  - Create and update governance policies.
  - Provide training and guidance to teams.

2. Standardize Through Automation

- **Infrastructure as Code (IaC):**
  - Use tools like Terraform, AWS CloudFormation, or Azure Resource Manager to enforce consistent configurations.
  - Example: Deploy a standard VPC template with preconfigured subnets, routing tables, and security groups.
- **Policy Enforcement Tools:**
  - Use tools like AWS Config, Azure Policy, or Google Config Validator to automate compliance checks.

3. Monitor and Report

- **Real-Time Monitoring:**
  - Track resource usage, compliance status, and security alerts using native tools (e.g., AWS CloudWatch, Azure Monitor).
- **Reporting:**
  - Generate regular reports on compliance, cost, and operational metrics for leadership review.

4. Empower Teams with Guardrails

- Allow teams to innovate within defined boundaries by using "guardrails."
- **Examples:**
  - Provide self-service resource provisioning but limit resource types to approved configurations.
  - Allow experimentation in development environments while enforcing strict controls in production.

Example: Building a Cloud Governance Framework

Scenario: A global retail company transitions to the cloud and needs a governance framework to manage multiple teams operating in different regions.

Steps:

1. **Define Policies:**
   - Naming conventions: `<Region>-<Team>-<ResourceType>-<Environment>` (e.g., `us-east-1-marketing-ec2-dev`).
   - Cost limits: Monthly budgets per team with alerts at 75%, 90%, and 100% thresholds.
   - Security rules: All storage must be encrypted, and public access must be disabled by default.
2. **Establish Controls:**
   - Use AWS Organizations to implement service control policies (SCPs) restricting unapproved services.
   - Enable Azure Blueprints to standardize configurations across regions.
3. **Automate Compliance:**
   - Configure AWS Config to audit compliance with tagging policies and security settings.
   - Set up automated cost reports using Google Cloud Billing.
4. **Monitor and Adjust:**
   - Use Splunk or Datadog for centralized monitoring and anomaly detection.
   - Conduct quarterly reviews to refine policies based on evolving needs.

Best Practices for Cloud Governance

1. **Start Small, Scale Gradually:**
   - Focus on core policies like security and cost management first, then expand to other areas.
2. **Use Multi-Cloud Tools for Consistency:**
   - Adopt tools like HashiCorp Terraform or Ansible to manage configurations across multiple cloud platforms.
3. **Train Teams Regularly:**
   - Provide ongoing training to ensure teams understand governance policies and their rationale.
4. **Review and Evolve:**
   - Revisit governance policies periodically to align with organizational growth and technological advancements.

By defining robust cloud governance frameworks, organizations can maintain control over their cloud environments while enabling innovation and agility. These frameworks serve as the foundation for secure, cost-effective, and scalable cloud operations.

Managing Risks in Cloud Deployments

Cloud deployments, while offering scalability and flexibility, come with their own set of risks that can threaten security, compliance, performance, and business continuity. This chapter explores how to identify and mitigate potential threats and introduces risk management frameworks and methodologies for ensuring secure and resilient cloud operations.

Identifying Potential Threats

The first step in managing risks is to identify vulnerabilities and potential threats that could impact cloud deployments. These can be categorized into several key areas:

1. Security Risks

- **Data Breaches:** Unauthorized access to sensitive data due to weak authentication or misconfigurations.
- **Insider Threats:** Malicious or accidental actions by employees or contractors that compromise cloud security.
- **Ransomware and Malware:** Malicious software targeting cloud-hosted systems.

2. Compliance Risks

- **Regulatory Violations:** Non-compliance with laws such as GDPR, HIPAA, or PCI DSS.
- **Data Residency:** Hosting data in regions with restrictive laws or inadequate protections.

3. Operational Risks

- **Downtime:** Service outages caused by misconfigurations, provider failures, or natural disasters.
- **Overprovisioning or Underprovisioning:** Inefficient resource management leading to increased costs or degraded performance.

4. Vendor Risks

- **Vendor Lock-In:** Difficulty in migrating workloads due to proprietary services or incompatible architectures.
- **Service Termination:** Sudden discontinuation of critical services by a cloud provider.

5. Financial Risks

- **Unexpected Costs:** Unplanned expenses due to resource mismanagement, overuse, or hidden fees.

Mitigating Potential Threats

Mitigation strategies aim to reduce the likelihood or impact of identified risks. Here are targeted approaches for each category:

1. Security Risk Mitigation

- **Enable Strong Authentication:** Require multi-factor authentication (MFA) for all accounts.
- **Encrypt Data:** Use encryption for data at rest and in transit.
- **Conduct Regular Penetration Testing:** Identify and address vulnerabilities in applications and infrastructure.
- **Automate Security Compliance Checks:** Use tools like AWS Config, Azure Policy, or Google Security Command Center to enforce security rules.

2. Compliance Risk Mitigation

- **Data Localization:** Store data in regions compliant with local laws (e.g., GDPR-compliant regions for EU data).
- **Auditing and Reporting:** Use tools like AWS CloudTrail or Azure Monitor to maintain detailed logs for audits.
- **Third-Party Assessments:** Engage external auditors to validate compliance.

3. Operational Risk Mitigation

- **Implement Redundancy:** Use multi-region deployments for high availability and disaster recovery.
- **Monitor Performance:** Track key metrics to detect issues before they escalate.

- **Enable Autoscaling:** Dynamically adjust resources to match demand.

4. Vendor Risk Mitigation

- **Adopt Open Standards:** Use open-source or standardized technologies to reduce lock-in.
- **Diversify Providers:** Implement a multi-cloud strategy to avoid over-reliance on a single vendor.
- **Negotiate SLAs:** Include stringent uptime and performance guarantees in contracts.

5. Financial Risk Mitigation

- **Set Budgets and Alerts:** Use tools like AWS Budgets or Azure Cost Management to track spending and prevent overruns.
- **Optimize Resources:** Regularly audit unused or underutilized resources.
- **Right-Size Workloads:** Match instance types and sizes to actual workload requirements.

Risk Management Frameworks and Methodologies

Adopting a structured approach to risk management ensures consistent practices across teams and projects. Common frameworks include:

1. NIST Risk Management Framework (RMF)

- **Purpose:** Provides guidelines for identifying, assessing, and mitigating risks in IT environments.
- **Steps:**
    1. **Categorize:** Define the system and its sensitivity.
    2. **Select Controls:** Choose appropriate security controls based on risk.
    3. **Implement Controls:** Apply selected controls.
    4. **Assess Effectiveness:** Verify that controls are functioning as intended.
    5. **Authorize Systems:** Approve the system for operation.
    6. **Monitor Continuously:** Track changes and reassess risks.

2. ISO 31000

- **Purpose:** Offers a generic framework for managing all types of organizational risks, including cloud-specific ones.
- **Steps:**
    - **Establish Context:** Define the scope and objectives of risk management.
    - **Identify Risks:** List potential risks and their sources.
    - **Analyze and Evaluate Risks:** Assess likelihood and impact.
    - **Treat Risks:** Develop mitigation strategies.
    - **Monitor and Review:** Continuously track risks and update strategies.

3. FAIR Model (Factor Analysis of Information Risk)

- **Purpose:** Focuses on quantifying information risk in financial terms.
- **Key Components:**
  - **Threat Event Frequency (TEF):** Likelihood of an attack.
  - **Vulnerability (V):** Probability that an attack will succeed.
  - **Loss Magnitude (LM):** Impact of the event.

4. Cloud-Specific Best Practices

- Use cloud-native tools for governance and security (e.g., AWS Well-Architected Framework, Azure Security Center).
- Establish a Cloud Center of Excellence (CCoE) to oversee governance and risk management.

Example: Implementing Risk Management in Practice

Scenario: A financial services company migrating to the cloud wants to ensure data security, compliance with PCI DSS, and minimal operational risks.

Steps:

1. **Identify Risks:**
   - **Data Breach:** Sensitive transaction data could be exposed.
   - **Downtime:** System outages could disrupt customer transactions.
   - **Vendor Lock-In:** Proprietary technologies could hinder future migration.
2. **Mitigate Risks:**
   - **Security Controls:**
     - Enable encryption for all storage and databases.
     - Use IAM roles to enforce least privilege access.
   - **Compliance Measures:**
     - Store payment data in PCI-compliant regions.
     - Enable detailed logging for audit trails.
   - **Operational Practices:**
     - Deploy across multiple regions for redundancy.
     - Implement automated failover mechanisms.
3. **Apply a Framework:**
   - Follow the **NIST RMF** to categorize sensitive systems, select and implement controls, and continuously monitor operations.
4. **Test and Monitor:**
   - Conduct quarterly disaster recovery drills.
   - Use AWS Trusted Advisor and Azure Policy for ongoing compliance checks.

Best Practices for Managing Risks in Cloud Deployments

1. **Adopt a Risk-First Mindset:**
   - Continuously identify and prioritize risks as environments evolve.
2. **Leverage Automation:**
   - Use automated tools for compliance, monitoring, and remediation to reduce human error.
3. **Train and Empower Teams:**
   - Regularly train staff on security best practices and risk management methodologies.
4. **Engage Stakeholders:**
   - Include legal, compliance, and business leaders in the risk management process.
5. **Continuously Monitor and Adapt:**
   - Use tools like SIEM platforms, anomaly detection, and cloud-native monitoring to stay ahead of emerging threats.

By systematically identifying and addressing risks, organizations can build secure, compliant, and resilient cloud environments that support long-term business goals.

Implementing Policies and Procedures

The success of any cloud operation lies in its ability to balance innovation with control. Policies and procedures provide this balance by offering a clear set of guidelines for managing resources, ensuring security, and maintaining operational consistency. Through the lens of real-world examples, this chapter demonstrates how access controls, auditing, and change management combine with automation to enforce policies across dynamic cloud environments.

Access Controls: The First Line of Defense

Scenario: A Startup's Wake-Up Call

A fintech startup launched a mobile payment app that gained rapid traction. In the excitement, development teams provisioned resources without much oversight, using shared credentials and granting broad access to critical systems. Everything worked fine—until it didn't.

One day, a malicious actor gained access to the company's cloud environment, exploiting a leaked key stored in a public repository. Sensitive customer data was at risk. The startup quickly realized they lacked robust access controls and scrambled to mitigate the damage.

What They Did:

1. **Defined Roles and Responsibilities:**
   - They adopted **Role-Based Access Control (RBAC)**, creating distinct roles for developers, administrators, and auditors.
   - IAM roles were defined with precise permissions, ensuring that developers could deploy code without touching production databases.

2. **Enabled Multi-Factor Authentication (MFA):**
   - MFA became mandatory for all users, adding a layer of protection against compromised credentials.
3. **Implemented Conditional Access:**
   - Using their cloud provider's tools, they restricted access based on IP address and geolocation.

Result:

- Within weeks, the startup transformed its access management practices. Each team member had only the access they needed, minimizing the attack surface and restoring confidence among customers and investors.

Auditing: Building a Culture of Accountability

Scenario: The Audit That Saved a Company

A mid-sized e-commerce company, expanding rapidly, decided to prepare for an ISO 27001 certification. During their internal audit, they discovered alarming gaps in their cloud environment:

- S3 buckets storing customer invoices were publicly accessible.
- Logs were not enabled for critical resources, making activity tracking impossible.

The audit, though stressful, proved invaluable.

What They Did:

1. **Enabled Comprehensive Logging:**
   - They turned on **AWS CloudTrail** to capture all API activity.
   - Log data was sent to a centralized **Amazon S3 bucket** with restricted access.
2. **Set Up Alerts for Anomalies:**
   - Using **AWS Config**, they created rules to detect and alert on public S3 buckets or untagged resources.
3. **Automated Compliance Reporting:**
   - The team used **Splunk** to generate reports for auditors, highlighting their adherence to ISO 27001 controls.

Result:

- The company not only passed its certification audit but also established a culture of accountability, with proactive measures to ensure compliance moving forward.

Change Management: From Chaos to Control

Scenario: A Retail Giant Learns the Value of Process

During a routine deployment, a developer at a major retailer accidentally overwrote a production database. With no immediate rollback strategy, the website went down for hours, resulting in lost revenue and a PR nightmare.

The incident was a turning point, prompting the organization to adopt a formal change management process.

What They Did:

1. **Introduced Approval Workflows:**
   - All changes required detailed documentation and review through **ServiceNow** before implementation.
   - Critical changes had to be approved by a change advisory board (CAB).
2. **Standardized CI/CD Pipelines:**
   - They integrated **Jenkins** pipelines with automated tests and rollbacks, ensuring changes were validated before reaching production.
3. **Implemented Deployment Strategies:**
   - Blue-green deployments became the norm, allowing seamless rollouts without disrupting the customer experience.
4. **Ran Regular Disaster Drills:**
   - Quarterly exercises simulated incidents, testing the organization's ability to respond and recover.

Result:

- The new processes drastically reduced incidents caused by human error. When an issue arose, rollback mechanisms ensured rapid recovery.

Policy Enforcement Through Automation: A Game Changer

Scenario: Scaling Governance Across Teams

A global healthcare provider operating in multiple regions faced the challenge of maintaining consistent policies across its cloud environments. Manual enforcement was impractical given the scale, leading to inconsistent configurations and non-compliance in some regions.

What They Did:

1. **Adopted Infrastructure as Code (IaC):**
   - Using **Terraform**, they created reusable templates for deploying resources with pre-defined security configurations.

    - Templates enforced tagging standards, encryption requirements, and network access controls.
2. **Enabled Automated Compliance Checks:**
    - Tools like **AWS Config** monitored configurations in real time, automatically correcting deviations (e.g., disabling public access to an S3 bucket).
3. **Integrated Compliance into CI/CD Pipelines:**
    - Before deploying infrastructure, **Checkov** scanned Terraform templates to detect and fix non-compliant configurations.
4. **Automated Remediation:**
    - **AWS Lambda** functions were set to handle common violations, such as adding missing tags or revoking open security group rules.

Result:

- Policy enforcement became seamless and scalable. Teams retained the agility to innovate while staying within guardrails.

Lessons Learned: The Power of Policies and Procedures

1. **Proactive Beats Reactive:**
    - Many organizations adopt policies after incidents. Instead, establish strong governance from the outset.
2. **Automation is Key:**
    - Manual enforcement is not scalable. Tools like AWS Config and Azure Policy enable consistent, real-time enforcement.
3. **Policies Evolve:**
    - Regularly revisit and update policies to address emerging risks, technologies, and business needs.
4. **Empower Teams with Guardrails:**
    - Governance doesn't have to stifle innovation. With guardrails, teams can experiment safely and responsibly.

By weaving access controls, auditing, and change management into their operations—and automating enforcement—organizations can build secure, compliant, and resilient cloud environments. These practices empower teams to innovate confidently while ensuring alignment with organizational goals.

Auditing Cloud Environments

Auditing a cloud environment is akin to shining a spotlight on an intricate machine, uncovering not only its vulnerabilities but also its strengths. In today's fast-paced digital landscape, where organizations depend on the cloud for agility and scalability, robust auditing practices ensure security, compliance, and operational integrity. This chapter delves deep into the art and science of cloud audits, illustrating the process with compelling narratives, practical examples, and actionable insights.

The Purpose of Cloud Audits

Auditing is not merely a box-checking exercise; it is a proactive strategy to identify weaknesses, mitigate risks, and align operations with industry standards. Organizations conduct cloud audits for several reasons:

- **Security:** To detect misconfigurations, unauthorized access, or vulnerabilities that could lead to breaches.
- **Compliance:** To demonstrate adherence to regulations like GDPR, HIPAA, or PCI DSS.
- **Cost Optimization:** To identify unused or underutilized resources that inflate expenses.
- **Operational Consistency:** To ensure configurations meet organizational standards across environments.

Consider a multinational corporation managing multiple cloud accounts across regions. Without periodic audits, each team could operate with varying configurations, introducing inefficiencies and risks. A robust audit brings these inconsistencies to light, fostering harmony across the organization.

The Auditing Process: From Discovery to Remediation

Imagine this: A cybersecurity team at a healthcare provider prepares for an annual HIPAA compliance audit. Patient trust and regulatory fines are on the line. The process begins with defining the scope of the audit and culminates in actionable reports.

1. Preparing for the Audit: Setting the Stage

The team starts by defining what the audit will cover. They outline objectives such as verifying encryption for patient data, ensuring access logs are enabled, and checking firewall rules for misconfigurations.

To streamline the process, they enable logging services:

- **AWS CloudTrail** records API activity.
- **VPC Flow Logs** capture network traffic.
- **GuardDuty** monitors for threats like unauthorized access or anomalous behavior.

By centralizing these logs in a SIEM platform, the team ensures they have a comprehensive view of their cloud environment.

2. Gathering Data: The Foundation of Insights

With the scope defined, the team collects data from various services:

- **IAM Policies:** Are any roles granting excessive permissions?
- **Storage Configurations:** Are all S3 buckets encrypted and private?

- **Network Security:** Are security groups overly permissive, allowing unnecessary inbound traffic?

Using tools like AWS Config and Azure Security Center, they quickly identify deviations from best practices. For example, they find an S3 bucket containing patient records is publicly accessible—a critical compliance violation.

3. Analyzing Findings: The Moment of Truth

The collected data undergoes meticulous analysis. The team prioritizes findings based on severity:

- **Critical:** Publicly accessible buckets with sensitive data.
- **High:** Unpatched servers vulnerable to exploitation.
- **Medium:** Lack of MFA enforcement for privileged accounts.

Each finding is cross-referenced against HIPAA requirements, ensuring the audit aligns with regulatory standards. For instance, they note that encryption is mandatory for patient data but is missing for 10% of their storage volumes.

Remediation: Turning Insights into Action

Discovering vulnerabilities is only the first step. Remediation ensures identified risks are mitigated effectively.

1. Fixing Misconfigurations The team begins with the critical issue of the exposed S3 bucket. They:

- Update the bucket policy to restrict access to authorized IAM roles.
- Enable server-side encryption with AWS Key Management Service (KMS).
- Implement a lifecycle policy to archive old data to a more secure storage class.

2. Automating Future Compliance To prevent similar issues, they deploy an AWS Config rule that automatically disables public access for newly created buckets. If a violation occurs, the rule triggers an AWS Lambda function to remediate the issue in real-time.

3. Patching Vulnerabilities Unpatched servers are updated through automated scripts in a CI/CD pipeline, minimizing downtime while ensuring compliance.

4. Strengthening Access Controls To address the lack of MFA, the team mandates its use for all privileged accounts. They use IAM Access Analyzer to monitor for unauthorized changes to roles and policies.

The Power of Reporting: Communicating the Findings

An audit's value lies in its ability to translate technical findings into actionable insights for stakeholders. The healthcare provider generates a detailed report with sections tailored to various audiences.

1. Executive Summary: For Leadership This section highlights:

- Key risks (e.g., "10% of storage volumes lack encryption").
- Business impact (e.g., "Non-compliance with HIPAA could result in fines up to $1 million").
- Mitigation actions and progress (e.g., "Encryption implemented for all critical storage").

2. Technical Details: For IT Teams Here, the team includes:

- A breakdown of vulnerabilities with affected resources.
- Steps taken to remediate each issue.
- Tools and methodologies used, such as the specific AWS Config rules enforced.

3. Compliance Overview: For Auditors This section maps findings to HIPAA requirements, demonstrating where the organization meets standards and highlighting ongoing improvements.

The report's visualizations, such as pie charts showing compliance status and graphs tracking remediation timelines, make the data accessible and actionable.

Real-World Narratives: Why Auditing Matters

A Crisis Averted At a financial institution, an audit revealed that 20% of its IAM roles granted excessive permissions, violating internal security policies. Before the issue could be exploited, the organization enforced the principle of least privilege, reducing its attack surface and avoiding potential fines under PCI DSS.

Turning Insight into Efficiency A media company's audit uncovered 500 unused EC2 instances, costing the business $20,000 monthly. After addressing the issue, they reinvested the savings into their content delivery strategy.

Best Practices for Effective Cloud Audits

1. **Automate Wherever Possible**
    - Use tools like AWS Security Hub or Google Security Command Center to streamline data collection and analysis.
2. **Regularly Schedule Audits**
    - Conduct audits quarterly or annually to ensure continuous compliance and operational efficiency.
3. **Collaborate Across Teams**

- Involve security, IT, and compliance teams to ensure audits address all organizational needs.

4. **Train Your Workforce**
   - Educate teams on audit objectives, methodologies, and tools to build a culture of accountability.
5. **Focus on Remediation**
   - Prioritize actionable insights over exhaustive lists of vulnerabilities.

The Value of Cloud Audits

Through a combination of meticulous data collection, insightful analysis, and actionable reporting, cloud audits enable organizations to secure their environments, ensure compliance, and optimize operations. By treating audits not as a burden but as a strategic opportunity, organizations can build resilient and scalable systems that inspire confidence among stakeholders and customers alike.

Aligning Cloud Practices with Organizational Goals

Cloud computing has revolutionized how organizations innovate and operate, enabling them to scale rapidly, improve efficiency, and reduce costs. However, aligning cloud practices with broader organizational goals requires balancing the drive for innovation with the need for effective risk management and governance. This chapter explores strategies for achieving alignment and supporting business objectives through robust cloud governance.

Balancing Innovation with Risk Management

Scenario: A Retailer's Race to Innovate

A global retailer sees an opportunity to revolutionize its customer experience through AI-driven recommendations. To move quickly, the development team deploys a machine learning platform directly into the cloud. While the project launches successfully, it soon becomes clear that security controls were overlooked. A misconfigured storage bucket containing customer data is inadvertently exposed, creating a crisis that stalls innovation and damages trust.

This scenario highlights the tension between innovation and risk management. Successful alignment requires striking a balance between speed and security, creativity and control.

1. Foster a Culture of Shared Responsibility

Innovation thrives when teams understand their roles in safeguarding organizational interests. To this end:

- **Encourage Collaboration:** Bring together developers, security professionals, and business leaders early in the project lifecycle.
- **Embed Security in the Development Workflow:** Adopt **DevSecOps** practices to integrate security checks into CI/CD pipelines.

Example: A financial services firm implements automated vulnerability scans in its CI/CD process, enabling developers to address security issues before deployment.

2. Implement Guardrails, Not Roadblocks

Rather than stifling innovation with rigid rules, provide flexible frameworks that empower teams while managing risks.

- **Automated Governance:** Use tools like **AWS Config** or **Azure Policy** to enforce critical controls (e.g., encryption or resource tagging) without manual intervention.
- **Role-Based Permissions:** Leverage IAM policies to ensure teams have the access they need—no more, no less.

Example: An e-commerce company allows developers to provision instances autonomously but ensures that all resources are automatically tagged with `ProjectName` and `Owner` for accountability.

3. Embrace Iterative Risk Management

In dynamic cloud environments, risk evolves alongside innovation. Adopt a proactive, iterative approach:

- **Continuous Monitoring:** Use tools like **Datadog** or **Splunk** to track real-time performance and security metrics.
- **Regular Audits:** Conduct quarterly reviews of configurations, costs, and compliance to identify and mitigate emerging risks.

Example: A media company identifies unoptimized workloads during a routine audit, saving 30% on cloud expenses through right-sizing.

Supporting Business Objectives Through Cloud Governance

Cloud governance ensures that cloud practices align with organizational goals, whether improving customer experience, accelerating time-to-market, or optimizing costs.

1. Align Governance with Strategic Goals

Effective governance begins with understanding how cloud initiatives support the organization's mission. For example:

- **Goal:** A healthcare provider aims to enhance patient care by implementing a telemedicine platform.
- **Governance:** Enforce HIPAA compliance, ensure high availability, and enable real-time analytics to support the platform's objectives.

Framework: Use the **AWS Well-Architected Framework** or similar methodologies to evaluate and align cloud architectures with business goals.

2. Enable Innovation Through Guardrails

Governance should guide teams toward responsible innovation:

- **Predefined Templates:** Use Infrastructure as Code (IaC) templates to standardize resource configurations.
- **Tagging Strategies:** Implement consistent tagging for cost tracking, ownership, and compliance.

Example: A global logistics firm uses **Terraform modules** to deploy pre-approved virtual networks, ensuring scalability and security across regions.

3. Support Cost Optimization

Managing cloud spend aligns directly with business goals by preserving resources for strategic investments. To achieve this:

- **Set Budgets and Alerts:** Use tools like **Azure Cost Management** or **AWS Budgets** to track and control spending.
- **Optimize Workloads:** Regularly analyze resource utilization and right-size or decommission underused assets.

Example: A software-as-a-service (SaaS) company saves 20% annually by scheduling non-critical workloads to run during off-peak hours.

4. Drive Business Agility

Cloud governance should empower teams to respond swiftly to changing business needs:

- **Dynamic Scaling:** Use autoscaling for applications to handle demand spikes during events like Black Friday.
- **Multi-Region Deployments:** Ensure global availability and disaster recovery for mission-critical applications.

Example: An entertainment company scales its streaming service across multiple AWS regions to ensure seamless performance during a new show's global premiere.

Case Study: A Technology Firm's Cloud Governance Journey

Challenge:
A fast-growing tech startup struggled with rising cloud costs, inconsistent configurations, and security vulnerabilities as it expanded globally.

Actions Taken:

1. **Defined Governance Policies:**
   - Established naming conventions, tagging standards, and cost control mechanisms.
   - Required encryption for all data at rest and in transit.
2. **Automated Policy Enforcement:**
   - Used **Google Cloud Policy Analyzer** to detect and remediate misconfigurations in real time.
   - Integrated security scans into CI/CD pipelines.
3. **Aligned Practices with Business Goals:**
   - Focused on reducing time-to-market by empowering teams to provision resources autonomously while adhering to compliance rules.

Outcome:

- Achieved a 30% reduction in cloud spending through resource optimization.
- Enhanced security posture by eliminating misconfigurations.
- Accelerated development cycles, enabling the company to launch features 20% faster.

Best Practices for Aligning Cloud Practices with Organizational Goals

1. **Engage Stakeholders Early:**
   - Include business leaders, developers, and security teams in governance discussions to ensure alignment with strategic objectives.
2. **Adopt Cloud-Native Tools:**
   - Leverage governance tools provided by cloud providers (e.g., AWS Organizations, Azure Blueprints) to automate and enforce policies.
3. **Regularly Reevaluate Governance:**
   - As the organization evolves, revisit policies and practices to ensure they remain aligned with goals.
4. **Foster a Learning Culture:**
   - Provide training and resources to help teams understand governance frameworks and their role in achieving business success.
5. **Measure and Report Outcomes:**
   - Track metrics like cost savings, compliance rates, and deployment times to demonstrate the impact of governance.

By aligning cloud practices with organizational goals, businesses can harness the power of the cloud to innovate responsibly, optimize costs, and deliver value to customers. Through balanced governance, organizations can empower teams to move fast while staying secure and compliant, creating a sustainable foundation for long-term success.

Chapter 10: Emerging Cloud Technologies

Emerging cloud technologies are transforming how organizations innovate and operate, driving efficiency, scalability, and sustainability. Serverless computing enables developers to focus on application logic without managing infrastructure, offering cost efficiency and faster time-to-market for use cases like data processing, IoT, and real-time analytics. Edge computing and IoT reduce latency by processing data closer to its source, enabling real-time decision-making for applications in smart cities, healthcare, and industrial automation. AI/ML services from providers like AWS, Azure, and Google Cloud democratize advanced analytics, making it easier to develop and deploy models for personalized recommendations, anomaly detection, and predictive insights. Additionally, green cloud initiatives focus on reducing the environmental impact of cloud operations through renewable energy, energy-efficient data centers, and resource optimization strategies.

Looking ahead, multi-cloud and hybrid cloud adoption will become standard as organizations leverage the strengths of multiple providers to optimize performance, cost, and compliance. Quantum computing, integrated with cloud platforms, is set to revolutionize industries like finance, healthcare, and logistics by solving complex problems at unprecedented speed. As these technologies evolve, businesses must remain agile, adopt open standards, and embrace sustainable practices to stay competitive. By harnessing the potential of these innovations, organizations can drive transformative outcomes, from improving operational efficiency to achieving environmental goals, while preparing for the next wave of digital transformation.

Serverless Computing

Serverless computing has transformed how applications are developed and deployed, enabling organizations to focus on code and innovation rather than infrastructure management. This chapter explores the benefits and use cases of serverless architectures, highlighting popular platforms like AWS Lambda and Azure Functions that power this paradigm.

What is Serverless Computing?

Serverless computing is a cloud-native model where developers write and deploy code without managing the underlying infrastructure. The term "serverless" doesn't mean there are no servers but rather that the cloud provider handles server management, scaling, and maintenance.

Key Characteristics:

1. **No Server Management:** Developers focus solely on application logic; the provider manages the hardware, operating system, and runtime.
2. **Event-Driven Execution:** Functions are triggered by specific events, such as HTTP requests, file uploads, or database changes.
3. **Auto-Scaling:** Resources automatically scale up or down based on demand.
4. **Pay-Per-Use Pricing:** Costs are based on the actual execution time and resource consumption, making it cost-effective for variable workloads.

Benefits of Serverless Architectures

1. Cost Efficiency

- **Pay for What You Use:** Organizations are billed only for the compute time consumed, with no charges for idle resources.
- **Reduced Operational Costs:** Serverless eliminates the need for infrastructure management, reducing overhead.

Example:

- A startup uses AWS Lambda to process image uploads. With no servers to manage, they save on hosting costs and only pay for the milliseconds their code runs.

2. Scalability

- **Automatic Scaling:** Functions scale dynamically to handle spikes in traffic without manual intervention.
- **Global Reach:** Deploy serverless functions close to users in multiple regions, reducing latency.

Example:

- An e-commerce platform uses Azure Functions to handle checkout requests during Black Friday sales. The functions scale automatically to accommodate the surge in traffic.

3. Faster Time to Market

- **Streamlined Development:** Developers focus on writing code instead of configuring servers.
- **Built-In Integration:** Serverless platforms offer seamless integration with other cloud services, like databases, APIs, and monitoring tools.

Example:

- A fintech company rapidly develops a payment gateway using Google Cloud Functions, reducing time-to-market by weeks.

4. Resilience and Availability

- **High Availability:** Serverless platforms are designed for fault tolerance, ensuring consistent performance.
- **Managed Maintenance:** Providers handle updates, patches, and infrastructure health.

Example:

- A social media platform uses AWS Lambda for user notifications, benefiting from the platform's built-in redundancy and high uptime.

Use Cases for Serverless Computing

1. Data Processing and Analytics

- **Scenario:** A media company processes millions of video uploads daily.
- **Solution:** Use AWS Lambda to transcode videos as they are uploaded to Amazon S3, enabling fast, scalable processing.

2. Backend for Mobile and Web Apps

- **Scenario:** A food delivery app needs a backend to handle user requests, such as order placement and status tracking.
- **Solution:** Azure Functions serve as a lightweight backend, interfacing with databases and APIs.

3. Real-Time Stream Processing

- **Scenario:** A financial firm processes stock market data in real time to provide live insights.
- **Solution:** Google Cloud Functions analyze data streams from Pub/Sub, triggering alerts for market anomalies.

4. Event-Driven Workflows

- **Scenario:** An e-commerce platform updates inventory after every purchase.
- **Solution:** AWS Lambda functions are triggered by DynamoDB changes to update inventory and notify suppliers.

5. Chatbots and Virtual Assistants

- **Scenario:** A retailer wants a chatbot to enhance customer support.
- **Solution:** Azure Functions integrate with AI services like Azure Cognitive Services to power the chatbot's natural language processing.

6. IoT Applications

- **Scenario:** A smart home system processes sensor data for temperature and lighting adjustments.
- **Solution:** AWS Lambda handles IoT data ingestion and triggers actions based on predefined rules.

Popular Serverless Platforms

1. AWS Lambda

- **Overview:** Pioneered serverless computing, offering seamless integration with AWS services.
- **Features:**
  - Supports multiple runtimes (Node.js, Python, Java, etc.).
  - Event sources include S3, DynamoDB, API Gateway, and CloudWatch.
  - Flexible memory and timeout settings for diverse workloads.
- **Example:**
  - A gaming company uses Lambda to analyze player activity and update leaderboards in real time.

2. Azure Functions

- **Overview:** Microsoft's serverless platform designed for integration with Azure services and beyond.
- **Features:**

    - Supports event triggers from Azure services like Blob Storage, Event Hubs, and Cosmos DB.
    - Offers a **Durable Functions** extension for stateful workflows.
    - Integrated development environment (IDE) support, including Visual Studio.
- **Example:**
    - A healthcare provider uses Azure Functions to process and store patient records in a secure, compliant manner.

3. Google Cloud Functions

- **Overview:** Google's serverless platform with strong integration into the Google Cloud ecosystem.
- **Features:**
    - Supports event-driven triggers from Pub/Sub, Cloud Storage, and Firebase.
    - Built-in monitoring with Google Cloud Operations Suite.
    - Supports popular languages like Node.js, Python, and Go.
- **Example:**
    - A media startup uses Cloud Functions to generate thumbnails for images uploaded to Google Cloud Storage.

4. IBM Cloud Functions

- **Overview:** Built on Apache OpenWhisk, offering flexibility for building serverless applications.
- **Features:**
    - Supports integrations with Watson AI and other IBM services.
    - Open-source and extensible.
- **Example:**
    - A research organization uses IBM Cloud Functions for scientific data analysis, leveraging Watson for AI-driven insights.

5. Other Notable Platforms

- **Oracle Functions:** Designed for enterprise applications with integration into Oracle Cloud.
- **Alibaba Cloud Function Compute:** Focused on scalability and cost efficiency for the Asia-Pacific market.

Challenges and Considerations

While serverless computing offers many benefits, organizations must navigate certain challenges:

1. **Cold Starts:**
    - Initial invocation of a function can introduce latency.
    - Mitigation: Use provisions like AWS Lambda's **Provisioned Concurrency**.

2. **Vendor Lock-In:**
    - Functions are tightly integrated with specific cloud services, complicating migration.
    - Mitigation: Adopt portable frameworks like **Serverless Framework** or **Knative**.
3. **Resource Limits:**
    - Execution time and memory are limited by the platform.
    - Mitigation: Divide workloads into smaller, modular functions.

Summary

Serverless computing empowers organizations to innovate quickly while reducing the burden of infrastructure management. With platforms like AWS Lambda, Azure Functions, and Google Cloud Functions, businesses can build scalable, resilient applications tailored to their needs. Whether processing data, powering mobile backends, or enabling IoT, serverless is the foundation of the next generation of cloud-native applications.

Edge Computing and IoT in the Cloud

Edge computing and the Internet of Things (IoT) are transforming how organizations interact with data, devices, and users. These technologies push computing closer to where data is generated, reducing latency and enabling real-time decision-making. This chapter explores the role of edge computing in minimizing latency and examines strategies for managing IoT devices in cloud environments.

The Role of Edge Computing in Reducing Latency

Edge computing is a distributed computing paradigm that brings computation and data storage closer to the sources of data, such as IoT devices, users, or sensors. Unlike traditional cloud architectures where data travels to centralized data centers, edge computing processes data near its origin, minimizing latency and improving performance.

1. Why Latency Matters

In many use cases, even milliseconds of delay can have significant consequences. Examples include:

- **Autonomous Vehicles:** Real-time decision-making is critical for safety.
- **Healthcare:** Remote monitoring devices need to alert medical staff instantly during emergencies.
- **Retail:** Smart checkout systems require immediate responses for seamless customer experiences.

Traditional cloud architectures can struggle with these latency-sensitive applications due to the time it takes for data to travel to and from centralized data centers. Edge computing addresses this by reducing the distance data needs to travel.

2. How Edge Computing Reduces Latency

Key Mechanisms:

1. **Local Data Processing:**
    - Computation occurs on or near the device generating the data.
    - Example: A factory uses an edge gateway to analyze sensor data locally for real-time equipment monitoring.
2. **Proximity to Users:**
    - Content is delivered from edge locations closer to end-users, improving performance.
    - Example: A video streaming service caches content in edge servers near viewers, reducing buffering.
3. **Offloading to Edge Devices:**
    - Certain workloads are handled by edge devices, reducing the burden on central cloud infrastructure.
    - Example: A smart city processes traffic sensor data locally to adjust signals in real time.

3. Cloud Providers and Edge Computing Solutions

Cloud providers have recognized the importance of edge computing and offer services to support it:

- **AWS:** AWS Outposts and AWS IoT Greengrass provide local processing capabilities integrated with the AWS ecosystem.
- **Microsoft Azure:** Azure Stack Edge allows on-premises data processing while integrating with Azure for centralized management.
- **Google Cloud:** Google Distributed Cloud provides edge solutions for latency-critical workloads.

Managing IoT Devices in Cloud Environments

IoT ecosystems consist of connected devices that generate, transmit, and analyze data. Managing these devices in cloud environments requires robust solutions for device provisioning, monitoring, and security.

1. Challenges in IoT Device Management

Scale:
IoT deployments can involve millions of devices, requiring scalable management solutions.

Diversity:
IoT devices often use varied hardware, operating systems, and communication protocols.

Security Risks:
IoT devices can be entry points for cyberattacks, making secure device management essential.

Latency Sensitivity:
Many IoT applications, such as predictive maintenance and smart grids, demand near-instantaneous responses.

2. Key Components of IoT Device Management

Device Provisioning and Onboarding

- **Definition:** Setting up devices to communicate with the cloud securely.
- **Best Practices:**
    - Use unique identifiers and secure certificates during provisioning.
    - Automate onboarding using tools like AWS IoT Core or Azure IoT Hub.

Example: A smart thermostat manufacturer uses AWS IoT Core to automate onboarding, assigning each device a unique certificate during production.

Monitoring and Maintenance

- **Definition:** Tracking device health, usage patterns, and firmware versions.
- **Best Practices:**
    - Implement telemetry to monitor device metrics like uptime, temperature, and network connectivity.
    - Use over-the-air (OTA) updates to patch vulnerabilities or add features.

Example: An agricultural company monitors IoT sensors in greenhouses using Azure IoT Hub, automatically updating firmware to address security patches.

Security Management

- **Definition:** Protecting IoT devices and their communication with the cloud.
- **Best Practices:**
    - Enforce encryption for data in transit and at rest.
    - Rotate keys and credentials regularly.
    - Segment networks to limit the blast radius of potential breaches.

Example: A utility provider uses Google Cloud IoT Core to encrypt communication between smart meters and the cloud, ensuring compliance with energy regulations.

Data Management

- **Definition:** Processing, storing, and analyzing data generated by IoT devices.
- **Best Practices:**
    - Process data locally when latency is critical, using edge devices or gateways.

- Send aggregated or processed data to the cloud for further analysis.

Example: A transportation company uses AWS IoT Greengrass to process sensor data locally on buses and sends summarized insights to AWS for fleet optimization.

3. Cloud Solutions for IoT Management

AWS IoT Core

- **Features:**
  - Device registry for tracking IoT devices.
  - Secure communication with TLS encryption.
  - Integration with AWS services like Lambda for automation.
- **Use Case:**
  - An oil company uses AWS IoT Core to monitor pipeline sensors and detect leaks.

Azure IoT Hub

- **Features:**
  - Bi-directional communication between devices and the cloud.
  - Integration with Azure Sphere for device security.
  - Supports OTA updates and telemetry data collection.
- **Use Case:**
  - A retailer uses Azure IoT Hub to manage in-store IoT devices, such as cameras and smart shelves.

Google Cloud IoT Core

- **Features:**
  - Pub/Sub integration for real-time data streaming.
  - Device telemetry and state monitoring.
  - Secure device-to-cloud communication.
- **Use Case:**
  - A logistics company uses Google Cloud IoT Core to monitor fleet locations and optimize delivery routes.

Real-World Applications

1. Smart Cities

- **Challenge:** Real-time management of traffic signals, surveillance cameras, and public safety sensors.
- **Solution:** Edge computing processes sensor data locally, while the cloud aggregates and analyzes city-wide data.

2. Healthcare

- **Challenge:** Remote patient monitoring devices must deliver real-time insights to caregivers.
- **Solution:** IoT devices send data to cloud platforms for storage and analysis, while edge devices handle immediate alerts.

3. Industrial IoT (IIoT)

- **Challenge:** Predictive maintenance for manufacturing equipment requires fast responses.
- **Solution:** Edge gateways analyze sensor data on-site to predict failures, reducing downtime.

Summary

Edge computing and IoT are redefining how organizations process data and manage devices. By reducing latency through localized processing and leveraging cloud platforms for scalable device management, businesses can unlock new possibilities in innovation and efficiency. Whether it's a smart city optimizing traffic flow or a healthcare provider monitoring patient vitals, edge computing and IoT are at the forefront of the digital transformation journey.

Artificial Intelligence and Machine Learning in Cloud Services

Artificial Intelligence (AI) and Machine Learning (ML) have become cornerstones of innovation across industries. Cloud services play a pivotal role in democratizing these technologies, providing scalable, cost-effective platforms for developing, training, and deploying AI/ML models. This chapter explores the AI/ML services offered by major cloud providers and outlines strategies for training and deploying models in the cloud.

Overview of AI/ML Services Offered by Major Cloud Providers

Cloud providers offer a wide array of AI/ML services, from pre-trained models for common use cases to robust infrastructure for custom model development. These services enable businesses to harness the power of AI/ML without the need for extensive in-house expertise or infrastructure.

1. AWS AI/ML Services

Amazon Web Services (AWS) offers a comprehensive suite of tools for AI/ML under the Amazon SageMaker umbrella, along with pre-built AI services.

- **Key Services:**
    - **Amazon SageMaker:** A fully managed service for building, training, and deploying ML models at scale.
    - **Rekognition:** Image and video analysis for object detection, facial recognition, and moderation.
    - **Comprehend:** Natural language processing (NLP) for sentiment analysis, entity recognition, and text categorization.
    - **Polly:** Text-to-speech service for converting text into lifelike speech.

    - **Lex:** Conversational AI for building chatbots.
- **Example Use Case:**
    - An e-commerce company uses **Amazon SageMaker** to develop a recommendation engine that personalizes product suggestions based on customer behavior.

2. Microsoft Azure AI/ML Services

Microsoft Azure offers AI/ML capabilities through its **Azure AI** platform, focusing on integration and ease of use.

- **Key Services:**
    - **Azure Machine Learning:** A comprehensive platform for training and deploying ML models, with support for AutoML and custom workflows.
    - **Cognitive Services:** APIs for vision, speech, language, and decision-making tasks.
        - **Computer Vision:** Image analysis and OCR.
        - **Azure OpenAI Service:** Advanced NLP capabilities powered by OpenAI's models.
    - **Azure Bot Services:** Tools for building and deploying intelligent chatbots.
- **Example Use Case:**
    - A healthcare provider uses **Azure Cognitive Services** to analyze medical images and assist doctors in diagnosing conditions.

3. Google Cloud AI/ML Services

Google Cloud leverages its expertise in AI research to offer cutting-edge tools and services for AI/ML.

- **Key Services:**
    - **Vertex AI:** An end-to-end platform for ML workflows, supporting training, evaluation, and deployment of models.
    - **Vision AI:** Image and video analysis, including facial recognition and object detection.
    - **Natural Language AI:** NLP capabilities for text analysis, including sentiment detection and entity recognition.
    - **AutoML:** Tools for training custom models without extensive ML expertise.
- **Example Use Case:**
    - A media company uses **Google Cloud Vision AI** to automate content tagging for large-scale video libraries.

4. Other Notable Platforms

- **IBM Watson:**
    - Offers AI services like Watson Assistant (chatbots) and Watson Natural Language Understanding for advanced text analysis.

    - Example: A legal firm uses Watson to analyze contracts and identify key clauses.
- **Oracle Cloud Infrastructure (OCI):**
    - Provides AI services for predictive analytics and custom model training.
    - Example: A financial institution uses OCI AI services to predict customer churn.

Training and Deploying AI/ML Models in the Cloud

The cloud simplifies the AI/ML lifecycle, from data preparation and model training to deployment and monitoring. Here's how organizations can leverage cloud platforms for each stage of the process.

1. Data Preparation

Step 1: Data Collection and Storage

- Store and manage data using cloud-native storage solutions like AWS S3, Azure Blob Storage, or Google Cloud Storage.
- Use services like **AWS Glue** or **Google Dataflow** to clean and transform raw data.

Example:

- A retail chain collects sales data from multiple stores and processes it in Azure Blob Storage before training an ML model.

Step 2: Data Annotation

- Annotate datasets for supervised learning using tools like **Amazon SageMaker Ground Truth** or **Google Data Labeling Service.**

2. Model Training

Step 1: Choose a Training Environment

- Use managed ML platforms like **Amazon SageMaker**, **Azure ML**, or **Google Vertex AI** for scalable model training.
- Choose from pre-configured environments for popular frameworks like TensorFlow, PyTorch, or Scikit-learn.

Step 2: Leverage Cloud Compute Resources

- Scale training workloads using GPUs or TPUs provided by cloud services.
    - AWS: P3 or G5 instances with NVIDIA GPUs.
    - Azure: NC-series VMs for GPU-accelerated training.
    - Google Cloud: TPU Pods for high-performance training.

Step 3: Automate Training

- Use AutoML tools like Google AutoML or Azure AutoML to train models without extensive ML expertise.

Example:

- A logistics company trains a predictive maintenance model using Google Vertex AI to forecast equipment failures.

3. Model Deployment

Step 1: Deploy Models as APIs

- Use managed services like **SageMaker Endpoints**, **Azure ML Endpoints**, or **Vertex AI Endpoints** to deploy models as REST APIs.

Step 2: Edge Deployment

- Deploy models to edge devices using tools like **AWS IoT Greengrass** or **Azure IoT Edge** for low-latency predictions.

Step 3: Real-Time Monitoring

- Monitor model performance using cloud-native tools like **Amazon CloudWatch** or **Google AI Platform Monitoring** to detect drift or performance degradation.

Example:

- A ride-sharing app deploys a dynamic pricing model to real-time endpoints using Azure ML, ensuring competitive pricing during high-demand periods.

4. Continuous Learning

Step 1: Collect Feedback

- Gather user feedback or new data to refine the model.
- Example: An online retailer collects feedback on product recommendations to improve its ML model.

Step 2: Retrain and Redeploy

- Automate the retraining process using CI/CD pipelines for ML (MLOps).
- Example Tools: **Kubeflow**, **MLflow**, or **Azure Machine Learning Pipelines.**

Real-World Applications

1. **Healthcare**
   - Predict disease outbreaks using AWS SageMaker to analyze public health data.
2. **Retail**
   - Personalize shopping experiences using Google Vertex AI for recommendation systems.
3. **Manufacturing**
   - Use Azure ML to detect anomalies in production lines, reducing downtime.
4. **Finance**
   - Deploy fraud detection models using IBM Watson to analyze transaction patterns in real time.

Challenges in AI/ML Adoption

1. **Data Privacy:**
   - Ensure compliance with regulations like GDPR when storing and processing sensitive data.
   - Mitigation: Use tools like Google Cloud DLP for data anonymization.
2. **Skill Gaps:**
   - ML expertise may be limited in some organizations.
   - Mitigation: Leverage AutoML and pre-trained models to lower the barrier to entry.
3. **Model Interpretability:**
   - Stakeholders may require explanations for AI-driven decisions.
   - Mitigation: Use tools like SHAP (SHapley Additive exPlanations) or Azure InterpretML.

Summary

Cloud platforms have made AI/ML accessible to businesses of all sizes, enabling them to drive innovation and gain competitive advantages. Whether training a custom model or leveraging pre-built AI services, the cloud provides the scalability, flexibility, and tools needed for success. By integrating AI/ML into their workflows, organizations can unlock new possibilities, from improving customer experiences to optimizing operations.

Green Cloud Computing

As cloud computing becomes the backbone of digital transformation, its environmental impact grows. Green cloud computing emphasizes sustainable practices to reduce the carbon footprint of cloud operations. This chapter explores strategies for minimizing environmental impact, highlights energy-efficient data centers, and outlines best practices for sustainability in the cloud.

The Need for Green Cloud Computing

Cloud computing accounts for a significant share of global energy consumption due to the massive infrastructure required to power and cool data centers. Without proactive measures, the environmental cost of cloud growth could become unsustainable.

Key Concerns:

1. **Energy Consumption:**
   - Data centers worldwide consume approximately 1% of global electricity, with demand rising as cloud adoption grows.
2. **Carbon Emissions:**
   - Non-renewable energy sources contribute to greenhouse gas emissions.
3. **Electronic Waste:**
   - The rapid obsolescence of hardware generates significant electronic waste.

Green cloud computing addresses these challenges by prioritizing energy efficiency, renewable energy adoption, and sustainable practices.

Strategies for Reducing Environmental Impact

1. Optimize Cloud Workloads

Efficient resource usage minimizes energy consumption. Cloud providers offer tools to help organizations optimize workloads:

- **Auto-Scaling:** Dynamically adjust compute resources based on demand to avoid overprovisioning.
- **Serverless Architectures:** Execute functions only when triggered, reducing idle resource usage.
- **Spot Instances:** Utilize unused cloud capacity at a lower cost and environmental impact.

Example: An e-commerce platform uses AWS Lambda to handle event-driven tasks, significantly reducing the resources needed for idle servers.

2. Leverage Cloud Provider Sustainability Features

Major cloud providers are investing heavily in sustainability:

- **AWS:**
  - Commitment to 100% renewable energy by 2025.
  - Offers **AWS Well-Architected Tool** with sustainability guidelines.
- **Microsoft Azure:**
  - Achieved carbon neutrality in 2012.
  - Provides a **Sustainability Calculator** to estimate carbon emissions.
- **Google Cloud:**

- First major cloud provider to match 100% of its electricity use with renewable energy.
- Introduced **carbon-intelligent computing**, which shifts workloads to times when renewable energy availability is highest.

Example: A media company uses Google Cloud's Sustainability Dashboard to monitor and reduce its carbon footprint by optimizing workloads during periods of peak renewable energy availability.

3. Adopt Energy-Efficient Practices

Organizations can take steps to improve efficiency and sustainability:

- **Virtualization:** Consolidate workloads onto fewer servers to reduce hardware requirements.
- **Data Storage Optimization:**
  - Implement lifecycle management to move infrequently accessed data to lower-energy storage tiers.
- **Energy-Aware Scheduling:**
  - Schedule non-critical workloads during off-peak hours when data center cooling requirements are lower.

Example: A logistics company archives infrequently accessed delivery data to Azure Cool Blob Storage, cutting energy consumption.

Energy-Efficient Data Centers

Modern data centers are at the forefront of green computing, employing innovative technologies to reduce energy use and environmental impact.

1. Design Innovations

Efficient Cooling Systems:

- **Liquid Cooling:** Replaces traditional air cooling for better heat transfer and lower energy usage.
- **Free Cooling:** Utilizes ambient air or water for cooling instead of mechanical systems.

Example: Facebook's data center in Sweden uses free cooling with chilled Arctic air, achieving a Power Usage Effectiveness (PUE) of 1.1.

Modular Data Centers:

- Prefabricated units that scale efficiently to meet demand.
- Designed to optimize airflow and reduce cooling requirements.

2. Renewable Energy Integration

Solar and Wind Energy:

- Data centers increasingly rely on renewable sources to power operations.
- Example: Google's data centers are powered by solar and wind farms, contributing to their carbon-neutral status.

On-Site Generation:

- Some facilities deploy solar panels or wind turbines directly on-site to generate renewable energy.

3. Advanced Hardware

Energy-Efficient Processors:

- Use of processors designed for lower power consumption, such as ARM-based chips.
- Example: AWS Graviton processors offer up to 40% better energy efficiency compared to traditional x86 processors.

Solid-State Drives (SSDs):

- Consume less power and generate less heat compared to traditional hard drives.

Sustainability Practices for Organizations

Organizations can adopt sustainable practices to reduce their environmental impact when using the cloud:

1. Embrace a Sustainability-First Mindset

- Include sustainability metrics in procurement and operations decisions.
- Partner with cloud providers that align with organizational sustainability goals.

2. Measure and Monitor Carbon Footprint

- Use tools like AWS Carbon Footprint Tool or Azure Sustainability Calculator to track emissions.

3. Optimize Resource Usage

- Regularly audit workloads to identify and decommission unused or underutilized resources.

4. Transition to Renewable Energy

- Advocate for cloud providers that invest in renewable energy or choose data centers powered by renewables.

5. Promote Circular Economy Practices

- Extend the lifecycle of IT equipment by using refurbished hardware and ensuring proper recycling at end-of-life.

Real-World Applications

1. Financial Services

- A global bank reduced energy consumption by 30% by moving to a cloud provider with a renewable energy commitment and using serverless technologies for transaction processing.

2. Healthcare

- A hospital system optimized its data analytics workloads by scheduling jobs during off-peak hours, reducing its reliance on non-renewable energy.

3. Retail

- A multinational retailer consolidated its legacy infrastructure into a single cloud platform powered by renewable energy, achieving carbon neutrality for its IT operations.

Challenges and Opportunities

While green cloud computing offers significant benefits, organizations face challenges such as:

- **Cost Considerations:** Implementing sustainable practices may initially increase costs.
- **Data Sovereignty:** Compliance requirements may limit workload mobility to regions with renewable energy.
- **Awareness:** Many organizations are unaware of the environmental impact of their cloud operations.

These challenges, however, present opportunities for innovation, education, and collaboration with cloud providers to achieve sustainability goals.

Summary

Green cloud computing is no longer optional—it is a critical component of responsible IT operations. By leveraging energy-efficient technologies, adopting renewable energy, and implementing sustainable practices, organizations can reduce their environmental impact while driving innovation and efficiency. As cloud providers continue to invest in green technologies, businesses that prioritize sustainability will not only contribute to a healthier planet but also gain a competitive edge in a world increasingly focused on environmental responsibility.

Trends and Predictions in Cloud Technology

Cloud computing continues to evolve, driving innovations that reshape industries and redefine possibilities. This chapter explores emerging trends in cloud technology, focusing on the future of multi-cloud and hybrid cloud adoption and the anticipated convergence of quantum computing with cloud platforms.

The Future of Multi-Cloud and Hybrid Cloud Adoption

1. The Rise of Multi-Cloud Strategies

Organizations are increasingly adopting multi-cloud strategies, leveraging the strengths of multiple cloud providers to optimize performance, cost, and resilience.

Key Drivers:

- **Avoiding Vendor Lock-In:** Diversifying providers reduces dependency on a single vendor, offering flexibility and bargaining power.
- **Tailored Solutions:** Different providers excel in specific areas—AWS for scalability, Azure for enterprise integration, and Google Cloud for AI/ML.
- **Global Reach:** Multi-cloud strategies enable organizations to deploy workloads in regions served by different providers, ensuring low latency and compliance with data residency laws.

Example: A global retail company uses AWS for e-commerce scalability, Azure for ERP systems, and Google Cloud for analytics, creating a unified multi-cloud architecture.

2. Hybrid Cloud Adoption

Hybrid cloud models, which combine private and public cloud infrastructures, are gaining momentum as organizations seek the best of both worlds.

Key Benefits:

- **Data Sovereignty and Compliance:** Sensitive data remains on-premises, while less critical workloads move to the public cloud.
- **Legacy System Integration:** Hybrid clouds enable businesses to modernize incrementally without replacing existing systems.
- **Enhanced Flexibility:** Organizations can choose the optimal environment for each workload.

Example: A financial institution runs customer-facing applications in a public cloud while maintaining core banking systems on private infrastructure to meet stringent regulatory requirements.

3. Emerging Multi-Cloud and Hybrid Tools

To manage the complexities of multi-cloud and hybrid cloud environments, new tools and platforms are emerging:

- **Kubernetes for Multi-Cloud:** Kubernetes has become the de facto standard for container orchestration, enabling portability across clouds.
- **Unified Management Platforms:** Tools like VMware Tanzu, Anthos (Google Cloud), and Azure Arc provide centralized management for multi-cloud and hybrid environments.
- **AI-Driven Optimization:** AI tools analyze workloads and recommend optimal cloud configurations, balancing performance and cost.

Prediction:
By 2030, multi-cloud and hybrid cloud adoption will become the default approach for enterprises, with seamless interoperability driven by open standards and robust orchestration tools.

Advances in Quantum Computing and Cloud Integration

Quantum computing, once a theoretical concept, is gradually transitioning into practical applications, with cloud providers playing a key role in making quantum technology accessible.

1. Quantum Computing in the Cloud

Leading cloud providers are integrating quantum computing into their platforms, offering quantum-as-a-service (QaaS) to developers and researchers.

Current Offerings:

- **AWS Braket:** A managed quantum computing service that provides access to quantum hardware from IonQ, Rigetti, and D-Wave.
- **Azure Quantum:** A comprehensive platform integrating quantum computing, machine learning, and optimization tools.
- **Google Quantum AI:** Focused on quantum supremacy and experimental research, accessible via Google Cloud.

Use Cases:

- **Pharmaceutical Research:** Simulating complex molecules for drug discovery.
- **Financial Modeling:** Optimizing portfolios and managing risk with quantum algorithms.

- **Supply Chain Optimization:** Solving logistics challenges using quantum annealing techniques.

Example: A logistics company uses AWS Braket to experiment with quantum algorithms, optimizing delivery routes and reducing costs.

2. Overcoming Challenges in Quantum Integration

Quantum computing faces challenges such as error rates, scalability, and the need for specialized knowledge. Cloud integration addresses these hurdles:

- **Simulators for Training:** Cloud platforms provide quantum simulators, enabling developers to experiment without access to physical quantum hardware.
- **Hybrid Workflows:** Quantum and classical computing are combined to solve problems where quantum computing excels, such as optimization, while classical systems handle routine tasks.

Example: An AI startup uses Azure Quantum to train hybrid models, leveraging quantum-inspired optimization for natural language processing (NLP).

3. Predictions for Quantum Cloud Integration

Near-Term (2025-2030):

- **Increased Accessibility:** Cloud platforms will make quantum computing more accessible through simplified APIs and SDKs.
- **Niche Applications:** Quantum computing will initially impact specialized fields like cryptography, healthcare, and aerospace.

Mid-Term (2030-2040):

- **Wider Adoption:** As quantum hardware matures, broader industries will adopt quantum-enhanced cloud solutions for complex problem-solving.
- **Quantum Security:** Quantum-resistant encryption methods will become essential, driven by advancements in quantum capabilities.

Long-Term (2040+):

- **Ubiquity of Quantum Computing:** Quantum computing will seamlessly integrate with cloud platforms, powering mainstream applications like AI, blockchain, and real-time analytics.

Real-World Narratives: Trends in Action

1. A Multi-Cloud Transformation A healthcare organization adopts a multi-cloud strategy to improve global patient care:

- AWS is used for scalable telemedicine services.
- Azure integrates electronic health records with AI-driven insights.
- Google Cloud powers research into disease patterns using advanced analytics.

Result:
The organization achieves faster service delivery, enhanced data security, and improved patient outcomes.

2. Quantum Cloud for Financial Modeling A multinational bank leverages quantum computing via Azure Quantum to optimize risk models:

- Quantum algorithms analyze massive datasets for better predictions.
- The bank reduces operational risks and improves profitability through advanced insights.

Result:
Quantum cloud integration provides a competitive edge in financial markets.

Best Practices for Adopting Future Cloud Trends

1. **Stay Agile:**
   - Regularly assess new cloud offerings and integrate innovative tools that align with business goals.
2. **Invest in Talent:**
   - Train teams on emerging technologies like quantum computing, Kubernetes, and AI-driven management tools.
3. **Embrace Open Standards:**
   - Prioritize platforms and tools that support interoperability for seamless multi-cloud and hybrid deployments.
4. **Adopt a Sustainability Mindset:**
   - Leverage green cloud practices to align with environmental goals while exploring advanced technologies.
5. **Experiment and Innovate:**
   - Use cloud-native sandboxes and quantum simulators to explore new possibilities without significant upfront costs.

The future of cloud technology is defined by flexibility, innovation, and convergence. Multi-cloud and hybrid cloud models will dominate enterprise strategies, providing scalability, resilience, and tailored solutions. Simultaneously, advances in quantum computing will open doors to unprecedented computational power, driving breakthroughs in industries from healthcare to logistics. Organizations that embrace these trends today will position themselves as leaders in the digital economy of tomorrow.

Chapter 11: Certification Preparation and Exam Strategies

The **CompTIA Cloud+ (CV0-004)** certification is an industry-recognized credential that validates your expertise in managing and deploying cloud infrastructure services. Preparing for this exam requires a strategic combination of understanding the exam structure, mastering core concepts, and gaining hands-on experience. This chapter is your roadmap to success, providing in-depth strategies for preparation, practical exercises, and tips for tackling the exam with confidence.

Mastering Cloud Technologies: Your Path to CompTIA Cloud+ Certification

The **CompTIA Cloud+ CV0-004** exam evaluates your ability to manage and maintain complex cloud environments, with a strong focus on multi-cloud and hybrid strategies, DevOps integration, security, and troubleshooting. Passing this exam demonstrates your expertise in handling real-world cloud challenges, including automation and operational efficiencies.

1. Exam Structure

- **Number of Questions**: The exam includes up to **90 questions**.
- **Question Types**:
  - **Multiple-Choice**: Includes single- and multiple-answer questions.
  - **Performance-Based Questions (PBQs)**: Hands-on scenarios testing practical skills like configuring or troubleshooting cloud systems.
- **Time Limit**: 90 minutes.
- **Passing Score**: 750 on a scale of 100–900.

Pro Tip: Manage your time effectively. Allocate about **1 minute per question**, leaving additional time for PBQs.

2. Key Content Areas

The CV0-004 exam includes six updated domains, reflecting the latest industry practices. The domain weightings are as follows:

Domain	Weighting
Cloud Architecture	16%
Cloud Deployment	20%
Cloud Security	19%
Operations	16%
Troubleshooting	19%
DevOps Fundamentals	10%

Focus Areas:

- Prioritize domains like **Cloud Deployment**, **Security**, and **Troubleshooting**, which together account for **58%** of the exam.
- Pay attention to the new **DevOps Fundamentals** domain, which introduces concepts like CI/CD pipelines and automation.

3. Importance of Performance-Based Questions (PBQs)

PBQs evaluate your ability to apply theoretical knowledge to real-world scenarios. Examples include:

- **Configuring a virtual private cloud (VPC)** with specific access control settings.

- **Troubleshooting multi-cloud connectivity issues** or deployment failures.

PBQ Preparation Tips:

- Practice using cloud platforms such as **AWS**, **Azure**, or **Google Cloud**.
- Focus on skills like deploying Infrastructure as Code (IaC), monitoring cloud environments, and securing data.
- Use virtual labs and sandboxes to simulate real-world scenarios.

Exam Objectives Breakdown

1. Cloud Architecture (16%)

- Evaluate cloud service and deployment models (IaaS, PaaS, SaaS, public, private, hybrid).
- Understand cost optimization and cloud-native design principles.
- Design resilient, scalable, and secure cloud architectures.

Example Scenario:

- Design a high-availability system with failover across multiple regions.

2. Cloud Deployment (20%)

- Deploy and configure compute, storage, and network resources.
- Automate deployments using Infrastructure as Code (IaC) tools like Terraform or AWS CloudFormation.
- Implement auto-scaling and load-balancing for fault tolerance and scalability.

Practical Task:

- Use Terraform to deploy a scalable web application across multiple regions with automated failover.

3. Cloud Security (19%)

- Implement advanced IAM policies, role-based access control (RBAC), and encryption.
- Manage security incidents and ensure compliance with standards like GDPR and PCI DSS.
- Use monitoring tools to detect and respond to vulnerabilities.

Hands-On Practice:

- Configure IAM roles to enforce least-privilege principles and encrypt data at rest in S3 buckets.

4. Operations (16%)

- Monitor resource performance using tools like **AWS CloudWatch** or **Azure Monitor**.
- Develop backup, disaster recovery, and business continuity plans.
- Optimize resource usage to reduce costs and improve efficiency.

Example Scenario:

- Create an automated backup schedule for critical databases and validate recovery procedures.

5. Troubleshooting (19%)

- Diagnose and resolve issues related to networking, storage, and application performance.
- Analyze logs and monitoring data to identify security and compliance breaches.
- Troubleshoot multi-cloud deployment failures and service outages.

Practical Task:

- Use logging tools to trace and resolve network latency between application tiers in a hybrid cloud.

6. DevOps Fundamentals (10%)

- Understand CI/CD pipelines and integrate automation into cloud workflows.
- Manage source control, orchestration, and containerization using tools like Jenkins, Git, and Kubernetes.
- Monitor and optimize application deployments with continuous feedback loops.

Hands-On Practice:

- Set up a CI/CD pipeline to deploy a containerized application using Kubernetes.

Practice Problem:
Resolve a performance issue by identifying and addressing an overloaded virtual machine.

Practice Questions and Simulations

1. Sample Multiple-Choice Questions

Here are **25 practice example questions and simulations** for the CompTIA Cloud+ CV0-004 exam, covering multiple-choice questions, performance-based questions, and practice scenarios.

1. Which deployment model allows sharing cloud resources across multiple organizations?

   A. Private
   B. Community
   C. Public
   D. Hybrid
   Answer: B. Community

2. Which of the following best describes Infrastructure as a Service (IaaS)?
   A. Provides a platform for developing applications.
   B. Offers complete control over the operating system, networking, and storage.
   C. Allows access to software applications over the internet.
   D. Provides hardware virtualization only.
   Answer: B. Offers complete control over the operating system, networking, and storage.
3. What is a key advantage of a hybrid cloud model?
   A. Unlimited scalability.
   B. Enhanced security through on-premises hosting.
   C. Full control over public infrastructure.
   D. Easier vendor management.
   Answer: B. Enhanced security through on-premises hosting.
4. What feature ensures high availability in a cloud environment?
   A. Fault tolerance.
   B. Encryption at rest.
   C. Resource tagging.
   D. On-demand self-service.
   Answer: A. Fault tolerance.
5. Which architecture type is best suited for reducing latency for global users?
   A. Serverless.
   B. Content Delivery Network (CDN).
   C. Monolithic.
   D. Edge Computing.
   Answer: B. Content Delivery Network (CDN).

6. What does the principle of least privilege entail?
   A. Granting minimal access rights for specific tasks.
   B. Providing administrative access to all users.
   C. Disabling all user roles by default.

D. Allowing public access to storage buckets.
Answer: A. Granting minimal access rights for specific tasks.

7. Which technology ensures secure data transmission between cloud instances?
    A. NAT Gateway.
    B. VPN.
    C. Public IP.
    D. Load Balancer.
    Answer: B. VPN.
8. What should be implemented to detect unauthorized access to cloud resources?
    A. Web Application Firewall (WAF).
    B. Intrusion Detection System (IDS).
    C. Multi-Factor Authentication (MFA).
    D. Autoscaling.
    Answer: B. Intrusion Detection System (IDS).
9. What is the main purpose of a security group in a cloud environment?
    A. To encrypt data at rest.
    B. To monitor application performance.
    C. To control inbound and outbound traffic to resources.
    D. To manage user authentication.
    Answer: C. To control inbound and outbound traffic to resources.
10. Which encryption standard is commonly used for securing data in transit?
    A. SHA-256.
    B. RSA.
    C. TLS.
    D. DES.
    Answer: C. TLS.

11. Which tool is commonly used for automating cloud infrastructure deployment?
    A. Terraform.
    B. Splunk.
    C. Tableau.
    D. Zabbix.
    Answer: A. Terraform.
12. What is the purpose of a load balancer in a cloud deployment?
    A. Distribute incoming traffic across multiple servers.
    B. Provide encryption for data in transit.
    C. Analyze application performance metrics.
    D. Scale virtual machines dynamically.
    Answer: A. Distribute incoming traffic across multiple servers.
13. What is a key advantage of using containers over virtual machines?
    A. Containers are hardware-independent.
    B. Containers have lower resource overhead.
    C. Containers offer persistent storage by default.

D. Containers require no orchestration.

Answer: B. Containers have lower resource overhead.

14. Which networking component allows communication between a private subnet and the internet?
    A. Internet Gateway.
    B. Virtual Private Gateway.
    C. Elastic Load Balancer.
    D. Security Group.

    Answer: A. Internet Gateway.
15. Which storage type is most appropriate for hosting an application requiring frequent random read/write operations?
    A. Object storage.
    B. Block storage.
    C. Cold storage.
    D. File storage.

    Answer: B. Block storage.

16. What tool provides visibility into the performance of cloud resources in AWS?
    A. CloudTrail.
    B. CloudWatch.
    C. Config.
    D. Lambda.

    Answer: B. CloudWatch.
17. What is the primary purpose of a backup strategy?
    A. Improve application latency.
    B. Protect against data loss.
    C. Scale application infrastructure.
    D. Monitor resource utilization.

    Answer: B. Protect against data loss.
18. Which disaster recovery approach has the shortest recovery time?
    A. Warm site.
    B. Hot site.
    C. Cold site.
    D. Backup-only site.

    Answer: B. Hot site.
19. What does Infrastructure as Code (IaC) enable?
    A. Manual infrastructure configuration.
    B. Automated deployment of resources using scripts.
    C. Enhanced resource encryption.
    D. Real-time traffic monitoring.

    Answer: B. Automated deployment of resources using scripts.
20. Which service can archive logs for compliance in Azure?
    A. Azure Monitor.
    B. Azure Blob Storage.
    C. Azure Key Vault.

D. Azure Policy.
Answer: B. Azure Blob Storage.

21. What is the first step in troubleshooting a network connectivity issue in a cloud environment?
    A. Reboot the server.
    B. Verify the security group rules.
    C. Increase instance size.
    D. Enable logging.
    Answer: B. Verify the security group rules.
22. Which log type is most helpful for identifying failed login attempts?
    A. Application logs.
    B. System logs.
    C. Audit logs.
    D. Performance logs.
    Answer: C. Audit logs.
23. What is the likely cause of an application crash under high load?
    A. Overutilized CPU.
    B. Insufficient encryption.
    C. Misconfigured IAM roles.
    D. Unoptimized logging.
    Answer: A. Overutilized CPU.
24. What tool can you use to identify misconfigurations in cloud resources?
    A. Terraform.
    B. AWS Config.
    C. Jenkins.
    D. Nagios.
    Answer: B. AWS Config.
25. Which scenario would likely require increasing the size of a virtual machine?
    A. High network latency.
    B. Consistently high memory usage.
    C. High packet loss.
    D. Decreasing application traffic.
    Answer: B. Consistently high memory usage.

Performance-Based Questions

1. Configure a VPC with a public and private subnet, enabling internet access for only the public subnet.
2. Set up a lifecycle policy to transition S3 objects to Glacier after 30 days.
3. Implement a security group allowing inbound HTTP traffic (port 80) and blocking all other traffic.

By mastering these questions and scenarios, you will build the confidence needed to excel in the CompTIA Cloud+ CV0-004 exam.

Final Tips for Exam Success

Success in the **CompTIA Cloud+ CV0-004 exam** requires not just knowledge and skills but also the right mindset and strategies to perform under pressure. This section provides expanded tips to help you approach the exam with confidence and maximize your chances of success.

1. Manage Your Time Effectively

Time management is crucial during the 90-minute exam, especially with performance-based questions (PBQs) that may require more time.

Key Strategies:

- **Allocate Time Wisely:**
  - Spend no more than 1 minute on multiple-choice questions.
  - Leave at least 20 minutes for PBQs.
- **Use the Mark-for-Review Option:**
  - If unsure about an answer, mark the question for review and move on. Return to it after addressing other questions.
- **Save PBQs for Last:**
  - Answer all multiple-choice questions first to ensure you capture easy points, then focus on PBQs.

Example Time Breakdown:

- Multiple-Choice Questions: 60 minutes.
- PBQs: 20 minutes.
- Review: 10 minutes.

2. Understand the Question Types

Familiarizing yourself with the types of questions in the exam can help reduce surprises and build confidence.

Multiple-Choice Tips:

- **Eliminate Obvious Wrong Answers:** Narrow your options to improve your chances of guessing correctly.
- **Watch for Absolute Words:** Options with words like "always" or "never" are often incorrect, as cloud scenarios can vary.
- **Read the Question Twice:** Ensure you fully understand what’s being asked before selecting an answer.

Performance-Based Questions (PBQs):

- **Follow the Instructions Precisely:** Read the prompt carefully and ensure you address all parts of the scenario.
- **Prioritize Simplicity:** Avoid overcomplicating configurations—stick to the basics unless explicitly instructed otherwise.
- **Validate Your Work:** Before moving on, verify that the configurations you made are working as intended.

3. Stay Calm and Focused Under Pressure

The high stakes of certification exams can induce stress, but staying calm is essential for clear thinking.

Before the Exam:

- **Rest Well:** Ensure you get at least 7–8 hours of sleep the night before.
- **Eat Smart:** Choose a light, balanced meal to maintain energy and avoid a mid-exam crash.
- **Arrive Early:** Plan to arrive at the testing center or log in to the online proctoring system at least 30 minutes early.

During the Exam:

- **Pause and Breathe:** If you feel overwhelmed, take a few deep breaths to reset your focus.
- **Don't Panic Over Tough Questions:** Skip difficult questions initially and revisit them later.
- **Visualize Success:** Remind yourself of your preparation and ability to succeed.

4. Use the Process of Elimination

For multiple-choice questions, eliminating incorrect answers can significantly improve your odds of selecting the correct one.

Example Strategy:

- **Step 1:** Read the question and identify keywords.
- **Step 2:** Eliminate options that don't align with the scenario or violate best practices.
- **Step 3:** Focus on the remaining choices and make an informed decision.

Example Question: *Which tool is most effective for automating cloud resource deployments?*

A. Zabbix
B. Terraform
C. Splunk
D. Tableau

Process:

Eliminate A (Zabbix is for monitoring), C (Splunk is for log analysis), and D (Tableau is for data visualization).

Correct Answer: **B. Terraform**.

5. Review and Double-Check Your Work

Taking a few minutes to review your answers can make a big difference, especially for flagged questions or PBQs.

Key Review Steps:

- **Revisit Marked Questions:** Reassess questions you flagged earlier, now with a clearer mind.
- **Verify PBQs:** Ensure that all configurations and setups are complete and functioning as expected.
- **Check for Misinterpretations:** Ensure you didn't misread questions or overlook key details.

Tip: Avoid second-guessing yourself unless you're confident in your revised answer. Your first instinct is often correct.

6. Prepare for Exam Day

Proper preparation on exam day ensures a smooth experience.

Checklist for Exam Day:

1. **Bring Necessary Documents:**
    - For in-person exams: Two forms of ID, including one government-issued photo ID.
    - For online exams: Ensure your workspace complies with proctoring rules.
2. **Test Your Equipment:**
    - For remote exams, check your internet connection, webcam, and microphone.
3. **Know the Rules:**

- Review CompTIA's testing policies, including breaks, prohibited items, and behavior guidelines.

Pro Tip: Familiarize yourself with the testing interface by taking practice exams in a simulated environment.

7. Emphasize Hands-On Practice

Performance-based questions require practical knowledge, not just theoretical understanding. Allocate significant time for hands-on labs.

Hands-On Practice Suggestions:

- **Set Up a Cloud Environment:** Use AWS Free Tier, Azure's free services, or Google Cloud's trial to practice deployments and configurations.
- **Simulate Real-World Scenarios:** For example, configure a load balancer, deploy a virtual machine, and monitor logs.
- **Use Online Labs:** Platforms like AWS Skill Builder, Azure Labs, and CompTIA CertMaster Labs offer guided exercises.

8. Take Care of Your Physical and Mental Well-Being

Staying physically and mentally prepared will enhance your performance.

Tips:

- **Stay Hydrated:** Bring a water bottle if allowed or hydrate before starting the exam.
- **Stretch During Breaks:** Brief physical activity can help reduce tension.
- **Positive Mindset:** Replace negative thoughts with affirmations like, "I've prepared for this, and I can do it."

9. Learn from Your Practice Exams

Practice exams are a powerful tool for gauging readiness and identifying areas for improvement.

Steps for Effective Use:

1. **Simulate Test Conditions:** Take practice exams in a quiet environment and adhere to the time limit.
2. **Analyze Results:** Review incorrect answers to understand why you missed them.
3. **Focus on Weak Areas:** Dedicate extra study time to domains where you scored poorly.

10. Trust Your Preparation

Confidence is key. By the time you reach exam day, trust the preparation and effort you've invested.

Motivational Reminder:

- "This exam is an opportunity to showcase what you've learned and achieve a milestone in your career."

Example Checklist: Day Before the Exam

1. Confirm your exam time and location (or online proctoring details).
2. Organize required materials (ID, testing equipment).
3. Review your notes, flashcards, or key concepts.
4. Take a light practice test for confidence but avoid overloading.
5. Relax with an activity that calms your mind—meditation, reading, or a walk.

By following these strategies, you'll approach the **CompTIA Cloud+ CV0-004 exam** well-prepared, confident, and ready to excel.

Case Study: A Candidate's Journey to Cloud+ Certification Success

Background

Meet Sarah:
Sarah is a mid-career IT professional with six years of experience in systems administration. Her responsibilities include managing virtual machines, monitoring server performance, and supporting on-premises applications. Recently, her organization began migrating to the cloud, and Sarah was tasked with leading this transition. While familiar with traditional IT environments, she realized her cloud knowledge was limited and decided to pursue the **CompTIA Cloud+ CV0-004 certification** to upskill and secure her role in the evolving IT landscape.

The Challenge

Initial Challenges Sarah Faced:

1. **Lack of Cloud Experience:**
    - Sarah had limited exposure to cloud platforms like AWS, Azure, or Google Cloud.
    - She was unfamiliar with cloud-native concepts such as containers, Infrastructure as Code (IaC), and serverless architectures.
2. **Time Constraints:**
    - Balancing her full-time job and family commitments made it challenging to dedicate consistent study time.
3. **Performance-Based Questions (PBQs):**
    - The hands-on nature of PBQs intimidated Sarah, as she had minimal experience configuring cloud environments.
4. **Exam Anxiety:**
    - She hadn't taken a certification exam in years and felt nervous about the process.

Mastering Cloud Technologies: Your Path to CompTIA Cloud+ Certification

Step 1: Setting Goals and Creating a Study Plan

Sarah started by creating a structured study plan tailored to her schedule and the exam objectives.

Actions Taken:

1. **Define Goals:**
    - Pass the CompTIA Cloud+ exam within three months.
    - Gain hands-on experience with cloud platforms during preparation.
2. **Break Down the Objectives:**
    - Sarah reviewed the CompTIA Cloud+ objectives and prioritized high-weighted domains like **Cloud Deployment (23%)** and **Troubleshooting (22%)**.
3. **Schedule Study Blocks:**
    - She allocated 1–2 hours daily for study and labs, with weekends reserved for practice exams and deep dives into challenging topics.
4. **Use Study Materials:**
    - Sarah invested in a mix of resources:
        - **Books:** CompTIA Cloud+ study guide.
        - **Videos:** Online courses from platforms like LinkedIn Learning and Udemy.
        - **Labs:** Access to AWS Free Tier and Azure trial accounts for practical exercises.

Step 2: Gaining Hands-On Experience

Sarah recognized the importance of hands-on skills, especially for PBQs, and incorporated labs into her study routine.

Practical Activities:

1. **Set Up a Cloud Environment:**
    - Sarah created accounts on AWS and Azure to familiarize herself with their management consoles.
2. **Deploy and Manage Resources:**
    - She practiced creating virtual machines, configuring storage, and setting up basic network components like security groups and VPCs.
3. **Automate Tasks:**
    - Using Terraform, Sarah automated the deployment of infrastructure, such as virtual machines with predefined configurations.
4. **Simulate Real-World Scenarios:**
    - Configured a load balancer in AWS to distribute traffic between multiple instances.
    - Deployed an application in Azure and monitored its performance using Azure Monitor.

Step 3: Joining Study Groups and Practice Exams

To overcome her exam anxiety and gain insights from peers, Sarah joined a study group and regularly took practice exams.

Actions Taken:

1. **Study Groups:**
   - Sarah joined a LinkedIn group for Cloud+ aspirants and participated in discussions on tricky topics like cloud security and disaster recovery.
2. **Practice Exams:**
   - She used mock exams from ExamCompass and Boson to simulate test conditions.
   - After each exam, Sarah analyzed her performance to identify weak areas.
3. **Collaborative Learning:**
   - In her study group, Sarah discussed PBQ strategies, such as configuring IAM roles or troubleshooting network connectivity issues.

Outcome:
By the second month, her practice exam scores improved from 65% to 85%.

Step 4: Tackling Performance-Based Questions

PBQs were Sarah's biggest concern, so she focused on building confidence through repetitive practice.

How She Prepared:

1. **Scenario-Based Labs:**
   - Sarah practiced scenarios such as:
     - Configuring S3 bucket policies to restrict public access.
     - Resolving a VM's inability to connect to the internet by modifying route tables and security group settings.
2. **Testing Automation Skills:**
   - She used Terraform to deploy infrastructure and troubleshoot deployment errors, mimicking real-world PBQ challenges.
3. **Time Management:**
   - During practice sessions, Sarah timed herself to ensure she could complete PBQs within 20 minutes.

Breakthrough Moment:
By the end of her preparation, Sarah could confidently complete PBQs, such as creating a high-availability architecture with a load balancer and auto-scaling groups.

Exam Day

On exam day, Sarah arrived at the testing center 30 minutes early, equipped with two forms of ID and a calm mindset.

How Sarah Managed Exam Day:

1. **Tackled Multiple-Choice Questions First:**
   - She answered all the straightforward multiple-choice questions within the first 50 minutes.
2. **Addressed PBQs Next:**
   - With 30 minutes remaining, Sarah moved to the PBQs. Her hands-on practice paid off, allowing her to complete them with confidence.
3. **Reviewed Answers:**
   - Sarah used the remaining time to revisit flagged questions and double-check her configurations in PBQs.

The Results

Sarah passed the **CompTIA Cloud+ CV0-004 exam** with a score of 820 (out of 900). Beyond certification, she gained valuable skills that she immediately applied at work.

Post-Certification Impact

1. **Workplace Contributions:**
   - Sarah led her company's migration to a hybrid cloud environment, designing scalable architectures and implementing disaster recovery solutions.
2. **Career Growth:**
   - She was promoted to **Cloud Infrastructure Specialist**, with a 20% salary increase.
3. **Confidence Boost:**
   - The certification bolstered Sarah's confidence, inspiring her to pursue further cloud certifications like AWS Certified Solutions Architect.

Key Takeaways from Sarah's Journey

1. **Set Realistic Goals:**
   - Define clear timelines and break study plans into manageable tasks.
2. **Emphasize Hands-On Practice:**
   - Practical experience with cloud platforms is essential, especially for PBQs.
3. **Leverage Community Resources:**
   - Study groups and online forums provide valuable insights and support.
4. **Simulate Test Conditions:**
   - Practice exams are critical for building confidence and improving time management.

5. **Stay Persistent:**
   - Consistency and dedication are key to overcoming challenges and achieving success.

By following Sarah's example, you can craft a structured, effective strategy to conquer the CompTIA Cloud+ exam and advance your career in cloud computing.

Appendix A: Important Terms

Below is a glossary of key terms and concepts you need to know for the CompTIA Cloud+ certification. These terms are grouped by relevance and cover foundational cloud computing topics, including architecture, security, and operational management.

A

API (Application Programming Interface):
A standardized interface that allows applications to communicate with each other. In cloud computing, APIs enable automation and interaction with cloud services. Examples include AWS SDKs, Azure REST APIs, and Google Cloud APIs.

Availability Zone:
A physically independent data center within a cloud provider's region, designed to be isolated from failures in other zones. Used to build high-availability and fault-tolerant systems. For instance, AWS has multiple availability zones in each region.

Automation:
The process of using scripts, tools, or software to perform tasks without human intervention. Common automation tools include Ansible, Chef, and Puppet, which are used to automate the deployment and configuration of cloud resources.

B

Backup:
The process of creating copies of data to ensure recoverability in the event of hardware failures, accidental deletions, or disasters. Azure Backup and AWS Backup provide managed backup solutions in cloud environments.

Block Storage:
Low-latency storage where data is stored in fixed-size blocks. Commonly used for database and virtual machine workloads. Examples include AWS Elastic Block Store (EBS) and Azure Managed Disks.

Bursting:
The ability to temporarily exceed allocated capacity to handle spikes in demand. This is common in compute and storage services, such as burstable VM types in AWS (e.g., t2.micro).

C

Cloud Deployment Models:

- **Public Cloud:** Resources are owned and operated by a third-party provider and shared across multiple tenants. Examples: AWS, Azure, Google Cloud.
- **Private Cloud:** Resources are dedicated to a single organization, often hosted on-premises or in a dedicated environment. Examples: VMware vSphere, Azure Stack.
- **Hybrid Cloud:** A mix of public and private cloud environments, enabling portability of workloads.
- **Community Cloud:** Shared by multiple organizations with similar needs, such as government agencies.

Cloud Service Models:

- **IaaS (Infrastructure as a Service):** Provides raw compute, storage, and networking resources. Example: Azure Virtual Machines.
- **PaaS (Platform as a Service):** Provides a platform for application development and deployment without managing the underlying infrastructure. Example: Azure App Service.
- **SaaS (Software as a Service):** Delivers ready-to-use applications over the internet. Example: Microsoft Office 365.

Cloud Storage:
A service that allows users to store data on remote servers accessed via the internet. Examples: AWS S3, Azure Blob Storage, and Google Cloud Storage.

D

Disaster Recovery (DR):
Strategies and solutions to restore systems and data after a failure or disaster. DR involves replication, backups, and failover systems. Example: Azure Site Recovery.

DNS (Domain Name System):
A service that translates domain names (e.g., www.example.com) into IP addresses. Cloud DNS services include AWS Route 53, Azure DNS, and Google Cloud DNS.

Data Sovereignty:
The legal regulations governing where data can be stored and processed based on geographic location. Examples include GDPR in Europe and CCPA in California.

E

Elasticity:
The ability to scale resources up or down dynamically based on demand. Elasticity is a key feature of cloud services like AWS Auto Scaling and Azure Scale Sets.

Encryption:
The process of encoding data to protect it from unauthorized access. Cloud providers offer tools to encrypt data in transit (e.g., TLS) and at rest (e.g., Azure Disk Encryption).

Edge Computing:
A distributed computing model where data processing occurs closer to the source or end-user to reduce latency. Examples include AWS Greengrass and Azure IoT Edge.

F

Fault Tolerance:
The capability of a system to continue functioning despite failures of one or more components. Redundancy and load balancing are common methods to achieve fault tolerance.

Firewall:
A security mechanism that monitors and controls incoming and outgoing network traffic. Examples include Azure NSG (Network Security Group) and AWS Security Groups.

Federated Identity:
A system where user authentication and authorization are shared across multiple systems, allowing Single Sign-On (SSO). Examples: Azure AD Federation Services and AWS Cognito.

H

High Availability (HA):
A design principle ensuring minimal downtime by distributing workloads across multiple instances or availability zones. Achieved using tools like Azure Load Balancer or AWS Elastic Load Balancer.

Hypervisor:
Software that enables virtualization by running multiple virtual machines on a single physical host. Examples include VMware ESXi, Microsoft Hyper-V, and KVM.

I

Identity and Access Management (IAM):
A framework for managing identities and permissions in a cloud environment. Examples include AWS IAM and Azure Active Directory.

Infrastructure as Code (IaC):
Managing and provisioning cloud infrastructure using code templates. Tools include Terraform, AWS CloudFormation, and Azure Resource Manager.

Instance:
A virtualized compute resource in the cloud. Examples include AWS EC2 and Azure Virtual Machines.

L

Load Balancer:
A device or service that distributes incoming traffic across multiple servers to improve performance and availability. Examples include Azure Load Balancer and AWS Elastic Load Balancer.

Latency:
The time delay between a request and a response in a network or system. Low latency is crucial for applications requiring real-time interaction.

M

Multi-Tenancy:
An architecture where multiple customers share the same physical infrastructure while maintaining logical separation of their data and configurations.

Monitoring:
The process of tracking resource performance and availability. Examples include Azure Monitor, AWS CloudWatch, and Google Cloud Operations Suite.

P

Provisioning:
The process of allocating and configuring cloud resources for use. For example, creating a virtual machine with specific CPU, memory, and storage settings.

Persistent Storage:
Storage that retains data even after the associated resource is stopped or deleted. Examples include Azure Managed Disks and AWS EBS.

R

Redundancy:
The duplication of components or systems to ensure availability in the event of a failure. Examples include redundant servers, power supplies, and network connections.

Regions:
Geographical locations where cloud providers have data centers. Examples: AWS US-East-1, Azure East US, and Google Cloud Europe-West-2.

Replication:
The process of copying data across multiple locations to ensure durability and availability. Examples: Azure Storage Replication and AWS S3 Replication.

S

Scalability:
The ability to increase or decrease resource capacity based on workload demands. Includes **vertical scaling** (increasing resource size) and **horizontal scaling** (adding more resources).

Service-Level Agreement (SLA):
A contractual agreement between a service provider and a customer outlining performance guarantees, such as uptime and response times.

Snapshot:
A point-in-time backup of a resource, such as a virtual machine disk. Useful for quick restoration and cloning.

T

Tenant:
An entity (organization or individual) using a shared cloud service. Each tenant's resources and data are isolated.

Traffic Shaping:
The management of data flow to ensure network bandwidth is allocated efficiently to maintain performance.

V

Virtual Private Cloud (VPC):
An isolated network within a public cloud, providing granular control over networking. Examples include AWS VPC and Azure Virtual Network.

Virtual Machine (VM):
A virtualized compute instance running an operating system and applications. Managed via platforms like Azure Virtual Machines and AWS EC2.

Appendix B: Practice Amazon Labs

Lab 1: Creating an AWS Account

Objective:
The goal of this lab is to guide you through the process of creating an AWS Free Tier account, which will serve as the foundation for future labs. By the end of this lab, you will have an AWS account ready to use and will verify successful completion by sharing a screenshot of your AWS Management Console dashboard.

Why This Lab is Important

AWS is one of the leading cloud service providers, offering a wide range of services under the Free Tier plan. The Free Tier allows you to explore and experiment with AWS services at no cost (within usage limits). Setting up an AWS account is essential for hands-on experience, making this lab the first step toward mastering cloud computing.

Prerequisites

- A valid email address.
- A payment method (credit or debit card) for identity verification.

Detailed Steps

Step 1: Access the AWS Free Tier Website

1. Open a web browser and navigate to the AWS Free Tier website. (https://aws.amazon.com/free/)
2. Review the benefits and limits of Free Tier usage. This includes:
    - **Compute**: 750 hours of Amazon EC2 usage.
    - **Storage**: 5GB of Amazon S3 storage.
    - **Databases**: 750 hours of Amazon RDS usage.
3. Click the **"Create an AWS Account"** button to start the registration process.

Step 2: Enter Email and Set Up a Root User

1. Enter your email address and create a strong password.
    - The password should include a mix of uppercase and lowercase letters, numbers, and special characters for security.
2. Enter a name for your AWS account. This name will help you identify your account if you manage multiple AWS environments.

Step 3: Provide Billing Information

1. AWS requires a credit card or debit card for identity verification, even though most Free Tier services are free.
2. Enter your billing details and review them for accuracy.
3. AWS will place a small charge (usually $1) to verify the card, which will be refunded shortly.

Step 4: Verify Identity

1. Enter your phone number for verification.
2. AWS will send a code via text message or voice call. Enter this code into the verification field on the website.
3. Once verified, proceed to the next step.

Step 5: Choose a Support Plan

1. Select the **Basic Plan**, which is free and includes 24/7 access to customer service.
   - Paid support plans are not necessary for this lab series but can be useful for enterprise-level projects.

Step 6: Sign In to the AWS Management Console

1. Use your root user email and password to log in to the AWS Management Console. (https://aws.amazon.com/console/)
2. Upon logging in, you will land on the **AWS Dashboard**, which provides a high-level overview of your AWS account and services.

Step 7: Explore the AWS Management Console

1. Familiarize yourself with the layout and navigation:
   - **Search Bar**: Quickly access services by typing their names.
   - **Services Menu**: Categorized list of all AWS services.
   - **Account Settings**: Located in the top-right corner, this menu lets you manage billing, security, and preferences.
2. Browse key services like **EC2**, **S3**, and **IAM** to get an overview of the AWS ecosystem.

Validation

- To confirm successful account creation, take a screenshot of the AWS Management Console dashboard.
- The screenshot should show your account name in the top-right corner and the main dashboard interface.

Best Practices for Your AWS Account

1. **Secure Your Root User Account**:
   - Enable Multi-Factor Authentication (MFA) for added security.
2. **Understand Free Tier Limits**:
   - Regularly monitor usage to avoid exceeding Free Tier limits, which could incur charges.
3. **Organize Billing Alerts**:
   - Set up billing alerts to track any unexpected costs.

Expected Outcome

By completing this lab, you will:

- Have an active AWS account.
- Be familiar with the AWS Management Console.
- Be ready to start exploring AWS services in subsequent labs.

Lab 2: Launching an EC2 Instance

Objective:
Learn how to launch, configure, and connect to a virtual machine (EC2 instance) in AWS using the Free Tier. By the end of this lab, you will have a running EC2 instance and understand the basics of configuring a cloud-based virtual machine.

Why This Lab is Important

Amazon EC2 (Elastic Compute Cloud) is a foundational service that provides scalable virtual servers in the cloud. It allows you to run applications, host websites, or experiment with cloud computing without needing physical hardware. This lab introduces the essential skills required to deploy and manage EC2 instances.

Prerequisites

- An AWS account (set up in Lab 1).
- Basic knowledge of SSH or familiarity with browser-based console access.
- A key pair for secure connection (created during this lab).

Detailed Steps

Step 1: Access the EC2 Dashboard

1. Log in to the AWS Management Console. (https://aws.amazon.com/console/)
2. Navigate to the **EC2** service by typing "EC2" in the search bar or selecting it from the "Compute" section in the Services menu.
3. Once on the EC2 Dashboard, take note of the following:
    - Instance Running: Displays the number of active EC2 instances.
    - Key Sections: "Instances," "Key Pairs," and "Launch Instance."

Step 2: Launch an Instance

1. Click **"Launch Instance"** to begin the setup process.
2. Provide a name for the instance, such as "MyFirstInstance."

Step 3: Choose an Amazon Machine Image (AMI)

1. Select **Amazon Linux 2** as the operating system (Free Tier eligible).
    - Amazon Linux 2 is optimized for AWS and includes tools for managing and scaling your instance.

Step 4: Select an Instance Type

1. Choose **t2.micro** (Free Tier eligible).
    - This instance type provides enough resources for small-scale tasks without incurring charges under the Free Tier.

Step 5: Configure Instance Settings

1. Keep the default settings for **VPC** and **Subnet**.
    - This ensures the instance is placed in the default VPC and is publicly accessible.
2. Optionally, configure advanced settings like user data to pre-install software during instance launch.

Step 6: Add Storage

1. Leave the default storage setting of **8GB** (Free Tier eligible).
    - You can increase storage if required, but ensure it remains within Free Tier limits.

Step 7: Create a Key Pair

1. In the "Key Pair" section, choose **"Create New Key Pair"**.
2. Name the key pair (e.g., "MyKeyPair").
3. Download the `.pem` file and store it in a secure location.
    - This file is critical for connecting to your instance via SSH.

Step 8: Configure Security Group

1. AWS automatically creates a security group for your instance.
2. Verify that **port 22 (SSH)** is allowed from your IP address.
3. Add rules for additional ports if required, such as port **80 (HTTP)** for web server access.

Step 9: Launch the Instance

1. Review all settings on the final screen and click **"Launch Instance"**.
2. Wait for the instance to initialize. This can take a few minutes.

Step 10: Connect to the Instance

1. Return to the EC2 Dashboard and find your running instance.
2. Copy the **Public IP Address** or **Public DNS** of the instance.
3. Connect to the instance using one of the following methods:

Option 1: SSH (Command Line)

- Open a terminal on your local machine.
- Navigate to the directory where your `.pem` file is stored.
- Run the following command:

```
bash
Copy code
ssh -i "MyKeyPair.pem" ec2-user@<Public_IP>
```

- Replace `<Public_IP>` with the actual IP address of your instance.

Option 2: Browser-Based Console

- In the EC2 Dashboard, select your instance and click **"Connect"**.
- Choose **"Session Manager"** or **"SSH Client"** to open a terminal directly in your browser.

Optional: Post-Launch Configuration

1. Update and install software:

```
bash
Copy code
sudo yum update -y
sudo yum install httpd -y
```

2. Start and enable the web server:

```
bash
Copy code
sudo systemctl start httpd
sudo systemctl enable httpd
```

3. Test connectivity by visiting the instance's public IP in a web browser.

Validation

- Verify the instance is running by checking its status in the EC2 Dashboard.
- Confirm connectivity by:
  - Successfully connecting via SSH or browser console.
  - Accessing a hosted web page, if configured.

Best Practices for Managing EC2 Instances

1. **Terminate Unused Instances**:
   - To avoid unnecessary charges, terminate instances when they are no longer needed.
2. **Secure Key Pair Files**:
   - Never share or lose your `.pem` file.
3. **Monitor Usage**:
   - Regularly check resource utilization to stay within Free Tier limits.

Expected Outcome

By completing this lab, you will:

- Have launched and configured a virtual machine in AWS.
- Understand how to connect to and interact with an EC2 instance.
- Be ready to use EC2 instances for various tasks in subsequent labs.

Lab 3: Setting Up an Amazon S3 Bucket

Objective:
In this lab, you will learn how to create, manage, and use an Amazon S3 bucket for cloud-based object storage. By the end of the lab, you will have successfully created an S3 bucket, uploaded files, set appropriate permissions, and retrieved a file using its object URL.

Why This Lab is Important

Amazon S3 (Simple Storage Service) is a cornerstone of AWS, providing scalable object storage for various use cases such as backups, data archives, and hosting static websites. Understanding how to create and manage S3 buckets is essential for managing cloud storage effectively.

Prerequisites

- An AWS account (set up in Lab 1).
- Basic understanding of file storage and retrieval.

Detailed Steps

Step 1: Access the S3 Dashboard

1. Log in to the AWS Management Console. (https://aws.amazon.com/console/)
2. Navigate to **S3** under the "Storage" section.
3. You will land on the S3 Dashboard, which lists your existing buckets (if any).

Step 2: Create a Bucket

1. Click the **"Create Bucket"** button.
2. Enter a unique bucket name:
   - Bucket names must be globally unique across AWS.
   - Use a name that reflects its purpose, e.g., `my-first-s3-bucket`
3. Select a region:
   - Choose a region closest to your location to reduce latency.
4. Keep the default settings for:
   - **Block Public Access**: Ensure all options are enabled to prevent unauthorized access.
   - **Versioning**: Leave disabled for now (can be enabled later for version tracking).
5. Click **"Create Bucket"** to finalize the setup.

Step 3: Upload a File

1. Open your newly created bucket from the list.
2. Click **"Upload"**, then drag and drop a file from your computer or use the **"Add files"** button.
   - Choose a small text file, image, or document for testing purposes.

3. Leave the default settings for storage class and encryption (Amazon S3 Standard and no encryption for now).
4. Click **"Upload"** to add the file to the bucket.

Step 4: Configure Object Permissions

1. Navigate to the file you just uploaded and select it.
2. Review the permissions:
    - By default, the object is private, meaning only you can access it.
3. (Optional) If you want the object to be publicly accessible:
    - Click **"Actions"** > **"Make public"**.
    - Confirm the change.

Step 5: Retrieve Object URL

1. With the file selected, find the **Object URL** in the details pane.
    - The URL format is usually: `https://<bucket-name>.s3.<region>.amazonaws.com/<file-name>`
2. Copy the URL and open it in a web browser.
    - If the object is public, it should display or download the file.
    - If the object is private, you will receive an "Access Denied" error.

Step 6: Explore Bucket Features (Optional)

1. **Versioning**:
    - Enable versioning to keep multiple versions of objects in the bucket.
    - Test by uploading a file with the same name and checking the version history.
2. **Lifecycle Rules**:
    - Set up lifecycle rules to automatically transition objects to cheaper storage classes or delete them after a specified time.
3. **Static Website Hosting**:
    - Enable static website hosting in the bucket settings to serve web pages directly from S3.

Validation

- Verify that the bucket appears in your S3 Dashboard.
- Confirm the uploaded file is listed in the bucket.
- Test the object URL to ensure the file is accessible (based on permissions set).

Best Practices for S3 Bucket Management

1. **Keep Buckets Private**:
    - Do not expose sensitive data by making buckets public unless necessary.
2. **Enable Logging**:
    - Turn on server access logging to track access requests for your bucket.

3. **Monitor Costs**:
   - Monitor storage usage to avoid exceeding Free Tier limits.

Expected Outcome

By completing this lab, you will:

- Have created and configured an S3 bucket.
- Successfully uploaded and retrieved files from the bucket.
- Understand the basics of permissions, object URLs, and bucket features.

Lab 4: Creating a Custom Virtual Private Cloud (VPC)

Objective:
Learn how to create and configure a Virtual Private Cloud (VPC) in AWS. By the end of this lab, you will have set up a custom VPC, created public and private subnets, configured route tables, and tested connectivity between resources in your VPC.

Why This Lab is Important

A VPC is a key AWS service that enables you to create a logically isolated section of the AWS cloud. It provides full control over networking, including IP addressing, subnets, routing, and security. This lab introduces the foundational concepts and steps to design a secure and scalable cloud network.

Prerequisites

- An AWS account (set up in Lab 1).
- Familiarity with basic networking concepts, such as IP addresses and subnets.

Detailed Steps

Step 1: Access the VPC Dashboard

1. Log in to the AWS Management Console. (https://aws.amazon.com/console/)
2. Navigate to **VPC** under the "Networking & Content Delivery" section.
3. The VPC Dashboard will display existing VPCs and resources.

Step 2: Create a VPC

1. Click **"Create VPC"**.
2. Choose the **VPC only** option (for full customization).
3. Provide the following details:
   - **Name tag**: Enter a descriptive name, such as `MyCustomVPC`.
   - **IPv4 CIDR block**: Enter a CIDR block for your VPC (e.g., `10.0.0.0/16` for a network with 65,536 IP addresses).
   - **Tenancy**: Select **Default** unless you need dedicated hardware.
4. Click **"Create VPC"**.

Step 3: Create Subnets

1. From the VPC Dashboard, navigate to **Subnets** and click **"Create Subnet"**.
2. Create a **Public Subnet**:
   - **Name tag**: Enter a name such as `PublicSubnet`.
   - **VPC**: Select the VPC you created earlier.
   - **Availability Zone**: Choose an availability zone (e.g., `us-east-1a`).
   - **IPv4 CIDR block**: Use a smaller range within your VPC's CIDR block (e.g., `10.0.1.0/24` for 256 IP addresses).

3. Create a **Private Subnet**:
    - Repeat the above steps but name it `PrivateSubnet` and use a different CIDR block (e.g., `10.0.2.0/24`).

Step 4: Configure Route Tables

1. Navigate to **Route Tables** and locate the default route table associated with your VPC.
2. Rename it as `PrivateRouteTable` for clarity.
3. Create a new route table:
    - Click **"Create Route Table"** and name it `PublicRouteTable`.
    - Associate it with your custom VPC.
4. Edit Routes for the Public Route Table:
    - Add a route for internet access:
        - **Destination**: `0.0.0.0/0`
        - **Target**: Select the **Internet Gateway** created in the next step.
    - Save changes.
5. Associate Subnets with Route Tables:
    - Attach the `PublicSubnet` to the `PublicRouteTable`.
    - Attach the `PrivateSubnet` to the `PrivateRouteTable`.

Step 5: Create and Attach an Internet Gateway

1. Navigate to **Internet Gateways** and click **"Create Internet Gateway"**.
2. Name it `MyInternetGateway` and click **"Create"**.
3. Attach the gateway to your VPC:
    - Select the gateway and click **"Actions"** > **"Attach to VPC"**.
    - Choose your custom VPC and confirm.

Step 6: Test Connectivity

1. Launch an EC2 instance in the **Public Subnet**:
    - Use the `t2.micro` instance type and Amazon Linux 2 AMI.
    - Configure the security group to allow SSH (port 22) and HTTP (port 80) from your IP address.
    - Connect to the instance via SSH and test internet connectivity by running:

    ```
    bash
    Copy code
    ping google.com
    ```

2. Launch an EC2 instance in the **Private Subnet**:
    - Use similar settings as the public instance but with no internet access.
    - Confirm that this instance cannot access the internet.

Step 7: Configure NAT Gateway (Optional)

1. If you want the private instance to access the internet, create a NAT Gateway:

- Navigate to **NAT Gateways** and click **"Create NAT Gateway"**.
- Assign it to the Public Subnet and allocate an Elastic IP.
- Update the `PrivateRouteTable` with a route:
  - **Destination**: `0.0.0.0/0`
  - **Target**: Select the NAT Gateway.

2. Test internet access from the private instance.

Validation

- Verify that the VPC and subnets appear in the VPC Dashboard.
- Confirm internet access for the public EC2 instance and restricted access for the private EC2 instance.
- Test the functionality of the NAT Gateway if configured.

Best Practices for VPC Management

1. **Use CIDR Blocks Wisely**:
   - Plan IP ranges to avoid conflicts with on-premises networks.
2. **Secure Subnets**:
   - Ensure public subnets are exposed only when necessary, and private subnets remain isolated.
3. **Enable Flow Logs**:
   - Use VPC Flow Logs to monitor traffic in and out of your VPC for troubleshooting and security.

Expected Outcome

By completing this lab, you will:

- Have a fully functional custom VPC.
- Understand subnet configuration and route table management.
- Be able to test and validate network connectivity within your VPC.

Lab 5: Configuring IAM Roles and Policies

Objective:
In this lab, you will learn how to configure users, groups, roles, and policies using AWS Identity and Access Management (IAM). By the end of this lab, you will have created IAM users with specific permissions, assigned them to groups, and implemented a role for secure and controlled access to AWS resources.

Why This Lab is Important

AWS IAM is a critical service for managing access to AWS resources. Proper configuration of users, groups, roles, and policies is essential for maintaining security and ensuring that resources are accessed only by authorized entities. This lab provides hands-on experience in creating a secure, scalable access management system.

Prerequisites

- An AWS account (set up in Lab 1).
- Basic understanding of access control concepts, such as users, groups, and permissions.

Detailed Steps

Step 1: Access the IAM Dashboard

1. Log in to the AWS Management Console. (https://aws.amazon.com/console/)
2. Navigate to **IAM** under the "Security, Identity & Compliance" section.
3. Familiarize yourself with the IAM Dashboard, which includes sections for users, groups, roles, and policies.

Step 2: Create an IAM User

1. From the IAM Dashboard, click **"Users"** in the left-hand menu
2. Click **"Add Users"**.
3. Enter a username, such as `TestUser`.
4. Select the type of access:
   - **Programmatic access**: Generates an access key ID and secret access key for CLI/API access.
   - **AWS Management Console access**: Allows the user to log in to the AWS Console. Set an initial password if enabling this option.
5. Click **"Next: Permissions"**.

Step 3: Create a Group and Attach Policies

1. On the permissions screen, choose **"Add user to group"** and click **"Create group"**.
2. Name the group, such as `S3Admins`.
3. Attach a policy to the group:
   - Search for the `AmazonS3FullAccess` policy and select it.

  - This policy grants full access to Amazon S3 resources.
4. Click **"Create group"**.
5. Add the user to the group and click **"Next: Tags"**.

Step 4: Assign Tags (Optional)

1. Add metadata to the user, such as `Department: IT` or `Project: CloudLab`.
2. Tags are optional but useful for organizing resources.
3. Click **"Next: Review"**.

Step 5: Review and Create the User

1. Review the user details, including the assigned group and policies.
2. Click **"Create user"**.
3. Save the access key ID and secret access key securely if programmatic access was enabled.

Step 6: Create an IAM Role

1. Navigate to **Roles** in the IAM Dashboard and click **"Create Role"**.
2. Choose the trusted entity:
   - Select **AWS Service**.
   - For this lab, choose **EC2** to allow an EC2 instance to assume the role.
3. Click **"Next: Permissions"**.

Step 7: Attach a Policy to the Role

1. Search for and select the `AmazonS3ReadOnlyAccess` policy.
   - This policy allows read-only access to S3 resources.
2. Click **"Next: Tags"**, then **"Next: Review"**.
3. Name the role, such as `S3ReadOnlyRole`, and click **"Create Role"**.

Step 8: Test the IAM Role

1. Launch an EC2 instance (refer to Lab 2 for details).
2. While launching the instance, under the **Configure Instance Details** step:
   - Assign the `S3ReadOnlyRole` to the instance.
3. Connect to the EC2 instance via SSH.
4. Verify role functionality by running the following commands:

   ```
   bash
   Copy code
   sudo yum install -y aws-cli
   aws s3 ls
   ```

   - This should list all S3 buckets in your account if the role is properly configured.

Step 9: Test IAM User Access

1. Log in to the AWS Management Console using the IAM user's credentials.
2. Verify the user can access S3 and perform actions (e.g., create a bucket) as allowed by the `AmazonS3FullAccess` policy.
3. Test logging in with incorrect permissions to ensure restricted access.

Optional: Create a Custom Policy

1. Navigate to **Policies** in the IAM Dashboard and click **"Create Policy"**.
2. Use the visual editor or JSON editor to define permissions:
   - Example policy to allow access to a specific bucket:

```
json
Copy code
{
  "Version": "2012-10-17",
  "Statement": [
    {
      "Effect": "Allow",
      "Action": "s3:*",
      "Resource": "arn:aws:s3:::example-bucket-name/*"
    }
  ]
}
```

3. Name the policy, such as `CustomS3Policy`, and attach it to a user, group, or role.

Validation

- Verify the IAM user's access by testing actions like creating S3 buckets.
- Confirm the IAM role is working by listing S3 buckets from the EC2 instance.
- Test the custom policy to ensure it allows or denies the intended actions.

Best Practices for IAM Configuration

1. **Follow the Principle of Least Privilege**:
   - Assign only the minimum permissions required for each user, group, or role.
2. **Enable Multi-Factor Authentication (MFA)**:
   - Use MFA for the root user and all IAM users with console access.
3. **Rotate Access Keys Regularly**:
   - Avoid using long-lived access keys. Rotate them periodically for security.
4. **Monitor IAM Activity**:
   - Use AWS CloudTrail to track changes and monitor usage.

Expected Outcome

By completing this lab, you will:

- Have created an IAM user, group, and role with appropriate permissions.
- Understand how to securely manage access to AWS resources.
- Be able to test and validate access controls using IAM.

Lab 6: Deploying and Managing CloudWatch Alarms

Objective:
In this lab, you will learn how to monitor AWS resources using Amazon CloudWatch by creating and managing alarms. These alarms will help track key metrics, such as CPU utilization for an EC2 instance. By the end of this lab, you will have set up a CloudWatch alarm and tested it to ensure it triggers under the specified conditions.

Why This Lab is Important

Monitoring cloud resources is essential for maintaining application performance and ensuring infrastructure stability. Amazon CloudWatch provides robust monitoring tools for collecting and analyzing metrics, setting alarms, and automating responses to system changes. This lab introduces foundational skills for effective cloud monitoring.

Prerequisites

- An AWS account (set up in Lab 1).
- A running EC2 instance (from Lab 2) with a web server installed, or the ability to launch a new instance.

Detailed Steps

Step 1: Launch or Use an EC2 Instance

1. If you do not already have a running EC2 instance:
   - Launch a **t2.micro** instance with the Amazon Linux 2 AMI (Free Tier eligible).
   - Install a web server to simulate traffic:

     ```
     bash
     Copy code
     sudo yum update -y
     sudo yum install httpd -y
     sudo systemctl start httpd
     sudo systemctl enable httpd
     echo "Welcome to CloudWatch Monitoring" | sudo tee
     /var/www/html/index.html
     ```

2. Ensure the instance is running and accessible. Verify connectivity by visiting the public IP address in your web browser.

Step 2: Access the CloudWatch Dashboard

1. Navigate to **CloudWatch** in the AWS Management Console. (https://aws.amazon.com/console/)
2. Explore the dashboard to familiarize yourself with the sections, including **Metrics**, **Alarms**, **Logs**, and **Insights**.

Step 3: Create a CloudWatch Alarm

1. From the left-hand menu, click **"Alarms"** and then **"Create alarm"**.
2. **Select a Metric**:
   - Click **"Select metric"** and choose **EC2** > **Per-Instance Metrics**.
   - Locate your instance and select the **CPUUtilization** metric.
3. **Define the Alarm Conditions**:
   - Specify the conditions for the alarm:
     - **Threshold type**: Static.
     - **Threshold value**: 70% (to trigger the alarm if CPU utilization exceeds 70%).
     - **Period**: 5 minutes.
4. Click **"Next"**.

Step 4: Configure Actions

1. **Notification**:
   - Set up a notification for when the alarm state changes (e.g., to "ALARM").
   - Create or select an Amazon Simple Notification Service (SNS) topic:
     - If creating a new topic, name it (e.g., `HighCPUAlarm`) and provide your email address for notifications.
     - Confirm the subscription by checking your email and clicking the confirmation link.
2. (Optional) Add additional actions, such as triggering an auto-scaling policy or stopping the instance.

Step 5: Name and Review the Alarm

1. Provide a descriptive name for the alarm, such as `HighCPUAlarm`.
2. Review the configuration details and click **"Create alarm"**.

Step 6: Test the Alarm

1. Simulate high CPU utilization:
   - Connect to your instance via SSH.
   - Install a stress testing tool:

```
bash
Copy code
sudo yum install stress -y
```

   - Run a CPU-intensive process:

```
bash
Copy code
stress --cpu 1 --timeout 300
```

   - Monitor the instance's CPU utilization in CloudWatch.
2. Wait for the alarm to transition to the **ALARM** state (this may take a few minutes).

Step 7: Test Notifications

1. Check your email for a notification from CloudWatch.
   - Ensure the message includes details about the alarm and its triggered condition.
2. Once CPU utilization returns to normal, verify that the alarm returns to the **OK** state and you receive another notification (if configured).

Step 8: Clean Up (Optional)

1. Delete the alarm if it is no longer needed:
   - Go to the CloudWatch dashboard, select the alarm, and click **"Actions"** > **"Delete"**.
2. Stop or terminate the EC2 instance to avoid unnecessary costs.

Validation

- Verify the alarm was triggered when CPU utilization exceeded 70%.
- Confirm notifications were received via the configured SNS topic.
- Ensure the alarm returned to the **OK** state after CPU usage normalized.

Best Practices for CloudWatch Monitoring

1. **Set Realistic Thresholds**:
   - Tailor alarm thresholds to your application's normal operating ranges.
2. **Use Multiple Metrics**:
   - Monitor additional metrics, such as disk I/O, memory usage, or network traffic, for a comprehensive view of resource performance.
3. **Automate Responses**:
   - Integrate CloudWatch alarms with auto-scaling policies or Lambda functions to automatically address performance issues.
4. **Enable Detailed Monitoring**:
   - For more granular data, enable detailed monitoring on EC2 instances (charges may apply).

Expected Outcome

By completing this lab, you will:

- Understand how to monitor AWS resources using CloudWatch.
- Have created and tested a CloudWatch alarm.
- Be able to configure notifications for key metrics and take automated actions based on alarm states.

Lab 7: Creating and Configuring a Load Balancer

Objective:
In this lab, you will learn how to set up an Elastic Load Balancer (ELB) in AWS. A load balancer distributes incoming traffic across multiple EC2 instances, ensuring high availability, fault tolerance, and improved application performance. By the end of this lab, you will have configured an Application Load Balancer (ALB) and verified its functionality.

Why This Lab is Important

Load balancing is a fundamental aspect of cloud infrastructure, enabling applications to handle varying levels of traffic by distributing requests efficiently. AWS Elastic Load Balancing provides a managed solution to ensure reliability and scalability for your applications. This lab introduces the steps to configure an ALB and test its effectiveness.

Prerequisites

- An AWS account (set up in Lab 1).
- At least two EC2 instances running in the same VPC (refer to Lab 2 for launching instances).
- A basic understanding of networking and web server configurations.

Detailed Steps

Step 1: Launch Two EC2 Instances

1. **Instance Configuration**:
   - Launch two **t2.micro** instances with the Amazon Linux 2 AMI (Free Tier eligible).
   - Assign them to the same VPC and select different subnets for redundancy.
2. **Install a Web Server**:
   - Connect to each instance via SSH and install a web server (e.g., Apache):

     ```
     bash
     Copy code
     sudo yum update -y
     sudo yum install httpd -y
     sudo systemctl start httpd
     sudo systemctl enable httpd
     ```

   - Create a simple HTML page on each instance to distinguish them:
     - On **Instance 1**:

       ```
       bash
       Copy code
       echo "This is Instance 1" | sudo tee
       /var/www/html/index.html
       ```

- On **Instance 2**:

```
bash
Copy code
echo "This is Instance 2" | sudo tee
/var/www/html/index.html
```

3. **Configure Security Groups**:
   - Ensure the security group for both instances allows inbound traffic on **port 80 (HTTP)** from all sources.

Step 2: Access the Load Balancer Dashboard

1. Navigate to **EC2** in the AWS Management Console.
2. In the left-hand menu, select **Load Balancers** under the "Load Balancing" section.
3. Click **"Create Load Balancer"**.

Step 3: Create an Application Load Balancer

1. **Load Balancer Type**:
   - Select **Application Load Balancer**.
2. **Basic Configuration**:
   - Name your load balancer, e.g., `MyApplicationLoadBalancer`.
   - Select **Internet-facing** as the scheme.
   - Choose IPv4 under **IP address type**.
3. **Listeners and Availability Zones**:
   - Ensure a listener on **port 80** (HTTP) is added.
   - Select the VPC that contains your EC2 instances.
   - Choose at least two subnets in different availability zones.

Step 4: Configure Security Groups

1. Select an existing security group or create a new one:
   - The security group should allow inbound traffic on **port 80 (HTTP)**.
2. Attach the security group to the load balancer.

Step 5: Configure the Target Group

1. **Target Group Details**:
   - Name the target group, e.g., `MyTargetGroup`.
   - Choose **Instances** as the target type.
2. **Health Check Settings**:
   - Set the **Path** to `/` to check the root of the web server.
   - Leave other settings as default (e.g., interval and timeout).
3. **Register Targets**:
   - Select the two EC2 instances you launched earlier and add them to the target group.

- Click **"Create Target Group"**.

Step 6: Review and Create the Load Balancer

1. Review all configurations, ensuring the correct VPC, subnets, and security group are selected.
2. Click **"Create Load Balancer"** and wait for the load balancer to become active (this may take a few minutes).

Step 7: Test the Load Balancer

1. Obtain the **DNS name** of the load balancer from the EC2 dashboard under **Load Balancers**.
2. Open a web browser and navigate to the DNS name:
    - Refresh the page multiple times to observe traffic alternating between the two instances.
    - You should see "This is Instance 1" and "This is Instance 2" appearing alternately.

Step 8: Explore Load Balancer Metrics (Optional)

1. Navigate to **CloudWatch** in the AWS Management Console.
2. View metrics for your load balancer under the **ELB namespace**, such as:
    - **Request count**: Total number of requests handled by the load balancer.
    - **Healthy host count**: Number of healthy targets in the target group.
3. Use these metrics to monitor the performance and health of your load balancer.

Validation

- Confirm that the load balancer distributes traffic between the two EC2 instances.
- Verify the health check status of targets in the target group (all targets should be healthy).
- Test the security group settings by accessing the load balancer from different locations.

Best Practices for Load Balancer Configuration

1. **Use Multiple Availability Zones**:
    - Distribute instances across multiple availability zones for improved fault tolerance.
2. **Secure the Load Balancer**:
    - Restrict access to the load balancer by configuring IP-based rules in the security group.
3. **Monitor and Scale**:
    - Use CloudWatch metrics to identify bottlenecks and scale your infrastructure accordingly.
4. **Enable HTTPS**:
    - For production environments, configure the load balancer to use HTTPS by attaching an SSL certificate.

Expected Outcome

By completing this lab, you will:

- Understand how to set up and configure an Application Load Balancer.
- Be able to distribute traffic across multiple EC2 instances.
- Gain experience in monitoring load balancer performance and health.

Lab 8: Deploying an AWS RDS Instance and Performing a Backup

Objective:
In this lab, you will learn how to deploy an Amazon Relational Database Service (RDS) instance and perform a manual backup. RDS provides a scalable and fully managed relational database solution, making it easy to set up and operate databases in the cloud. By the end of this lab, you will have a running RDS instance and a snapshot backup for disaster recovery.

Why This Lab is Important

Amazon RDS simplifies database management by automating tasks such as provisioning, backups, and patching. Understanding how to deploy and back up an RDS instance is essential for ensuring data availability and reliability in cloud environments.

Prerequisites

- An AWS account (set up in Lab 1).
- Basic knowledge of relational databases and SQL.

Detailed Steps

Step 1: Access the RDS Console

1. Log in to the AWS Management Console. (https://aws.amazon.com/console/)
2. Navigate to **RDS** under the "Database" section.
3. Explore the dashboard to familiarize yourself with the sections, such as **Databases**, **Snapshots**, and **Parameter Groups**.

Step 2: Create an RDS Instance

1. Click **"Create Database"**.
2. **Choose a Database Creation Method**:
   - Select **Standard Create** for a customizable setup.
3. **Engine Options**:
   - Choose a database engine, such as:
     - **Amazon Aurora** (preferred for high performance and scalability).
     - **MySQL** (Free Tier eligible and widely used).
4. **Edition**:
   - If using MySQL, select the latest version for better features and security.

Step 3: Configure the RDS Instance

1. **DB Instance Size**:
   - Choose **db.t2.micro** (Free Tier eligible) for low-cost testing and development.
2. **Settings**:
   - DB Instance Identifier: Name your database, e.g., `MyRDSInstance`.
   - Master Username: Set a username, such as `admin`.

- Master Password: Create a strong password and confirm it.

3. **Storage**:
   - Select **General Purpose (SSD)** storage with 20GB (Free Tier eligible).
   - Enable **storage autoscaling** to allow automatic adjustment of storage capacity.

Step 4: Network and Security

1. **VPC**:
   - Choose the default VPC or a custom VPC if configured in earlier labs.
2. **Subnet Group**:
   - Select the default subnet group.
3. **Public Access**:
   - Set **Publicly Accessible** to **Yes** if you want to connect from your local machine. Otherwise, set it to **No** for enhanced security.
4. **Security Group**:
   - Create or select a security group that allows inbound traffic on the database port (e.g., **3306** for MySQL).
   - Restrict access to your IP address for security.

Step 5: Additional Configurations

1. **Database Options**:
   - Set the initial database name (e.g., `labdb`).
2. **Backup**:
   - Enable automatic backups with a retention period of 7 days.
3. **Monitoring**:
   - Enable Enhanced Monitoring for detailed performance metrics (optional).
4. **Maintenance**:
   - Keep default settings for automatic minor version upgrades and maintenance windows.

Step 6: Launch the RDS Instance

1. Review the configuration and click **"Create Database"**.
2. Wait for the instance status to change to **Available**. This may take a few minutes.

Step 7: Connect to the RDS Instance

1. Copy the **Endpoint** of the RDS instance from the database details page.
2. Use a MySQL client (e.g., MySQL Workbench or the `mysql` CLI) to connect:

```
bash
Copy code
mysql -h <RDS_ENDPOINT> -P 3306 -u admin -p
```

   - Replace `<RDS_ENDPOINT>` with your instance's endpoint.
3. Test the connection by creating a database and table:

```
sql
Copy code
CREATE DATABASE labdb;
USE labdb;
CREATE TABLE students (
    id INT PRIMARY KEY,
    name VARCHAR(50)
);
```

Step 8: Perform a Manual Backup

1. Navigate to the RDS console and select your instance.
2. Click **"Actions"** > **"Take Snapshot"**.
3. Provide a name for the snapshot, such as `MyFirstBackup`, and confirm.
4. Wait for the snapshot status to change to **Available**.

Step 9: Restore from Snapshot (Optional)

1. Select the snapshot you created and click **"Actions"** > **"Restore Snapshot"**.
2. Configure a new DB instance name (e.g., `RestoredRDSInstance`).
3. Complete the restoration process and test connectivity to the restored database.

Validation

- Verify the RDS instance is **Available** in the console.
- Confirm the ability to connect to the database using a MySQL client.
- Ensure the snapshot is created and visible in the **Snapshots** section.

Best Practices for Managing RDS Instances

1. **Secure Access**:
   - Always restrict security group rules to specific IP ranges or VPCs.
2. **Monitor Performance**:
   - Use Amazon CloudWatch to track metrics such as CPU utilization, disk I/O, and connections.
3. **Automate Backups**:
   - Enable automatic backups to ensure data recovery in case of failures.
4. **Optimize Costs**:
   - Choose the appropriate instance type and storage options based on workload requirements.

Expected Outcome

By completing this lab, you will:

- Deploy a fully functional Amazon RDS instance.
- Understand how to connect to and manage a relational database in AWS.
- Create a manual snapshot backup for disaster recovery.

Lab 9: Configuring EC2 Auto Scaling

Objective:
In this lab, you will set up an Auto Scaling Group (ASG) for EC2 instances to automatically adjust the number of running instances based on demand. This ensures high availability, cost efficiency, and optimal performance of applications. By the end of this lab, you will have a fully functional Auto Scaling Group that can scale in and out based on CPU utilization.

Why This Lab is Important

Auto Scaling is essential for managing variable workloads in cloud environments. It ensures that applications remain available during peak demand and reduces costs during low usage periods by scaling resources dynamically. This lab demonstrates how to configure and test AWS Auto Scaling.

Prerequisites

- An AWS account (set up in Lab 1).
- A basic understanding of EC2 instances and Amazon Machine Images (AMIs).
- An Application Load Balancer (ALB) configured in Lab 7 (optional but recommended).

Detailed Steps

Step 1: Create a Launch Template

1. Navigate to **EC2** in the AWS Management Console. (https://aws.amazon.com/console/)
2. In the left-hand menu, select **Launch Templates** and click **"Create Launch Template"**.
3. **Template Details**:
   - **Name**: Enter a name such as `AutoScalingTemplate`.
   - **Template Version**: Keep the default version.
4. **AMI**:
   - Select the Amazon Linux 2 AMI (Free Tier eligible).
5. **Instance Type**:
   - Choose **t2.micro** (Free Tier eligible).
6. **Key Pair**:
   - Select an existing key pair or create a new one.
7. **Network Settings**:
   - Leave the default VPC and subnet settings.
8. **User Data (Optional)**:
   - Add a script to configure a web server during instance initialization:

```
bash
Copy code
#!/bin/bash
sudo yum update -y
sudo yum install httpd -y
sudo systemctl start httpd
sudo systemctl enable httpd
```

```
echo "Welcome to Auto Scaling Instance" | sudo tee
/var/www/html/index.html
```

9. Click **"Create Launch Template"**.

Step 2: Create an Auto Scaling Group

1. Navigate to **Auto Scaling Groups** in the EC2 Dashboard and click **"Create Auto Scaling Group"**.
2. **Basic Configuration**:
   - **Name**: Enter a name such as `MyAutoScalingGroup`.
   - **Launch Template**: Select the launch template created in Step 1.
3. **Instance Purchase Options**:
   - Use the default option for On-Demand Instances.
4. **VPC and Subnets**:
   - Select the VPC and at least two subnets in different availability zones for high availability.

Step 3: Configure Scaling Policies

1. Set the desired capacity:
   - **Desired Instances**: 1.
   - **Minimum Instances**: 1.
   - **Maximum Instances**: 3.
2. Add a scaling policy:
   - **Scale Out** (Add Instances):
     - Trigger: When CPU utilization exceeds 70% for 2 consecutive periods of 1 minute.
   - **Scale In** (Remove Instances):
     - Trigger: When CPU utilization falls below 30% for 2 consecutive periods of 1 minute.

Step 4: Attach a Load Balancer (Optional)

1. If you configured an ALB in Lab 7:
   - Select the ALB to distribute incoming traffic across instances.
   - Attach the target group associated with the ALB.

Step 5: Review and Create the Auto Scaling Group

1. Review all settings to ensure accuracy.
2. Click **"Create Auto Scaling Group"**.

Step 6: Test Auto Scaling

1. Simulate High CPU Utilization:
   - Connect to an instance in the Auto Scaling Group via SSH.

- Install a stress testing tool:

```
bash
Copy code
sudo yum install stress -y
```

- Run a CPU-intensive process:

```
bash
Copy code
stress --cpu 1 --timeout 300
```

- Monitor the Auto Scaling Group in the AWS Management Console. A new instance should be launched as CPU utilization exceeds 70%.

2. Simulate Low CPU Utilization:
   - Stop the stress process and allow CPU usage to drop.
   - Monitor the Auto Scaling Group. Instances should terminate as utilization falls below 30%.

Step 7: Explore Auto Scaling Metrics

1. Navigate to **CloudWatch** in the AWS Management Console.
2. Review metrics such as:
   - **GroupInServiceInstances**: Number of running instances.
   - **GroupDesiredCapacity**: Target number of instances.
   - **GroupMinSize** and **GroupMaxSize**: Minimum and maximum instance limits.
3. Create CloudWatch alarms to monitor Auto Scaling activity, if desired.

Validation

- Confirm that the Auto Scaling Group launches additional instances when CPU utilization exceeds the threshold.
- Verify that instances are terminated when CPU utilization drops below the threshold.
- Test the optional ALB integration by accessing the ALB's DNS name and observing traffic distribution across instances.

Best Practices for Auto Scaling

1. **Use Predictive Scaling**:
   - Enable predictive scaling for better forecasting of demand trends.
2. **Monitor Costs**:
   - Regularly review scaling activity to optimize costs and ensure scaling policies align with workload patterns.
3. **Enable Termination Protection**:
   - For critical instances, enable termination protection to prevent accidental termination.
4. **Test Policies**:

- Periodically simulate scaling conditions to ensure policies behave as expected.

Expected Outcome

By completing this lab, you will:

- Have configured an Auto Scaling Group to dynamically scale EC2 instances based on demand.
- Understand how to test and monitor Auto Scaling behavior.
- Be able to integrate Auto Scaling with an Application Load Balancer for improved traffic distribution.

Lab 10: Setting Up AWS Lambda Functions

Objective:
In this lab, you will learn how to create, deploy, and test an AWS Lambda function. AWS Lambda allows you to run code without provisioning or managing servers, enabling you to focus on application development rather than infrastructure management. By the end of this lab, you will have a functional Lambda function that responds to events and can optionally integrate with other AWS services.

Why This Lab is Important

Serverless computing with AWS Lambda is a cost-effective and scalable way to run code in response to events such as API requests, file uploads, or scheduled tasks. Understanding Lambda is essential for building modern, event-driven architectures in the cloud.

Prerequisites

- An AWS account (set up in Lab 1).
- Familiarity with basic programming concepts in Python or another supported language.

Detailed Steps

Step 1: Access the Lambda Console

1. Log in to the AWS Management Console. (https://aws.amazon.com/console/)
2. Navigate to **Lambda** under the "Compute" section.
3. Explore the Lambda Dashboard to familiarize yourself with its features.

Step 2: Create a New Lambda Function

1. Click **"Create function"**.
2. **Author from Scratch**:
   - Function name: Enter a descriptive name, such as `MyFirstLambdaFunction`.
   - Runtime: Select **Python 3.9** (or another supported language of your choice).
   - Execution role: Choose one of the following:
     - **Create a new role with basic Lambda permissions**: AWS will create a role with minimal permissions to execute the function.
     - **Use an existing role**: Select a previously created role with the necessary permissions.
3. Click **"Create function"**.

Step 3: Write the Lambda Function Code

1. In the Lambda function editor, enter the following sample Python code:

```
python
Copy code
```

```
import json

def lambda_handler(event, context):
    return {
        'statusCode': 200,
        'body': json.dumps('Hello from AWS Lambda!')
    }
```

2. Save the function by clicking **"Deploy"**.

Step 4: Test the Lambda Function

1. Click **"Test"** in the Lambda console.
2. **Create a Test Event**:
    - Event template: Select **"Hello World"**.
    - Event name: Enter a name, such as `TestLambdaFunction`.
3. Save the event and click **"Test"** to invoke the function.
4. Review the output in the **Execution result** section. It should display:

```
json
Copy code
{
    "statusCode": 200,
    "body": "\"Hello from AWS Lambda!\""
}
```

Step 5: Set Up an S3 Trigger (Optional)

1. Navigate to the **"Configuration"** tab and select **"Triggers"**.
2. Click **"Add trigger"** and choose **S3**.
3. Configure the trigger:
    - Bucket: Select an existing S3 bucket or create a new one.
    - Event type: Choose **ObjectCreated (All)** to trigger the function whenever a file is uploaded to the bucket.
4. Save the trigger.

Step 6: Test the S3 Trigger (Optional)

1. Upload a file to the S3 bucket.
2. Monitor the **Monitor** tab in the Lambda console to view invocation metrics and logs.
3. View detailed logs in **Amazon CloudWatch Logs** to ensure the function executed correctly.

Step 7: Explore Environment Variables (Optional)

1. Navigate to the **"Configuration"** tab and select **"Environment variables"**.
2. Add a key-value pair:
    - Key: `GREETING`
    - Value: `Welcome to AWS Lambda`

3. Update the function code to use the environment variable:

```
python
Copy code
import os
import json

def lambda_handler(event, context):
    greeting = os.getenv('GREETING', 'Hello from AWS Lambda!')
    return {
        'statusCode': 200,
        'body': json.dumps(greeting)
    }
```

4. Deploy and test the updated function.

Step 8: Schedule the Lambda Function (Optional)

1. Navigate to the **"Configuration"** tab and select **"Triggers"**.
2. Add a **CloudWatch Events** trigger to schedule the function:
    - Rule name: `DailyTrigger`.
    - Schedule expression: `rate(1 day)` (runs the function once a day).
3. Save the trigger and monitor the function for scheduled executions.

Validation

- Verify the Lambda function runs successfully with the test event.
- Confirm the function is triggered by S3 uploads (if configured).
- Check the CloudWatch Logs for execution details and errors.
- Test optional features, such as environment variables and scheduled triggers.

Best Practices for Lambda Functions

1. **Minimize Function Size**:
    - Use lightweight libraries and minimize dependencies to reduce cold start times.
2. **Optimize Runtime Performance**:
    - Use efficient code and monitor execution times to keep costs low.
3. **Secure Permissions**:
    - Use IAM roles to grant the least privileges necessary for the function to execute.
4. **Monitor and Debug**:
    - Enable logging in CloudWatch and use AWS X-Ray for tracing function invocations.
5. **Test Extensively**:
    - Test Lambda functions with various input events to ensure robust handling.

Expected Outcome

By completing this lab, you will:

- Understand how to create, deploy, and test AWS Lambda functions.
- Learn how to integrate Lambda with other AWS services, such as S3 and CloudWatch.
- Be able to implement serverless solutions for event-driven use cases.

Appendix C: Practice Microsoft Azure Labs

Lab 1: Creating a Microsoft Azure Account

Objective:
This lab guides you through the process of creating a Microsoft Azure Free Account, which will serve as the foundation for future labs. By the end of this lab, you will have an active Azure account with access to Azure services and will verify successful setup by accessing the Azure Portal.

Why This Lab is Important

Microsoft Azure is a leading cloud service provider offering a broad range of services for computing, storage, networking, and more. Setting up an Azure account is the first step toward gaining hands-on experience in cloud computing and exploring the Azure ecosystem.

Prerequisites

- A valid email address.
- A payment method (credit or debit card) for identity verification.

Detailed Steps

Step 1: Access the Azure Free Account Sign-Up Page

1. Open a web browser and navigate to the Azure Free Account page. (https://azure.microsoft.com/free/)
2. Review the benefits of the Azure Free Account, which includes:
   - **$200 credit** for 30 days to explore paid services.
   - Access to **popular free services** for 12 months, such as Azure Virtual Machines, Blob Storage, and SQL Database.
   - Always free services like Azure Functions and Event Grid.

Step 2: Start the Account Creation Process

1. Click the **"Start free"** button on the Azure Free Account page.
2. Sign in with your Microsoft account. If you don't have one, click **"Create one!"** and follow the steps to set up a Microsoft account.

Step 3: Verify Identity and Provide Details

1. Enter your personal information:
   - Name
   - Country/Region
   - Phone number
2. Complete phone verification:
   - Enter your phone number and select text or call verification.
   - Enter the code received to verify your phone number.
3. Provide payment information:

- Add a credit or debit card for identity verification. Azure may place a small temporary hold on the card, which will be refunded shortly.
- Note: Azure will not charge you unless you explicitly upgrade to a paid subscription.

Step 4: Agree to Terms and Activate the Subscription

1. Review the subscription agreement and Microsoft's privacy statement.
2. Accept the terms and click **"Sign up"** to activate your Azure Free Account.

Step 5: Access the Azure Portal

1. Once your account is created, navigate to the Azure Portal. (https://portal.azure.com/)
2. Sign in using your Microsoft account credentials.
3. Take a moment to familiarize yourself with the Azure Portal, including:
   - **Search bar**: Quickly find resources and services.
   - **Dashboard**: Displays an overview of your resources and services.
   - **All Services**: Lists all Azure services categorized by type.

Step 6: Explore Core Azure Services

1. Access key services to understand the Azure ecosystem:
   - **Compute**: Navigate to "Virtual Machines" to view or create VMs.
   - **Storage**: Explore "Storage Accounts" to understand Azure's storage solutions.
   - **Networking**: Visit "Virtual Networks" to see networking capabilities.
2. Ensure your Azure account reflects the available Free Tier services and $200 credit.

Validation

- Confirm that you can log in to the Azure Portal and access the dashboard.
- Verify that the $200 free credit is visible in your subscription details.
- Optionally, take a screenshot of the Azure Portal dashboard showing your account name for documentation.

Best Practices for Managing Your Azure Account

1. **Enable Cost Management**:
   - Use Azure Cost Management to monitor your spending and avoid exceeding your free credit.
2. **Secure Your Account**:
   - Enable Multi-Factor Authentication (MFA) for added security.
3. **Explore Free Resources**:
   - Focus on Free Tier services to maximize learning without incurring charges.
4. **Set Spending Alerts**:
   - Configure spending alerts to notify you if you approach your free credit limit.

Expected Outcome

By completing this lab, you will:

- Have an active Microsoft Azure Free Account.
- Be familiar with the Azure Portal and its key features.
- Be ready to explore and deploy Azure services in subsequent labs.

Lab 2: Launching a Virtual Machine (VM) in Microsoft Azure

Objective:
This lab guides you through the process of creating and configuring a virtual machine (VM) in Microsoft Azure. By the end of this lab, you will have deployed a VM, accessed it remotely, and performed basic configurations.

Why This Lab is Important

Azure Virtual Machines provide scalable and flexible compute resources in the cloud. Deploying and configuring VMs is a foundational skill for cloud computing, enabling you to host applications, test environments, and more.

Prerequisites

- A Microsoft Azure account (set up in Lab 1).
- Familiarity with basic networking concepts and remote access protocols.

Detailed Steps

Step 1: Access the Azure Portal

1. Log in to the Azure Portal. (https://portal.azure.com/)
2. Navigate to **Virtual Machines** by searching for "Virtual Machines" in the search bar or selecting it from the **All Services** menu under "Compute."

Step 2: Create a Virtual Machine

1. Click **"Create"** and select **"Azure Virtual Machine"**.
2. **Basics** Tab:
    - **Subscription**: Ensure your Free Trial or active subscription is selected.
    - **Resource Group**: Create a new resource group (e.g., `LabVMGroup`) or use an existing one.
    - **Virtual Machine Name**: Enter a descriptive name (e.g., `MyFirstVM`).
    - **Region**: Choose a region close to your location for better performance.
    - **Availability Options**: Select **No infrastructure redundancy required**.
    - **Image**: Choose **Ubuntu Server 20.04 LTS** or another preferred OS.
    - **Size**: Select **Standard_B1ls** (Free Tier eligible, if available) or **Standard_B1s**.
    - **Administrator Account**:
        - **Authentication Type**: Choose **SSH public key** or **Password**.
        - **Username**: Enter a username (e.g., `azureuser`).
        - **Password** or **SSH Key**:
            - For **Password**: Set a strong password.
            - For **SSH**: Paste your public key (generate one if you don't have it).

Step 3: Configure Networking

1. Under the **Networking** tab:
   - **Virtual Network**: Select the default virtual network or create a new one.
   - **Subnet**: Use the default or create a new subnet.
   - **Public IP**: Ensure a new public IP address is created.
   - **Inbound Port Rules**: Allow **SSH (22)** for Linux VMs or **RDP (3389)** for Windows VMs.
2. Leave other networking settings as default.

Step 4: Configure Management Options (Optional)

1. Under the **Management** tab:
   - Enable **Boot Diagnostics** for troubleshooting.
   - Leave other settings as default.
2. Click **Next** to skip the advanced settings and move to the **Review + Create** tab.

Step 5: Review and Create the VM

1. Review all the configurations to ensure they are correct.
2. Click **"Create"** to deploy the VM. Azure will take a few minutes to provision the VM.

Step 6: Connect to the VM

1. Once the VM is deployed, navigate to the **Virtual Machines** section in the Azure Portal and select your VM.
2. **For Linux VMs**:
   - Copy the public IP address of the VM.
   - Connect using SSH from your terminal:

     ```
     bash
     Copy code
     ssh azureuser@<Public_IP>
     ```

     Replace <Public_IP> with the actual IP address of the VM.

3. **For Windows VMs**:
   - Download the RDP file from the **Connect** tab.
   - Open the RDP file and log in with your credentials.

Step 7: Configure the VM (Optional)

1. **For Linux VMs**:
   - Update the system:

     ```
     bash
     Copy code
     ```

```
sudo apt update && sudo apt upgrade -y
```

- Install a web server (e.g., Nginx):

```
bash
Copy code
sudo apt install nginx -y
sudo systemctl start nginx
```

- Test the web server by visiting the VM's public IP in a browser.

2. **For Windows VMs**:
   - Install IIS via the **Server Manager** for testing purposes.

Step 8: Stop or Delete the VM

1. To avoid charges, stop or delete the VM after completing the lab:
   - Navigate to the **Virtual Machines** section.
   - Select your VM and click **"Stop"** or **"Delete"**.

Validation

- Confirm the VM is running by accessing it via SSH (Linux) or RDP (Windows).
- Verify any additional configurations, such as running a web server.
- Test network connectivity to the VM using its public IP address.

Best Practices for Azure Virtual Machines

1. **Monitor Costs**:
   - Regularly monitor resource usage in the **Cost Management + Billing** section.
2. **Use Tags**:
   - Apply tags to resources for better organization and cost tracking.
3. **Secure Access**:
   - Restrict inbound traffic to specific IP addresses for SSH or RDP.
   - Use Azure Bastion for secure, browser-based access without exposing ports.
4. **Enable Backups**:
   - Configure Azure Backup to protect your VM's data.

Expected Outcome

By completing this lab, you will:

- Deploy and configure a virtual machine in Microsoft Azure.
- Understand how to connect to and manage the VM.
- Be ready to use VMs for hosting applications, testing environments, or other workloads in future labs.

Lab 3: Setting Up a Storage Account and Blob Storage in Microsoft Azure

Objective:
This lab will guide you through creating a storage account in Microsoft Azure and configuring a Blob Storage container. By the end of this lab, you will understand how to create, upload, and manage files in Azure Blob Storage.

Why This Lab is Important

Azure Blob Storage provides scalable object storage for unstructured data, such as images, videos, backups, and logs. It's a foundational Azure service used in numerous scenarios, including cloud-native applications, data archiving, and big data analytics.

Prerequisites

- A Microsoft Azure account (set up in Lab 1).
- Familiarity with basic file storage concepts.

Detailed Steps

Step 1: Access the Azure Portal

1. Log in to the Azure Portal. (https://portal.azure.com/)
2. Navigate to **Storage Accounts** by searching for "Storage Accounts" in the search bar or selecting it from the **All Services** menu under "Storage."

Step 2: Create a Storage Account

1. Click **"Create"** to start setting up a new storage account.
2. **Basics** Tab:
   - **Subscription**: Ensure your Free Trial or active subscription is selected.
   - **Resource Group**: Create a new resource group (e.g., `StorageLabGroup`) or use an existing one.
   - **Storage Account Name**: Enter a globally unique name (e.g., `mystoragelab123`).
   - **Region**: Choose a region close to your location.
   - **Performance**: Select **Standard** (cost-effective for general purposes).
   - **Redundancy**: Choose **Locally-redundant storage (LRS)** for single-region replication.
3. Click **"Next"** to configure additional settings.

Step 3: Configure Advanced Options (Optional)

1. Under the **Advanced** tab:
   - **Blob access tier (default)**: Choose **Hot** for frequent access.
   - Leave other settings as default unless specific configurations are needed.
2. Click **"Review + Create"**, review the settings, and click **"Create"**.
3. Wait for the storage account deployment to complete.

Step 4: Create a Blob Storage Container

1. Navigate to your newly created storage account.
2. In the left-hand menu, select **Containers** under the **Data Storage** section.
3. Click **"+ Container"**:
   - **Name**: Enter a name for the container (e.g., `myblobcontainer`).
   - **Public Access Level**:
     - **Private**: Only authorized users can access blobs.
     - **Blob**: Public read access for blobs only (ideal for testing file accessibility).
   - Click **"Create"**.

Step 5: Upload a File to Blob Storage

1. Open the container you just created.
2. Click **"Upload"**:
   - Select a file from your computer (e.g., a text file or image).
   - Leave the default settings.
   - Click **"Upload"** to add the file to the container.
3. Verify that the file appears in the container.

Step 6: Access the Blob

1. Click on the uploaded file to view its properties.
2. If you set the container's access level to **Blob**, copy the **Blob URL**.
3. Paste the Blob URL into a web browser:
   - If the container is public, the file will be accessible.
   - If the container is private, you will see an access error.

Step 7: Test with Azure Storage Explorer (Optional)

1. Download and install Azure Storage Explorer. (https://azure.microsoft.com/features/storage-explorer/)
2. Sign in to your Azure account in Storage Explorer.
3. Navigate to your storage account and container.
4. Upload, download, and manage files directly from Storage Explorer.

Validation

- Verify that the storage account and container appear in the Azure Portal.
- Confirm that the file is uploaded to the Blob Storage container.
- Test accessibility by accessing the Blob URL in a browser (if public).

Best Practices for Azure Blob Storage

1. **Secure Data**:

    - Use private containers for sensitive data and shared access signatures (SAS) for controlled access.
2. **Monitor Costs**:
    - Keep track of data usage and access frequency to optimize storage costs.
3. **Use Access Tiers**:
    - Assign **Hot**, **Cool**, or **Archive** tiers based on data access patterns.
4. **Enable Logging**:
    - Use Azure Monitor to track storage access and diagnose issues.

Expected Outcome

By completing this lab, you will:

- Have a working Azure storage account and Blob Storage container.
- Understand how to upload, manage, and access files in Azure Blob Storage.
- Be ready to use Blob Storage for scalable object storage in future projects.

Lab 4: Creating and Configuring a Virtual Network (VNet) in Microsoft Azure

Objective:
This lab will guide you through creating and configuring a Virtual Network (VNet) in Azure, including setting up subnets, network security groups, and testing connectivity. By the end of this lab, you will have a custom VNet with public and private subnets for secure network isolation.

Why This Lab is Important

Virtual Networks (VNets) are the backbone of Azure networking, allowing you to create logically isolated networks for your resources. VNets enable you to control IP addressing, subnets, routing, and security, making them essential for secure and scalable cloud architectures.

Prerequisites

- A Microsoft Azure account (set up in Lab 1).
- Basic understanding of networking concepts, such as IP addresses and subnets.

Detailed Steps

Step 1: Access the Azure Portal

1. Log in to the Azure Portal. (https://portal.azure.com/)
2. Navigate to **Virtual Networks** by searching for "Virtual Networks" in the search bar or selecting it from the **All Services** menu under "Networking."

Step 2: Create a Virtual Network

1. Click **"Create"** and select **Virtual Network**.
2. **Basics** Tab:
    - **Subscription**: Ensure your Free Trial or active subscription is selected.
    - **Resource Group**: Create a new resource group (e.g., `NetworkingLabGroup`) or use an existing one.
    - **Name**: Enter a name for the VNet, such as `MyCustomVNet`.
    - **Region**: Choose a region close to your location.
3. Click **"Next: IP Addresses"**.

Step 3: Configure IP Address Space

1. Under the **IP Addresses** tab:
    - **IPv4 Address Space**: Enter a CIDR block, such as `10.0.0.0/16`.
    - **Subnets**:
        - Create a **Public Subnet**:
            - Name: `PublicSubnet`.
            - Subnet Address Range: `10.0.1.0/24`.
        - Create a **Private Subnet**:

        - Name: `PrivateSubnet`.
        - Subnet Address Range: `10.0.2.0/24`.
    - Click **Add Subnet** for each entry.

Step 4: Configure Security

1. **Security Tab**:
    - **DDos Protection**: Select **Basic** (free tier).
    - Leave **Firewall** disabled for now.
2. Click **Next: Tags**, then **Review + Create** to validate the configuration.
3. Click **Create** to deploy the VNet.

Step 5: Create a Network Security Group (NSG)

1. Navigate to **Network Security Groups** in the Azure Portal.
2. Click **"Create"**.
3. **Basics** Tab:
    - **Name**: Enter a name for the NSG, such as `PublicNSG`.
    - **Resource Group**: Select the same resource group as your VNet.
4. Click **Review + Create**, then **Create**.
5. After deployment, navigate to the NSG and configure inbound rules:
    - **Allow SSH (Linux) or RDP (Windows)**:
        - Port: `22` (SSH) or `3389` (RDP).
        - Source: Select **My IP** for security.
    - **Allow HTTP/HTTPS (Optional)**:
        - Ports: `80` and `443` for web traffic.

Step 6: Associate Subnets with NSGs

1. Go to the **Subnets** section of the VNet.
2. Select the **PublicSubnet** and associate it with the `PublicNSG`.
3. (Optional) Create a separate NSG for the `PrivateSubnet` with stricter rules (e.g., block all inbound traffic except from the PublicSubnet).

Step 7: Test the VNet

1. Launch an **Azure Virtual Machine** in the Public Subnet (refer to Lab 2 for VM deployment details).
2. Connect to the VM using SSH (Linux) or RDP (Windows).
3. Verify internet connectivity from the Public Subnet:

```
bash
Copy code
ping google.com
```

4. Launch another VM in the Private Subnet and test connectivity between the two VMs:
    - SSH or RDP into the public VM.

- Ping the private VM's IP address from the public VM.

Step 8: Configure a NAT Gateway for Private Subnet (Optional)

1. Navigate to **NAT Gateways** in the Azure Portal.
2. Click **"Create"**:
    - **Name**: Enter a name for the NAT Gateway (e.g., `PrivateNAT`).
    - **Public IP**: Create a new public IP address.
    - **Subnet Association**: Associate the NAT Gateway with the `PrivateSubnet`.
3. Save and test internet access from the private VM.

Validation

- Verify that the VNet, subnets, and NSG are correctly configured in the Azure Portal.
- Confirm internet connectivity from the public VM and restricted access for the private VM.
- Test communication between resources in the VNet.

Best Practices for Azure VNets

1. **Use Subnet Segmentation**:
    - Segment workloads into different subnets (e.g., public, private, database).
2. **Apply Security Rules**:
    - Use NSGs to enforce least-privilege access.
3. **Monitor Network Traffic**:
    - Enable Network Watcher to monitor and troubleshoot network connectivity.
4. **Plan IP Addressing**:
    - Use well-organized CIDR ranges to avoid conflicts when integrating with other networks.

Expected Outcome

By completing this lab, you will:

- Understand how to create and configure a Virtual Network in Azure.
- Deploy and test a secure networking environment with public and private subnets.
- Be prepared to design and manage scalable cloud networks in future projects.

Lab 5: Configuring Azure Role-Based Access Control (RBAC) and Policies

Objective:
This lab will guide you through configuring Role-Based Access Control (RBAC) in Azure by creating users, assigning roles, and applying policies. By the end of this lab, you will have created secure access controls to manage Azure resources effectively.

Why This Lab is Important

Azure Role-Based Access Control (RBAC) and policies provide fine-grained access management for Azure resources. Proper configuration ensures that only authorized users can perform specific actions, enhancing security and governance across your cloud environment.

Prerequisites

- A Microsoft Azure account (set up in Lab 1).
- Basic understanding of access control concepts like users, roles, and permissions.

Detailed Steps

Step 1: Access the Azure Portal

1. Log in to the Azure Portal. (https://portal.azure.com/)
2. Navigate to **Azure Active Directory** by searching for it in the search bar.

Step 2: Create a New User

1. In the Azure Active Directory menu, click **"Users"** > **"New user"**.
2. **User Details**:
   - **User Type**: Choose **User**.
   - **Name**: Enter a name (e.g., `Test User`).
   - **Username**: Provide a unique username (e.g., `testuser@yourdomain.onmicrosoft.com`).
   - **Password**: Use the autogenerated password or set a custom one. Note the password for future use.
3. Click **"Create"** to add the user.

Step 3: Assign a Role to the User

1. Navigate to the resource (e.g., a Virtual Machine or Resource Group) you want to grant access to.
2. In the left-hand menu, select **Access Control (IAM)**.
3. Click **"Add"** > **"Add role assignment"**.
4. **Role Assignment**:
   - **Role**: Select a predefined role, such as **Reader** (read-only access) or **Contributor** (create/manage resources but no access to billing).
   - **Assign access to**: Select **User, group, or service principal**.

   - **Select**: Search for the user created in Step 2 and select them.
5. Click **"Save"** to assign the role.

Step 4: Test the Assigned Role

1. Log out of the Azure Portal and log in as the new user using the username and password created in Step 2.
2. Attempt to access the assigned resource and perform actions:
   - For a **Reader** role, verify that the user can view but not modify resources.
   - For a **Contributor** role, verify that the user can create or modify resources within the assigned scope.

Step 5: Create a Custom Role (Optional)

1. Navigate to **Subscriptions** in the Azure Portal and select your subscription.
2. Click **Access Control (IAM)** > **Roles** > **"Add custom role"**.
3. **Role Details**:
   - Name the role (e.g., `CustomStorageReader`).
   - Add a description (e.g., "Read-only access to storage accounts").
4. **Permissions**:
   - Click **"JSON"** and add the following:

```
json
Copy code
{
  "Name": "CustomStorageReader",
  "IsCustom": true,
  "Description": "Read-only access to storage accounts.",
  "Actions": [
    "Microsoft.Storage/storageAccounts/read"
  ],
  "NotActions": [],
  "AssignableScopes": [
    "/subscriptions/<your-subscription-id>"
  ]
}
```

   Replace `<your-subscription-id>` with your actual subscription ID.

5. Save and assign this role to a user.

Step 6: Create and Apply Azure Policy

1. Navigate to **Policy** in the Azure Portal.
2. Click **Definitions** > **"Create policy definition"**.
3. **Policy Definition Details**:
   - **Definition Location**: Select a subscription or management group.
   - **Display Name**: Enter a name (e.g., `Deny Public IP Creation`).
   - **Policy Rule**:

```
json
Copy code
{
  "if": {
    "field": "type",
    "equals": "Microsoft.Network/publicIPAddresses"
  },
  "then": {
    "effect": "deny"
  }
}
```

4. Save the policy definition.
5. **Assign the Policy**:
    - Click **Assignments** > **"Assign policy"**.
    - Select the policy definition and assign it to a subscription or resource group.
    - Click **"Review + Create"** to activate the policy.

Validation

- Verify that the assigned roles allow or restrict access as expected.
- Test the custom role by accessing resources under its scope.
- Confirm that the policy prevents users from creating public IP addresses or performing restricted actions.

Best Practices for RBAC and Policies

1. **Follow Least Privilege Principle**:
    - Assign users only the permissions necessary to perform their tasks.
2. **Use Resource Groups**:
    - Assign roles at the resource group level to simplify access management.
3. **Monitor Access**:
    - Use Azure Monitor or Activity Logs to track role assignments and resource access.
4. **Test Policies**:
    - Apply policies in non-production environments to verify their impact before deployment.

Expected Outcome

By completing this lab, you will:

- Understand how to configure and test RBAC roles in Azure.
- Be able to create and assign custom roles for tailored access control.
- Apply policies to enforce governance and compliance across your Azure environment.

Lab 6: Monitoring Resources and Configuring Alerts in Microsoft Azure

Objective:
This lab will guide you through monitoring Azure resources using Azure Monitor and configuring alerts to track key metrics such as CPU utilization for a virtual machine. By the end of this lab, you will understand how to use Azure Monitor to observe resource performance and configure alerts for proactive management.

Why This Lab is Important

Azure Monitor provides a comprehensive solution for collecting, analyzing, and acting on telemetry from your Azure resources. Alerts enable you to automate responses to specific conditions, ensuring your applications remain available and performant.

Prerequisites

- A Microsoft Azure account (set up in Lab 1).
- A running Azure Virtual Machine (created in Lab 2).
- Basic knowledge of Azure resource monitoring concepts.

Detailed Steps

Step 1: Access Azure Monitor

1. Log in to the Azure Portal. (https://portal.azure.com/)
2. Navigate to **Azure Monitor** by searching for it in the search bar or selecting it from the **All Services** menu under "Management & Governance."
3. Familiarize yourself with key sections in Azure Monitor:
   - **Insights**: Provides monitoring dashboards for resources.
   - **Metrics**: Tracks performance metrics for Azure resources.
   - **Alerts**: Allows you to create and manage alerts.

Step 2: Enable Monitoring for the Virtual Machine

1. Navigate to your virtual machine in the Azure Portal.
2. In the left-hand menu, click **Insights** under the **Monitoring** section.
3. Enable monitoring if it's not already configured. This will allow Azure Monitor to collect and display performance metrics for your VM.
4. Verify that metrics such as CPU utilization, memory usage, and disk I/O are visible.

Step 3: Configure Metrics in Azure Monitor

1. Navigate to **Metrics** in Azure Monitor.
2. Select your virtual machine as the **Resource**.
3. In the **Metric Namespace**, choose **Virtual Machine Host**.
4. Select a **Metric**, such as **Percentage CPU**.
5. Customize the graph:

   - Set **Aggregation** to **Average**.
   - Adjust the time range to view recent performance data (e.g., last 6 hours).
6. Save the chart to a custom dashboard by clicking **"Pin to dashboard"**.

Step 4: Create an Alert Rule

1. Navigate to **Alerts** in Azure Monitor.
2. Click **"New Alert Rule"**.
3. **Scope**:
   - Select your virtual machine as the resource.
4. **Condition**:
   - Click **"Add condition"**.
   - Choose the **Percentage CPU** metric.
   - Set a threshold condition:
     - Operator: **Greater than**.
     - Threshold value: **70** (triggers an alert if CPU utilization exceeds 70%).
5. **Action Group**:
   - Click **"Create Action Group"**.
   - **Action Group Name**: Enter a name (e.g., `HighCPUAlertGroup`).
   - **Notification Type**: Choose **Email/SMS/Push/Voice**.
   - Add your email address for notifications.
   - Click **OK** to save the action group.
6. **Alert Details**:
   - Name the alert rule (e.g., `HighCPUAlert`).
   - Set the severity (e.g., **2 – Warning**).
7. Click **"Create Alert Rule"**.

Step 5: Test the Alert

1. Connect to your virtual machine via SSH or RDP.
2. Simulate high CPU usage:
   - **For Linux VMs**:

     ```
     bash
     Copy code
     sudo apt install stress -y
     stress --cpu 1 --timeout 300
     ```

   - **For Windows VMs**: Run a CPU-intensive application (e.g., opening multiple instances of Resource Monitor).
3. Monitor the Azure Portal for alert activity.
4. Check your email or notification channel for the alert.

Step 6: Explore Logs in Azure Monitor

1. Navigate to **Logs** in Azure Monitor.
2. Use KQL (Kusto Query Language) to query logs:

- Example query to view CPU utilization over time:

```
kql
Copy code
InsightsMetrics
| where Origin == "vm.azm.ms"
| where Name == "Percentage CPU"
| summarize avg(Value) by bin(TimeGenerated, 1m)
| render timechart
```

3. Review the query results to analyze trends and patterns.

Step 7: (Optional) Automate Responses with Action Groups

1. Configure an automation response for the alert:
   - Add an Azure Logic App to the Action Group.
   - Example: Automatically scale the VM if CPU usage exceeds a threshold.
2. Create and deploy the Logic App to trigger scaling actions.

Validation

- Verify that the alert is triggered when CPU utilization exceeds 70%.
- Confirm that notifications are received via email or the selected channel.
- Review the alert activity log to ensure proper functionality.

Best Practices for Monitoring and Alerts

1. **Set Meaningful Thresholds**:
   - Tailor thresholds to your application's normal operating ranges.
2. **Use Action Groups**:
   - Combine email, SMS, and automation responses in action groups for comprehensive alert handling.
3. **Enable Diagnostic Settings**:
   - Forward logs to a storage account, Log Analytics, or Event Hub for long-term retention and analysis.
4. **Monitor Costs**:
   - Use Azure Cost Management to track monitoring-related costs.

Expected Outcome

By completing this lab, you will:

- Understand how to use Azure Monitor for tracking resource performance.
- Configure and test alert rules for proactive resource management.
- Gain insights into using metrics and logs for resource optimization.

Lab 7: Creating and Configuring an Azure Load Balancer

Objective:
This lab will guide you through setting up an Azure Load Balancer to distribute traffic across multiple virtual machines (VMs). By the end of this lab, you will have configured a load balancer, tested traffic distribution, and understood its importance in ensuring high availability and fault tolerance.

Why This Lab is Important

Azure Load Balancer is a critical component for building scalable and highly available cloud applications. It distributes incoming network traffic evenly across backend resources, ensuring reliability and performance for applications during varying traffic conditions.

Prerequisites

- A Microsoft Azure account (set up in Lab 1).
- At least two running Azure Virtual Machines (created in Lab 2).
- Basic understanding of networking concepts.

Detailed Steps

Step 1: Access the Azure Portal

1. Log in to the Azure Portal. (https://portal.azure.com/)
2. Navigate to **Load Balancers** by searching for it in the search bar or selecting it from the **All Services** menu under "Networking."

Step 2: Create a Load Balancer

1. Click **"Create"** to start the load balancer configuration.
2. **Basics** Tab:
   - **Subscription**: Ensure your Free Trial or active subscription is selected.
   - **Resource Group**: Create a new resource group (e.g., `LoadBalancerLabGroup`) or use an existing one.
   - **Name**: Enter a name for the load balancer (e.g., `MyLoadBalancer`).
   - **Region**: Choose the same region as your VMs.
   - **Type**: Select **Public** for internet-facing traffic or **Internal** for internal-only traffic.
   - **SKU**: Select **Basic** (cost-effective for small-scale testing) or **Standard** for production environments.
3. Click **Next: Frontend IP Configuration**.

Step 3: Configure the Frontend IP

1. **Frontend IP Configuration**:
   - Name: Enter a name (e.g., `FrontendIP`).
   - Public IP Address:

        - Select **Create new**.
        - Name the public IP (e.g., `MyLBPublicIP`) and click **OK**.
2. Click **Next: Backend Pools**.

Step 4: Configure the Backend Pool

1. **Backend Pool**:
    - Click **Add a backend pool**.
    - Name: Enter a name for the backend pool (e.g., `BackendPool`).
    - **Backend Pool Configuration**:
        - Select **Virtual Machines** as the backend resource type.
        - Add your VMs to the backend pool.
    - Click **Add** and then **Next: Health Probes**.

Step 5: Create a Health Probe

1. **Health Probe**:
    - Click **Add a health probe**.
    - Name: Enter a name (e.g., `HTTPHealthProbe`).
    - Protocol: Select **HTTP**.
    - Port: Enter `80`.
    - Path: Set `/` (the root path of the web server).
    - Interval: Set the frequency of health checks (default is 5 seconds).
    - Unhealthy Threshold: Specify how many consecutive failures mark a backend as unhealthy (default is 2).
2. Click **Add** and then **Next: Load Balancing Rules**.

Step 6: Configure a Load Balancing Rule

1. **Load Balancing Rule**:
    - Click **Add a load balancing rule**.
    - Name: Enter a name (e.g., `HTTPRule`).
    - Frontend IP Address: Select the frontend IP configuration created earlier.
    - Backend Pool: Select the backend pool created earlier.
    - Protocol: Select **TCP**.
    - Port:
        - Frontend Port: Enter `80`.
        - Backend Port: Enter `80`.
    - Session Persistence: Select **None** or **Client IP** for sticky sessions.
    - Idle Timeout: Leave the default value (4 minutes).
    - Enable Floating IP: Leave disabled for basic configurations.
2. Click **Add** and then **Review + Create** to deploy the load balancer.

Step 7: Test the Load Balancer

1. Obtain the public IP address of the load balancer from the **Frontend IP Configuration**.

2. Open a web browser and enter the public IP address:
   - The load balancer should route traffic to one of the backend VMs.
   - Refresh the page multiple times to observe traffic alternating between VMs (you can distinguish them using unique content on each VM's web server, e.g., `This is VM1` and `This is VM2`).

Step 8: Monitor the Load Balancer

1. Navigate to the **Metrics** section of the load balancer.
2. Review key metrics such as:
   - **Data Path Availability**: Indicates the overall health of the load balancer.
   - **Total Requests**: Tracks the number of incoming requests.
3. Use Azure Monitor to set up alerts for unusual traffic patterns or performance issues.

Step 9: Clean Up Resources

1. To avoid unnecessary charges, delete the load balancer and associated resources if they are no longer needed:
   - Navigate to the **Resource Group**.
   - Select **Delete resource group** and confirm.

Validation

- Verify that traffic is evenly distributed between backend VMs.
- Confirm that the health probe correctly identifies healthy and unhealthy backend resources.
- Test failover by stopping one VM and observing traffic routing to the remaining healthy VM.

Best Practices for Azure Load Balancers

1. **Use Health Probes Effectively**:
   - Configure probes based on your application's critical endpoints for accurate health monitoring.
2. **Leverage Standard SKU for Production**:
   - The Standard SKU provides advanced features like availability zones and better security.
3. **Secure Frontend Access**:
   - Use Azure Firewall or Network Security Groups (NSGs) to restrict inbound traffic to the load balancer.
4. **Monitor Performance**:
   - Regularly review metrics and set up alerts in Azure Monitor to proactively address issues.

Expected Outcome

By completing this lab, you will:

- Understand how to create and configure an Azure Load Balancer.
- Learn to distribute traffic across multiple virtual machines.
- Be able to monitor and manage the load balancer for performance and fault tolerance.

Lab 8: Deploying an Azure SQL Database and Performing a Backup

Objective:
This lab will guide you through deploying an Azure SQL Database and performing a backup. Azure SQL Database is a fully managed relational database service that provides high availability, scalability, and security. By the end of this lab, you will have a running Azure SQL Database and a backup to ensure data protection.

Why This Lab is Important

Azure SQL Database automates routine database management tasks such as backups, scaling, and patching, enabling you to focus on application development. Learning to deploy and back up an Azure SQL Database is critical for building robust, data-driven applications.

Prerequisites

- A Microsoft Azure account (set up in Lab 1).
- Basic knowledge of relational databases and SQL.

Detailed Steps

Step 1: Access the Azure Portal

1. Log in to the Azure Portal. (https://portal.azure.com/)
2. Navigate to **SQL Databases** by searching for it in the search bar or selecting it from the **All Services** menu under "Databases."

Step 2: Create an Azure SQL Database

1. Click **"Create"** to start the database creation process.
2. **Basics** Tab:
   - **Subscription**: Ensure your Free Trial or active subscription is selected.
   - **Resource Group**: Create a new resource group (e.g., `SQLLabGroup`) or use an existing one.
   - **Database Name**: Enter a name for the database (e.g., `MyFirstSQLDatabase`).
   - **Server**: Click **"Create new"** to create a new server:
     - **Server Name**: Enter a unique name (e.g., `MySQLServerLab`).
     - **Region**: Select a region close to your location.
     - **Authentication Method**: Use **SQL Authentication**.
     - **Server Admin Login**: Enter an admin username (e.g., `sqladmin`).
     - **Password**: Create and confirm a strong password.
     - Click **OK** to create the server.
   - **Compute + Storage**: Select the **Basic** service tier (cost-effective for testing).
3. Click **Next: Networking**.

Step 3: Configure Networking

1. **Networking Options**:
   - Choose **Public Endpoint** to enable access over the internet.
   - Select **Allow Azure services and resources to access this server**.
   - Add your current IP address to the firewall rules to allow database access.
2. Click **Next: Additional Settings**.

Step 4: Configure Database Settings

1. **Use Existing Data**:
   - For simplicity, select **Sample** to use a pre-populated AdventureWorksLT database.
2. **Backup Storage Redundancy**:
   - Leave the default **Geo-Redundant Storage (RA-GRS)** for backup resiliency.
3. Click **Review + Create** to validate the configuration, and then click **Create**.

Step 5: Connect to the Database

1. Once the deployment is complete, navigate to the database resource in the Azure Portal.
2. Copy the **Server Name** (FQDN) from the database overview page.
3. Use a SQL client (e.g., Azure Data Studio or SQL Server Management Studio) to connect:
   - **Server Type**: Database Engine.
   - **Server Name**: Paste the FQDN.
   - **Authentication**: SQL Server Authentication.
   - **Login**: Use the admin username and password created earlier.
4. Test the connection by running a query:

   ```
   sql
   Copy code
   SELECT TOP 10 * FROM SalesLT.Product;
   ```

Step 6: Perform a Manual Backup

1. Azure SQL Database automatically performs backups, but you can create a **Point-in-Time Restore**:
   - Navigate to the **Overview** tab of the database in the Azure Portal.
   - Click **Restore**.
   - Select a backup point from the timeline and provide a new database name (e.g., `MySQLDatabaseRestore`).
   - Click **OK** to start the restoration process.
2. Once restored, verify the new database by connecting to it using your SQL client.

Step 7: Explore Automatic Backups

1. Navigate to the **Backup Management** section of the database.
2. Review the backup retention settings:

  - **Point-in-Time Restore**: Retention varies based on the service tier (e.g., 7 days for Basic).
  - **Long-Term Retention**: Configure long-term retention for up to 10 years if needed.
3. Test restoring the database from an automatic backup.

Validation

- Verify that the Azure SQL Database is accessible via a SQL client.
- Confirm that sample data is present in the database.
- Test the backup by restoring the database and validating the restored data.

Best Practices for Azure SQL Databases

1. **Secure Your Database**:
   - Use **Private Endpoints** for secure communication.
   - Enable **Advanced Threat Protection** to detect suspicious activities.
2. **Monitor Performance**:
   - Use **Query Performance Insights** to analyze and optimize database performance.
3. **Automate Scaling**:
   - Enable **Autoscale** to adjust the database performance tier based on workload demands.
4. **Plan for Disaster Recovery**:
   - Configure **Geo-Replication** for high availability across regions.

Expected Outcome

By completing this lab, you will:

- Deploy and configure an Azure SQL Database.
- Connect to the database using a SQL client and perform queries.
- Perform manual and automatic backups to ensure data availability.

Lab 9: Configuring Auto-Scaling for Virtual Machines in Microsoft Azure

Objective:
This lab will guide you through setting up and testing auto-scaling for Azure Virtual Machines (VMs) using a Virtual Machine Scale Set (VMSS). By the end of this lab, you will have configured an auto-scaling group that dynamically adjusts the number of VMs based on workload demands.

Why This Lab is Important

Auto-scaling ensures that your applications can handle variable workloads while optimizing costs. By automatically adding or removing VMs based on resource usage, Azure Virtual Machine Scale Sets (VMSS) provide high availability and cost efficiency.

Prerequisites

- A Microsoft Azure account (set up in Lab 1).
- Familiarity with Azure Virtual Machines and basic networking concepts.
- A working Azure Load Balancer (optional, created in Lab 7).

Detailed Steps

Step 1: Access the Azure Portal

1. Log in to the Azure Portal. (https://portal.azure.com/)
2. Navigate to **Virtual Machine Scale Sets** by searching for it in the search bar or selecting it from the **All Services** menu under "Compute."

Step 2: Create a Virtual Machine Scale Set

1. Click **"Create"** and select **Virtual Machine Scale Set**.
2. **Basics** Tab:
   - **Subscription**: Ensure your Free Trial or active subscription is selected.
   - **Resource Group**: Create a new resource group (e.g., `AutoScaleLabGroup`) or use an existing one.
   - **Name**: Enter a name for the scale set (e.g., `MyAutoScaleSet`).
   - **Region**: Select a region close to your location.
   - **Image**: Choose **Ubuntu Server 20.04 LTS** or another preferred OS.
   - **Authentication Type**: Select **Password** or **SSH Public Key**.
   - **Username and Password/SSH Key**: Enter credentials for connecting to the VMs.
3. **Instance Details**:
   - VM size: Select **Standard_B1ls** (Free Tier eligible) or **Standard_B2s** for more resources.

Step 3: Configure Scaling

1. **Scaling Options**:
   - **Initial Instance Count**: Set to `1`.
   - **Orchestration Mode**: Select **Uniform**.
2. **Auto-scaling**:
   - Enable auto-scaling.
   - Minimum Number of VMs: `1`.
   - Maximum Number of VMs: `3`.
   - Scaling Policy:
     - **Scale Out**: Add instances when CPU utilization is above 70% for 5 minutes.
     - **Scale In**: Remove instances when CPU utilization is below 30% for 5 minutes.
3. Click **Next: Networking**.

Step 4: Configure Networking

1. **Networking Options**:
   - **Virtual Network**: Select an existing virtual network or create a new one.
   - **Subnet**: Use a subnet within the selected virtual network.
   - **Public IP Address**: Enable public IP for load balancer integration.
   - **Load Balancing**: Select an existing load balancer (if created in Lab 7) or create a new one.
2. Click **Next: Advanced**.

Step 5: Configure Advanced Settings (Optional)

1. **Diagnostics**:
   - Enable boot diagnostics and set a storage account for logs.
2. **Custom Script (Optional)**:
   - Add a custom script to initialize VMs (e.g., install a web server):

     ```
     bash
     Copy code
     #!/bin/bash
     sudo apt update -y
     sudo apt install nginx -y
     sudo systemctl start nginx
     ```

3. Click **Next: Review + Create**, then **Create**.

Step 6: Test Auto-Scaling

1. Navigate to the **Virtual Machine Scale Set** in the Azure Portal.
2. **Simulate High CPU Utilization**:
   - Connect to an instance using SSH or RDP.

- Install a CPU stress testing tool:

```
bash
Copy code
sudo apt install stress -y
stress --cpu 1 --timeout 300
```

- Monitor the **Instances** tab in the scale set. Additional instances should be created as CPU utilization exceeds the threshold.

3. **Simulate Low CPU Utilization**:
   - Stop the stress process and monitor the scale set as it reduces instances.

Step 7: Monitor Metrics and Alerts

1. Navigate to **Metrics** in the scale set overview.
2. Review key metrics, such as:
   - **CPU Percentage**: Tracks average CPU utilization across instances.
   - **Instance Count**: Displays the number of running instances over time.
3. Set up an alert to notify you when the number of instances changes:
   - Go to **Alerts** and click **New Alert Rule**.
   - Add a condition for **Instance Count** changes.
   - Configure an action group to send notifications via email or SMS.

Step 8: Clean Up Resources

1. To avoid unnecessary costs, delete the scale set and associated resources:
   - Navigate to the **Resource Group**.
   - Select **Delete resource group** and confirm.

Validation

- Verify that additional instances are created when CPU utilization exceeds the threshold.
- Confirm that instances are terminated when CPU utilization falls below the threshold.
- Test load balancing by accessing the public IP of the load balancer (if configured) and observing traffic distribution across instances.

Best Practices for Auto-Scaling

1. **Set Meaningful Thresholds**:
   - Configure scaling thresholds based on application-specific performance metrics.
2. **Use Predictive Scaling**:
   - Enable predictive scaling to anticipate workload trends and optimize resource allocation.
3. **Monitor Costs**:
   - Regularly review scaling activity to ensure cost efficiency.
4. **Secure Access**:
   - Use Azure Bastion or NSGs to restrict access to VMs in the scale set.

Expected Outcome

By completing this lab, you will:

- Understand how to configure and test auto-scaling in Azure using a Virtual Machine Scale Set.
- Learn to monitor and manage scale sets for dynamic workloads.
- Be able to integrate auto-scaling with load balancing for high availability.

Lab 10: Setting Up and Testing Azure Functions

Objective:
This lab will guide you through creating, deploying, and testing an Azure Function, a serverless compute service that allows you to run code without provisioning or managing infrastructure. By the end of this lab, you will have a functional Azure Function triggered by HTTP requests and optionally connected to other Azure services.

Why This Lab is Important

Azure Functions enable event-driven architectures by executing code in response to triggers, such as HTTP requests, database updates, or timer schedules. This serverless approach is cost-effective, scalable, and perfect for building lightweight cloud applications.

Prerequisites

- A Microsoft Azure account (set up in Lab 1).
- Basic knowledge of programming (e.g., Python, C#, or JavaScript).
- Azure CLI installed locally (optional for deployment from your machine).

Detailed Steps

Step 1: Access the Azure Portal

1. Log in to the Azure Portal. (https://portal.azure.com/)
2. Navigate to **Azure Functions** by searching for it in the search bar or selecting it from the **All Services** menu under "Compute."

Step 2: Create an Azure Function App

1. Click **"Create"** to start setting up the Function App.
2. **Basics** Tab:
    - **Subscription**: Ensure your Free Trial or active subscription is selected.
    - **Resource Group**: Create a new resource group (e.g., `FunctionLabGroup`) or use an existing one.
    - **Function App Name**: Enter a unique name (e.g., `MyFirstFunctionApp`).
    - **Region**: Choose a region close to your location.
    - **Runtime Stack**: Select your preferred language runtime (e.g., Python, .NET, Node.js, or Java).
    - **Version**: Choose the latest available version.
    - **Operating System**: Choose Windows or Linux.
3. Click **Next: Hosting**.

Step 3: Configure Hosting

1. **Storage**:
    - Create a new storage account or select an existing one.

2. **Plan Type**:
   - Select **Consumption (Serverless)** for cost-effective, on-demand scaling.
3. Click **Next: Monitoring**.

Step 4: Enable Monitoring

1. Enable **Application Insights** to monitor the performance of your Azure Function.
2. Click **Next: Tags** and then **Review + Create**.
3. After reviewing the configuration, click **Create** to deploy the Function App.

Step 5: Create an HTTP Trigger Function

1. Once the Function App is deployed, navigate to it in the Azure Portal.
2. In the left-hand menu, click **Functions** and then **Create**.
3. **Add Function**:
   - Choose **HTTP trigger**.
   - Function Name: Enter a name (e.g., `MyHttpFunction`).
   - Authorization Level: Select **Function** for secure access or **Anonymous** for public access.
4. Click **Create** to generate the function.

Step 6: Edit the Function Code

1. Navigate to the **Code + Test** section of the function.
2. Modify the default code to return a custom response:
   - **For Python**:

```
python
Copy code
import logging
import azure.functions as func

def main(req: func.HttpRequest) -> func.HttpResponse:
    logging.info('HTTP trigger function processed a request.')

    name = req.params.get('name')
    if not name:
        try:
            req_body = req.get_json()
        except ValueError:
            pass
        else:
            name = req_body.get('name')

    if name:
        return func.HttpResponse(f"Hello, {name}!")
    else:
        return func.HttpResponse(
            "Please pass a name in the query string or in the
request body.",
            status_code=400
```

)

- Save the changes and click **Test/Run** to test the function.

Step 7: Test the Function

1. In the **Test/Run** window:
   - Set the HTTP method to **GET**.
   - Add a query parameter, such as `?name=Azure`, to the URL.
   - Click **Run** and verify the output:

     ```
     Copy code
     Hello, Azure!
     ```

2. Copy the **Function URL** and test it in your browser or with a tool like Postman:
   - For example: `https://<FunctionAppName>.azurewebsites.net/api/MyHttpFunction?name=Azure`.

Step 8: Add a Trigger (Optional)

1. Navigate to **Functions** and create a new function with a different trigger, such as:
   - **Blob Trigger**: Executes when a file is uploaded to a Blob Storage container.
   - **Timer Trigger**: Executes at regular intervals (e.g., `0 */5 * * * *` for every 5 minutes).
2. Configure the trigger and test it by performing the associated event (e.g., uploading a file for a Blob Trigger).

Step 9: Monitor and Scale the Function

1. Navigate to the **Monitor** section to view function execution logs.
2. Use **Application Insights** to analyze performance metrics and detect issues.
3. Configure scaling:
   - The Consumption Plan automatically scales based on demand.
   - For greater control, consider switching to a Premium or Dedicated App Service Plan.

Validation

- Verify the HTTP trigger function returns the expected response.
- Test optional triggers, such as Blob or Timer, and confirm their execution.
- Review logs in the **Monitor** section to ensure proper function execution.

Best Practices for Azure Functions

1. **Optimize Cold Starts**:
   - Use the Premium Plan for reduced latency in critical applications.

2. **Secure Access**:
   - Use Function-level authentication or API keys to restrict access.
3. **Monitor Costs**:
   - Review execution metrics and optimize functions to minimize unnecessary invocations.
4. **Use Durable Functions**:
   - For long-running workflows, implement Durable Functions to manage state and dependencies.

Expected Outcome

By completing this lab, you will:

- Understand how to create and deploy serverless Azure Functions.
- Learn to trigger and test functions using HTTP requests.
- Be able to integrate Azure Functions with other Azure services.

Appendix D: Practice Questions

Question 1
An engineer made a change to an application and needs to select a deployment strategy that meets the following requirements: is simple and fast, can be performed on two identical platforms. Which of the following strategies should the engineer use?

A. Blue-green
B. Canary
C. Rolling
D. In-place

Question 2
The change control board received a request to approve a configuration change to deploy in the cloud production environment. Which of the following should have already been completed?

A. Penetration test
B. End-to-end security testing
C. Cost benefit analysis
D. User acceptance testing

Question 3
A customer is migrating applications to the cloud and wants to grant authorization based on the classification levels of each system. Which of the following should the customer implement to ensure authorization to systems is granted when the user and system classification properties match? (Select two)

A. Resource tagging
B. Role-based access control
C. Multifactor authentication
D. Role-based access control

Question 4
A system surpasses 75% to 80% of resource consumption. Which of the following scaling approaches is the most appropriate?

A. Trending
B. Manual
C. Load
D. Scheduled

Question 5
A network administrator is building a site-to-site VPN tunnel from the company's headquarters office to the company's public cloud development network. The network administrator confirms the following: - The VPN tunnel is established on the headquarters office firewall.- While inside the office, developers report that they cannot connect to the development network resources.- While outside the office on a client VPN, developers report that they can connect to the development network resources.- The office and the client VPN have different IP subnet ranges.- The firewall flow logs show VPN traffic is reaching the development network from the office. Which of the following is the next step the network administrator should take to troubleshoot the VPN tunnel?

A. Review the development network routing table
B. Change the ciphers on the site-to-site VPN
C. Restart the site-to-site VPN tunnel
D. Check the ACLs on the development workloads

Question 6
A company's main web application is no longer accessible via the internet. The cloud administrator investigates and discovers the application is accessible locally and only via an IP address. Which of the following was misconfigured?

A. IP
B. DHCP
C. NAT
D. DNS.

Question 7
A cloud engineer is provisioning a new application that requires access to the organization's public cloud resources. Which of the following is the best way for the cloud engineer to authenticate the application?

A. Access key
B. API
C. MFA token
D. Username and password

Question 8
A security engineer identifies a vulnerability in a containerized application. The vulnerability can be exploited by a privileged process to read the content of the host's memory. Which of the following is the best solution to prevent similar exploits by privileged processes?

A. Adding the user myappuser instruction
B. Patching the host running the Docker daemon
C. Changing from alpine:3.17 to from alpine:latest
D. Running the container with the read-only filesystem configuration

Question 9
A cross-site request forgery vulnerability exploited a web application that was hosted in a public IaaS network. A security engineer determined that deploying a WAF in blocking mode at a CDN would prevent the application from being exploited again. However, a week after implementing the WAF, the application was exploited again. Which of the following should the security engineer do to make the WAF control effective?

A. Configure the DDoS protection on the CDN
B. Install endpoint protection software on the VMs
C. Add an ACL to the VM subnet
D. Deploy an IDS on the IaaS network

Question 10
A cloud engineer wants containers to run the latest version of a container base image to reduce the number of vulnerabilities. The applications in use require Python 3.10 and are not compatible with any other version. Given the container Dockerfile below, which of the following actions will achieve the objectives with the least effort?

A. Perform docker pull before executing docker run
B. Execute docker update using a local cron to get the latest container version
C. Change the image to use python:latest on the image build process
D. Update the Dockerfile to pin the source image version

Question 11
An engineer wants to scale several cloud workloads on demand. Which of the following approaches is the most suitable?

A. Load
B. Scheduled
C. Manual
D. Trending

Question 12
A software engineer is integrating an application to the cloud that is WebSocket-based. Which of the following applications is the engineer most likely deploying?

A. Image-sharing
B. Data visualization
C. Chat
D. File transfer

Question 13
A manager wants information about which users signed in to a certain VM during the past month. Which of the following can the cloud administrator use to obtain this information?

A. Retention
B. Alerting
C. Aggregation
D. Collection

Question 14
A cloud engineer is reviewing the following Dockerfile to deploy a Python web application: Which of the following changes should the engineer make to the file to improve container security?

A. Add the instruction 'USER nonroot.'
B. Change the version from latest to 3.11.
C. Remove the entrypoint instruction.
D. Ensure myapp/main.py is owned by root.

Question 15
A company has decided to adopt a microservices architecture for its applications that are deployed to the cloud. Which of the following is a major advantage of this type of architecture?

A. Increased security
B. Simplified communication
C. Reduced server cost
D. Rapid feature deployment

Question 16
A company wants to optimize cloud resources and lower the overhead caused by managing multiple operating systems. Which of the following compute resources would be best to help achieve this goal?

A. VM
B. Containers
C. Remote desktops
D. Bare-metal servers

Question 17
A developer is deploying a new version of a containerized application. The DevOps team wants: no disruption, no performance degradation, cost-effective deployment, and minimal deployment time. Which of the following is the best deployment strategy given the requirements?

A. Canary
B. In-place
C. Blue-green
D. Rolling

Question 18
A DevOps engineer is receiving reports that users can no longer access the company's web application after hardening of a web server. The users are receiving the following error: ERR_SSL_VERSION_OR_CIPHER_MISMATCH. Which of the following actions should the engineer take to resolve the issue?

A. Restart the web server.
B. Configure TLS 1.2 or newer.
C. Update the web server.
D. Review logs on the WAF.

Question 19
A healthcare organization must follow strict compliance requirements to ensure that PII is not leaked. The cloud administrator needs to ensure the cloud email system can support this requirement. Which of the following should the organization enable?

A. IPS
B. DLP
C. ACL
D. WAF

Question 20
A cloud engineer wants to implement a monitoring solution to detect cryptojacking and other cryptomining malware on cloud instances. Which of the following metrics would most likely be used to identify the activity?

A. Disk I/O
B. Network packets
C. Average memory utilization
D. Percent of CPU utilization

Question 21
A developer is testing code that will be used to deploy a web farm in a public cloud. The main code block is a function to create a load balancer and a loop to create 1,000 web servers. The developer runs the code against the company's cloud account and observes that the load balancer is successfully created, but only 100 web servers have been created. Which of the following should the developer do to fix this issue?

A. Request an increase of instance quota
B. Run the code multiple times until all servers are created.
C. Check the my_web_server() function to ensure it is using the right credentials.
D. Place the my_load_balancer() function after the loop.

Question 22
A cloud networking engineer is troubleshooting the corporate office's network configuration. Employees in the IT and operations departments are unable to resolve IP addresses on all devices, and the IT department cannot establish a connection to other departments' subnets. Which of the following actions meet the IP addressing and routing requirements?

A. Modifying the subnet mask to 255.255.254.0 for IT and operations departments
B. Configuring static routing to allow access from each subnet to 10.1.40.1
C. Modifying the BYOD policy to reduce the volume of devices that are allowed to connect to the network
D. Configuring static routing to allow access from 10.1.30.1 to each subnet

Question 23
A cloud developer is creating a static website that customers will be accessing globally. Which of the following services will help reduce latency?

A. VPC
B. Application load balancer
C. CDN
D. API gateway

Question 24
An administrator needs to adhere to the following requirements when moving a customer's data to the cloud:
- The new service must be geographically dispersed.
- The customer should have local access to data.
- Legacy applications should be accessible.
Which of the following cloud deployment models is most suitable?

A. On-premises
B. Private
C. Hybrid
D. Public

Question 25
A technician receives an email from a vendor requesting payment of an invoice for human resources services. The email contains a request for bank account numbers. Which of the following types of attacks does this behavior most likely indicate?

A. Malware
B. Cryptojacking
C. Ransomware
D. Phishing

Question 26
Which of the following best explains the concept of migrating from on-premises to the cloud?

A. The configuration of a dedicated pipeline to transfer content to a remote location
B. The creation of virtual instances in an external provider to transfer operations of selected servers
C. The physical transportation, installation, and configuration of company IT equipment in a cloud
D. The extension of company IT infrastructure to a managed service provider

Question 27
Which of the following service options would provide the best availability for critical applications in the event of a disaster?

A. Edge computing
B. Cloud bursting
C. Availability zones
D. Multicloud tenancy

Question 28
A newly configured VM fails to run application updates despite having internet access. The updates download automatically from a third-party network. Which of the following troubleshooting steps would be best to take?

A. Checking DNS configurations
B. Reconfiguring routing protocols
C. Testing the IP address configuration
D. Running a trace to the router

Question 29
A company migrated its CRM system to a SaaS solution. The security team is updating the RACI matrix for the newly migrated CRM. Which of the following responsibility assignments best aligns with the shared responsibility model for the new CRM?

A. Data-center security
B. CRM software security
C. CRM server patching
D. CRM development life cycle

Question 30
A social networking company operates globally. Some users from Brazil and Argentina are reporting the following error: Website address was not found. Which of the following is the most likely cause of this outage?

A. Client DNS misconfiguration
B. Regional DNS provider outage
C. DNS server misconfiguration
D. DNS propagation issues

Question 31
A cloud engineer is designing a cloud-native, three-tier application. The engineer must adhere to the following security best practices:
- Minimal services should run on all layers of the stack.
- The solution should be vendor-agnostic.
- Virtualization could be used over physical hardware.
Which of the following concepts should the engineer use to design the system to best meet these requirements?

A. Virtual machine
B. Microservices
C. Fan-out
D. Cloud-provided managed services

Question 32
A high-usage cloud resource needs to be monitored in real time on specific events to guarantee its availability. Which of the following actions should be used to meet this requirement?

A. Configure a ping command to identify when the cloud instance is out of service.
B. Create a dashboard with visualizations to filter the status of critical activities.
C. Collect all the daily activity from the cloud instance and create a dump file for analysis.
D. Schedule an hourly scan of the network to check for the availability of the resource.

Question 33
A junior cloud administrator was recently promoted to cloud administrator and has been added to the cloud administrator group. The cloud administrator group is the only one that can access the engineering VM. The new administrator unsuccessfully attempts to access the engineering VM. However, the other administrators can access it without issue. Which of the following is the best way to identify the root cause?

A. Rebooting the engineering VM
B. Reviewing the administrator's permissions to access the engineering VM
C. Allowing connections from 0.0.0.0/0 to the engineering VM
D. Performing a packet capture on the engineering VM

Question 34
A cloud solutions architect is designing a VM-based solution that requires reducing the cost as much as possible. Which of the following solutions will best satisfy this requirement?

A. Using ephemeral storage on replicated VMs
B. Creating spot VMs in one availability zone
C. Spreading the VMs across different regions
D. Using provisioned IOPS storage

Question 35
A critical security patch is required on a network load balancer in a public cloud. The organization has a major sales conference next week, and the Chief Executive Officer does not want any interruptions during the demonstration of an application behind the load balancer. Which of the following approaches should the cloud security engineer take?

A. Ask the management team to delay the conference.
B. Apply the security patch after the event.
C. Ask the upper management team to approve an emergency patch window.
D. Apply the security patch immediately before the conference.

Question 36
A newly configured VM fails to run application updates despite having internet access. The updates download automatically from a third-party network. Given the following output, which of the following troubleshooting steps would be best to take?

A. Checking DNS configurations
B. Reconfiguring routing protocols
C. Testing the IP address configuration
D. Running a trace to the router

Question 37
A company migrated its CRM system to a SaaS solution. The security team is updating the RACI matrix for the newly migrated CRM. Which of the following responsibility assignments best aligns with the shared responsibility model for the new CRM?

A. Data-center security
B. CRM software security
C. CRM server patching
D. CRM development life cycle

Question 38
A social networking company operates globally. Some users from Brazil and Argentina are reporting the following error: 'Website address was not found.' Which of the following is the most likely cause of this outage?

A. Client DNS misconfiguration
B. Regional DNS provider outage
C. DNS server misconfiguration
D. DNS propagation issues

Question 39
A cloud engineer is designing a cloud-native, three-tier application. The engineer must adhere to the following security best practices:
- Minimal services should run on all layers of the stack.
- The solution should be vendor agnostic.
- Virtualization could be used over physical hardware.
Which of the following concepts should the engineer use to design the system to best meet these requirements?

A. Virtual machine
B. Microservices
C. Fan-out
D. Cloud-provided managed services

Question 40
A high-usage cloud resource needs to be monitored in real-time on specific events to guarantee its availability. Which of the following actions should be used to meet this requirement?

A. Configure a ping command to identify when the cloud instance is out of service.
B. Create a dashboard with visualizations to filter the status of critical activities.
C. Collect all the daily activity from the cloud instance and create a dump file for analysis.
D. Schedule an hourly scan of the network to check for the availability of the resource.

Question 41
A junior cloud administrator was recently promoted to cloud administrator and has been added to the cloud administrator group. The cloud administrator group is the only one that can access the engineering VM. The new administrator unsuccessfully attempts to access the engineering VM. However, the other administrators can access it without issue. Which of the following is the best way to identify the root cause?

A. Rebooting the engineering VM
B. Reviewing the administrator's permissions to access the engineering VM
C. Allowing connections from 0.0.0.0/0 to the engineering VM
D. Performing a packet capture on the engineering VM

Question 42
A cloud solutions architect is designing a VM-based solution that requires reducing the cost as much as possible. Which of the following solutions will best satisfy this requirement?

A. Using ephemeral storage on replicated VMs
B. Creating spot VMs in one availability zone
C. Spreading the VMs across different regions
D. Using provisioned IOPS storage

Question 43
A critical security patch is required on a network load balancer in a public cloud. The organization has a major sales conference next week, and the Chief Executive Officer does not want any interruptions during the demonstration of an application behind the load balancer. Which of the following approaches should the cloud security engineer take?

A. Ask the management team to delay the conference.
B. Apply the security patch after the event.
C. Ask the upper management team to approve an emergency patch window.
D. Apply the security patch immediately before the conference.

Question 44
A cloud engineer has provisioned a VM for a high-frequency trading application. After the VM is put into production, users report high latency in trades. The engineer checks the last six hours of VM metrics and sees the following:
- CPU utilization is between 30% to 60%.
- NetworkIn is between 50kbps and 70kbps.
- NetworkOut is between 3,000kbps and 5,000kbps.
- DiskReadOps is at 30.
- DiskWriteOps is at 70.
- Memory utilization is between 50% and 70%.

Which of the following steps should the engineer take next to solve the latency issue?

A. Move to a network-optimized instance type as the network throughput is not enough.
B. Modify the disk IOPS to a higher value as the disk IO is being bottlenecked at 100 IOPS.
C. Increase the memory of the instance as the high-frequency trading application requires more memory.
D. Increase the instance size to allocate more vCPUs as the CPU utilization is very high.

Question 45
A cloud engineer was deploying the company's payment processing application, but it failed with the following error log:
ERROR:root: transaction failed HTTP 429 response, please try again.
Which of the following are the most likely causes for this error? (Select two)

A. API throttling
B. API gateway outage
C. Web server outage
D. Oversubscription
E. Unauthorized access
F. Insufficient quota

Question 46
An organization's web application experiences periodic bursts of traffic when a new video is launched. Users are reporting poor performance in the middle of the month. Which of the following scaling approaches should the organization use to scale based on forecasted traffic?

A. Scheduled
B. Manual
C. Event
D. Load

Question 47
A critical security patch is required on a network load balancer in a public cloud. The organization has a major sales conference next week, and the Chief Executive Officer does not want any interruptions during the demonstration of an application behind the load balancer. Which of the following approaches should the cloud security engineer take?

A. Ask the management team to delay the conference.
B. Apply the security patch after the event.
C. Ask the upper management team to approve an emergency patch window.
D. Apply the security patch immediately before the conference.

Question 48
A cloud engineer has provisioned a VM for a high-frequency trading application. After the VM is put into production, users report high latency in trades. The engineer checks the last six hours of VM metrics and sees the following:
- CPU utilization is between 30% to 60%.
- NetworkIn is between 50kbps and 70kbps.
- NetworkOut is between 3,000kbps and 5,000kbps.
- DiskReadOps is at 30.
- DiskWriteOps is at 70.
- Memory utilization is between 50% and 70%.
Which of the following steps should the engineer take next to solve the latency issue?

A. Move to a network-optimized instance type as the network throughput is not enough.
B. Modify the disk IOPS to a higher value as the disk IO is being bottlenecked at 100 IOPS.
C. Increase the memory of the instance as the high-frequency trading application requires more memory.
D. Increase the instance size to allocate more vCPUs as the CPU utilization is very high.

Question 49
A cloud engineer was deploying the company's payment processing application, but it failed with the following error log:
ERROR:root: transaction failed HTTP 429 response, please try again.
Which of the following are the most likely causes for this error? (Select two)

A. API throttling
B. API gateway outage
C. Web server outage
D. Oversubscription
E. Unauthorized access
F. Insufficient quota

Question 50
An organization's web application experiences periodic bursts of traffic when a new video is launched. Users are reporting poor performance in the middle of the month. Which of the following scaling approaches should the organization use to scale based on forecasted traffic?

A. Scheduled
B. Manual
C. Event
D. Load

Question 51
A company uses containers stored in Docker Hub to deploy workloads for its IaaS infrastructure. The development team releases changes to the containers several times per hour. Which of the following should a cloud engineer do to prevent the proprietary code from being exposed to third parties?

A. Use IaC to deploy the IaaS infrastructure.
B. Convert the containers to VMs.
C. Deploy the containers over SSH.
D. Use private repositories for the containers.

Question 52
Which of the following is an auditing procedure that ensures service providers securely manage the data to protect the interests of the organization and the privacy of its clients?

A. CIS
B. ITIL
C. SOC2
D. ISO 27001

Question 53
A cloud engineer wants to replace the current on-premises, unstructured data storage with a solution in the cloud. The new solution needs to be cost-effective and highly scalable. Which of the following types of storage would be best to use?

A. File
B. Block
C. Object
D. SAN

Question 54
A security analyst reviews the daily logs and notices the following suspicious activity:
The analyst investigates the firewall logs and identifies the following:
Which of the following steps should the security analyst take next to resolve this issue? (Select two)

A. Submit an IT support ticket and request Kali Linux be uninstalled from John Smith's computer
B. Block all inbound connections on port 4444 and block the IP address 201.101.25.121.
C. Contact John Smith and request the Ethernet cable attached to the desktop be unplugged
D. Check the running processes to confirm if a backdoor connection has been established.
E. Upgrade the Windows x64 operating system on John Smith's computer to the latest version
F. Block all outbound connections from the IP address 10.150.71.151.

Question 55
A security analyst confirms a zero-day vulnerability was exploited by hackers who gained access to confidential customer data and installed ransomware on the server. Which of the following steps should the security analyst take? (Select two)

A. Contact the customers to inform them about the data breach.
B. Contact the hackers to negotiate payment to unlock the server.
C. Send a global communication to inform all impacted users.
D. Inform the management and legal teams about the data breach.
E. Delete confidential data used on other servers that might be compromised.
F. Modify the firewall rules to block the IP addresses and update the ports.

Question 56
Which of the following types of storage provides the greatest performance advantage for a traditional relational database?

A. File
B. Object
C. Block
D. Ephemeral

Question 57
Which of the following is used to detect signals and measure physical properties, such as the temperature of the human body?

A. Beacon
B. Transmission protocols
C. Sensors
D. Gateways

Question 58
A company wants to combine solutions in a central and scalable environment to achieve the following: control, visibility, automation, and cost efficiency. Which of the following best describes what the company should implement?

A. Batch processing
B. Workload orchestration
C. Containerization
D. Application modernization

Question 59
Which of the following requirements are core considerations when migrating a small business's on-premises applications to the cloud? (Select two)

A. Availability
B. Hybrid
C. Testing
D. Networking
E. Compute
F. Logs

Question 60
The performance of an e-commerce website decreases dramatically during random periods. The IT team is evaluating available resources to mitigate the situation. Which of the following is the best approach to effectively manage this scenario?

A. Migrating to a dedicated host
B. Purchasing additional servers
C. Scheduling resource allocation
D. Configuring automatic elasticity

Appendix E: Practice Questions with Answers

Question 1
An engineer made a change to an application and needs to select a deployment strategy that meets the following requirements: is simple and fast, can be performed on two identical platforms. Which of the following strategies should the engineer use?

A. Blue-green
B. Canary
C. Rolling
D. In-place

Correct Answer: A
Justification: The blue-green strategy is simple, fast, and suitable for identical platforms, meeting the requirements specified.

Question 2
The change control board received a request to approve a configuration change to deploy in the cloud production environment. Which of the following should have already been completed?

A. Penetration test
B. End-to-end security testing
C. Cost benefit analysis
D. User acceptance testing

Correct Answer: D
Justification: User acceptance testing ensures the change is ready for deployment and meets the intended business needs.

Question 3
A customer is migrating applications to the cloud and wants to grant authorization based on the classification levels of each system. Which of the following should the customer implement to ensure authorization to systems is granted when the user and system classification properties match? (Select two)

A. Resource tagging
B. Role-based access control
C. Multifactor authentication
D. Role-based access control

Correct Answer: B, D
Justification: Role-based access control and classification levels ensure proper authorization based on user and system properties.

Question 4
A system surpasses 75% to 80% of resource consumption. Which of the following scaling approaches is the most appropriate?

A. Trending
B. Manual
C. Load
D. Scheduled

Correct Answer: C
Justification: Load scaling dynamically adjusts resources in response to usage metrics, aligning with system demands.

Question 5
A network administrator is building a site-to-site VPN tunnel from the company's headquarters office to the company's public cloud development network. The network administrator confirms the following: - The VPN tunnel is established on the headquarters office firewall.- While inside the office, developers report that they cannot connect to the development network resources.- While outside the office on a client VPN, developers report that they can connect to the development network resources. The office and the client VPN have different IP subnet ranges.- The firewall flow logs show VPN traffic is reaching the development network from the office. Which of the following is the next step the network administrator should take to troubleshoot the VPN tunnel?

A. Review the development network routing table
B. Change the ciphers on the site-to-site VPN
C. Restart the site-to-site VPN tunnel
D. Check the ACLs on the development workloads

Correct Answer: A
Justification: Reviewing the routing table ensures traffic is correctly routed, addressing connectivity issues.

Question 6
A company's main web application is no longer accessible via the internet. The cloud administrator investigates and discovers the application is accessible locally and only via an IP address. Which of the following was misconfigured?

A. IP
B. DHCP
C. NAT
D. DNS

Correct Answer: D
Justification: DNS misconfiguration prevents proper resolution of domain names to IP addresses, limiting internet accessibility.

Question 7
A cloud engineer is provisioning a new application that requires access to the organization's public cloud resources. Which of the following is the best way for the cloud engineer to authenticate the application?

A. Access key
B. API
C. MFA token
D. Username and password

Correct Answer: A
Justification: Access keys are specifically designed for programmatic access, offering a secure and efficient solution.

Question 8
A security engineer identifies a vulnerability in a containerized application. The vulnerability can be exploited by a privileged process to read the content of the host's memory. Which of the following is the best solution to prevent similar exploits by privileged processes?

A. Adding the user myappuser instruction
B. Patching the host running the Docker daemon
C. Changing from alpine:3.17 to from alpine:latest
D. Running the container with the read-only filesystem configuration

Correct Answer: A
Justification: Adding a non-root user prevents privileged processes from exploiting host vulnerabilities.

Question 9
A cross-site request forgery vulnerability exploited a web application that was hosted in a public IaaS network. A security engineer determined that deploying a WAF in blocking mode at a CDN would prevent the application from being exploited again. However, a week after implementing the WAF, the application was exploited again. Which of the following should the security engineer do to make the WAF control effective?

A. Configure the DDoS protection on the CDN
B. Install endpoint protection software on the VMs
C. Add an ACL to the VM subnet
D. Deploy an IDS on the IaaS network

Correct Answer: C
Justification: Adding an ACL to the subnet provides an additional layer of access control, preventing unauthorized traffic.

Question 10
A cloud engineer wants containers to run the latest version of a container base image to reduce the number of vulnerabilities. The applications in use require Python 3.10 and are not compatible with any other version. Given the container Dockerfile below, which of the following actions will achieve the objectives with the least effort?

A. Perform docker pull before executing docker run
B. Execute docker update using a local cron to get the latest container version
C. Change the image to use python:latest on the image build process
D. Update the Dockerfile to pin the source image version

Correct Answer: A
Justification: Pulling the latest image ensures up-to-date patches while retaining compatibility with Python 3.10.

Question 11
An engineer wants to scale several cloud workloads on demand. Which of the following approaches is the most suitable?

A. Load
B. Scheduled
C. Manual
D. Trending

Correct Answer: A
Justification: Load-based scaling dynamically adjusts resources in response to demand, ensuring efficient performance.

Question 12
A software engineer is integrating an application to the cloud that is WebSocket-based. Which of the following applications is the engineer most likely deploying?

A. Image-sharing
B. Data visualization
C. Chat
D. File transfer

Correct Answer: C
Justification: WebSocket-based applications are often used for real-time communication, such as chat applications.

Question 13
A manager wants information about which users signed in to a certain VM during the past month. Which of the following can the cloud administrator use to obtain this information?

A. Retention
B. Alerting
C. Aggregation
D. Collection

Correct Answer: D
Justification: Collection processes gather and store data, enabling historical access logs for user activity.

Question 14
A cloud engineer is reviewing the following Dockerfile to deploy a Python web application: Which of the following changes should the engineer make to the file to improve container security?

A. Add the instruction 'USER nonroot.'
B. Change the version from latest to 3.11.
C. Remove the entrypoint instruction.
D. Ensure myapp/main.py is owned by root.

Correct Answer: A
Justification: Running containers as a non-root user enhances security by minimizing privileges.

Question 15
A company has decided to adopt a microservices architecture for its applications that are deployed to the cloud. Which of the following is a major advantage of this type of architecture?

A. Increased security
B. Simplified communication
C. Reduced server cost
D. Rapid feature deployment

Correct Answer: D
Justification: Microservices enable rapid and independent updates, supporting quick feature deployment.

Question 16
A company wants to optimize cloud resources and lower the overhead caused by managing multiple operating systems. Which of the following compute resources would be best to help achieve this goal?

A. VM
B. Containers
C. Remote desktops
D. Bare-metal servers

Correct Answer: B
Justification: Containers minimize OS overhead by sharing the host OS kernel, optimizing resource use.

Question 17
A developer is deploying a new version of a containerized application. The DevOps team wants: no disruption, no performance degradation, cost-effective deployment, and minimal deployment time. Which of the following is the best deployment strategy given the requirements?

A. Canary
B. In-place
C. Blue-green
D. Rolling

Correct Answer: C
Justification: The blue-green deployment strategy minimizes disruption and performance degradation while being cost-effective.

Question 18
A DevOps engineer is receiving reports that users can no longer access the company's web application after hardening of a web server. The users are receiving the following error: ERR_SSL_VERSION_OR_CIPHER_MISMATCH. Which of the following actions should the engineer take to resolve the issue?

A. Restart the web server.
B. Configure TLS 1.2 or newer.
C. Update the web server.
D. Review logs on the WAF.

Correct Answer: B
Justification: Ensuring the use of TLS 1.2 or newer resolves compatibility issues with SSL versions.

Question 19
A healthcare organization must follow strict compliance requirements to ensure that PII is not leaked. The cloud administrator needs to ensure the cloud email system can support this requirement. Which of the following should the organization enable?

A. IPS
B. DLP
C. ACL
D. WAF

Correct Answer: B
Justification: Data Loss Prevention (DLP) systems help enforce compliance by protecting sensitive information like PII.

Question 20
A cloud engineer wants to implement a monitoring solution to detect cryptojacking and other cryptomining malware on cloud instances. Which of the following metrics would most likely be used to identify the activity?

A. Disk I/O
B. Network packets
C. Average memory utilization
D. Percent of CPU utilization

Correct Answer: D
Justification: Cryptojacking typically leads to unusually high CPU usage, making CPU utilization a key detection metric.

Question 21
A developer is testing code that will be used to deploy a web farm in a public cloud. The main code block is a function to create a load balancer and a loop to create 1,000 web servers. The developer runs the code against the company's cloud account and observes that the load balancer is successfully created, but only 100 web servers have been created. Which of the following should the developer do to fix this issue?

A. Request an increase of instance quota
B. Run the code multiple times until all servers are created.
C. Check the my_web_server() function to ensure it is using the right credentials.
D. Place the my_load_balancer() function after the loop.

Correct Answer: A
Justification: Instance quota limits restrict the number of web servers created. Increasing the quota resolves the issue.

Question 22
A cloud networking engineer is troubleshooting the corporate office's network configuration. Employees in the IT and operations departments are unable to resolve IP addresses on all devices, and the IT department cannot establish a connection to other departments' subnets. Which of the following actions meet the IP addressing and routing requirements?

A. Modifying the subnet mask to 255.255.254.0 for IT and operations departments
B. Configuring static routing to allow access from each subnet to 10.1.40.1
C. Modifying the BYOD policy to reduce the volume of devices that are allowed to connect to the network
D. Configuring static routing to allow access from 10.1.30.1 to each subnet

Correct Answer: D, F
Justification: Static routing and subnet mask modifications ensure proper connectivity while maintaining segregation.

Question 23
A cloud developer is creating a static website that customers will be accessing globally. Which of the following services will help reduce latency?

A. VPC
B. Application load balancer
C. CDN
D. API gateway

Correct Answer: C
Justification: Content Delivery Networks (CDNs) cache content at edge locations, reducing latency for global access.

Question 24
An administrator needs to adhere to the following requirements when moving a customer's data to the cloud:
- The new service must be geographically dispersed.
- The customer should have local access to data.
- Legacy applications should be accessible.
Which of the following cloud deployment models is most suitable?

A. On-premises
B. Private
C. Hybrid
D. Public

Correct Answer: C
Justification: Hybrid cloud models provide local access and support legacy systems while leveraging cloud capabilities.

Question 25
A technician receives an email from a vendor requesting payment of an invoice for human resources services. The email contains a request for bank account numbers. Which of the following types of attacks does this behavior most likely indicate?

A. Malware
B. Cryptojacking
C. Ransomware
D. Phishing

Correct Answer: D
Justification: Phishing attempts involve fraudulent requests for sensitive information like bank details.

Question 26
Which of the following best explains the concept of migrating from on-premises to the cloud?

A. The configuration of a dedicated pipeline to transfer content to a remote location
B. The creation of virtual instances in an external provider to transfer operations of selected servers
C. The physical transportation, installation, and configuration of company IT equipment in a cloud
D. The extension of company IT infrastructure to a managed service provider

Correct Answer: B
Justification: Virtual instances enable seamless migration of server operations to the cloud without physical transportation.

Question 27
Which of the following service options would provide the best availability for critical applications in the event of a disaster?

A. Edge computing
B. Cloud bursting
C. Availability zones
D. Multicloud tenancy

Correct Answer: C
Justification: Availability zones offer redundancy and fault tolerance, ensuring high availability for critical applications.

Question 28
A newly configured VM fails to run application updates despite having internet access. The updates download automatically from a third-party network. Which of the following troubleshooting steps would be best to take?

A. Checking DNS configurations
B. Reconfiguring routing protocols
C. Testing the IP address configuration
D. Running a trace to the router

Correct Answer: A
Justification: DNS misconfigurations can prevent resolution of third-party network addresses, affecting updates.

Question 29
A company migrated its CRM system to a SaaS solution. The security team is updating the RACI matrix for the newly migrated CRM. Which of the following responsibility assignments best aligns with the shared responsibility model for the new CRM?

A. Data-center security
B. CRM software security
C. CRM server patching
D. CRM development life cycle

Correct Answer: A
Justification: The provider handles data-center security in the SaaS model, aligning with shared responsibility.

Question 30
A social networking company operates globally. Some users from Brazil and Argentina are reporting the following error: Website address was not found. Which of the following is the most likely cause of this outage?

A. Client DNS misconfiguration
B. Regional DNS provider outage
C. DNS server misconfiguration
D. DNS propagation issues

Correct Answer: B
Justification: A regional DNS outage could cause localized issues for users in specific regions.

Question 31
A cloud engineer is designing a cloud-native, three-tier application. The engineer must adhere to the following security best practices:
- Minimal services should run on all layers of the stack.
- The solution should be vendor-agnostic.
- Virtualization could be used over physical hardware.
Which of the following concepts should the engineer use to design the system to best meet these requirements?

A. Virtual machine
B. Microservices
C. Fan-out
D. Cloud-provided managed services

Correct Answer: B
Justification: Microservices align with minimal services and vendor-agnostic principles for secure, scalable architectures.

Question 32
A high-usage cloud resource needs to be monitored in real time on specific events to guarantee its availability. Which of the following actions should be used to meet this requirement?

A. Configure a ping command to identify when the cloud instance is out of service.
B. Create a dashboard with visualizations to filter the status of critical activities.
C. Collect all the daily activity from the cloud instance and create a dump file for analysis.
D. Schedule an hourly scan of the network to check for the availability of the resource.

Correct Answer: B
Justification: Dashboards provide real-time monitoring and visibility into the status of critical resources.

Question 33
A junior cloud administrator was recently promoted to cloud administrator and has been added to the cloud administrator group. The cloud administrator group is the only one that can access the engineering VM. The new administrator unsuccessfully attempts to access the engineering VM. However, the other administrators can access it without issue. Which of the following is the best way to identify the root cause?

A. Rebooting the engineering VM
B. Reviewing the administrator's permissions to access the engineering VM
C. Allowing connections from 0.0.0.0/0 to the engineering VM
D. Performing a packet capture on the engineering VM

Correct Answer: B
Justification: Permission issues are likely preventing access; reviewing permissions is the most logical step.

Question 34
A cloud solutions architect is designing a VM-based solution that requires reducing the cost as much as possible. Which of the following solutions will best satisfy this requirement?

A. Using ephemeral storage on replicated VMs
B. Creating spot VMs in one availability zone
C. Spreading the VMs across different regions
D. Using provisioned IOPS storage

Correct Answer: B
Justification: Spot VMs are cost-effective options for non-critical workloads, offering significant savings.

Question 35
A critical security patch is required on a network load balancer in a public cloud. The organization has a major sales conference next week, and the Chief Executive Officer does not want any interruptions during the demonstration of an application behind the load balancer. Which of the following approaches should the cloud security engineer take?

A. Ask the management team to delay the conference.
B. Apply the security patch after the event.
C. Ask the upper management team to approve an emergency patch window.
D. Apply the security patch immediately before the conference.

Correct Answer: C
Justification: An emergency patch window ensures the system is secure without impacting critical business events.

Question 36
A newly configured VM fails to run application updates despite having internet access. The updates download automatically from a third-party network. Given the following output, which of the following troubleshooting steps would be best to take?

A. Checking DNS configurations
B. Reconfiguring routing protocols
C. Testing the IP address configuration
D. Running a trace to the router

Correct Answer: A
Justification: Incorrect DNS configurations can prevent updates from resolving and downloading properly.

Question 37
A company migrated its CRM system to a SaaS solution. The security team is updating the RACI matrix for the newly migrated CRM. Which of the following responsibility assignments best aligns with the shared responsibility model for the new CRM?

A. Data-center security
B. CRM software security
C. CRM server patching
D. CRM development life cycle

Correct Answer: A
Justification: In a SaaS model, the provider is responsible for infrastructure-level security, including the data center.

Question 38
A social networking company operates globally. Some users from Brazil and Argentina are reporting the following error: 'Website address was not found.' Which of the following is the most likely cause of this outage?

A. Client DNS misconfiguration
B. Regional DNS provider outage
C. DNS server misconfiguration
D. DNS propagation issues

Correct Answer: B
Justification: A regional DNS provider outage can lead to localized issues in resolving website addresses.

Question 39
A cloud engineer is designing a cloud-native, three-tier application. The engineer must adhere to the following security best practices:
- Minimal services should run on all layers of the stack.
- The solution should be vendor agnostic.
- Virtualization could be used over physical hardware.
Which of the following concepts should the engineer use to design the system to best meet these requirements?

A. Virtual machine
B. Microservices
C. Fan-out
D. Cloud-provided managed services

Correct Answer: B
Justification: Microservices enable minimal service requirements, flexibility, and vendor-agnostic solutions.

Question 40
A high-usage cloud resource needs to be monitored in real-time on specific events to guarantee its availability. Which of the following actions should be used to meet this requirement?

A. Configure a ping command to identify when the cloud instance is out of service.
B. Create a dashboard with visualizations to filter the status of critical activities.
C. Collect all the daily activity from the cloud instance and create a dump file for analysis.
D. Schedule an hourly scan of the network to check for the availability of the resource.

Correct Answer: B
Justification: Dashboards provide real-time monitoring and visualization of critical metrics to ensure resource availability.

Question 41
A junior cloud administrator was recently promoted to cloud administrator and has been added to the cloud administrator group. The cloud administrator group is the only one that can access the engineering VM. The new administrator unsuccessfully attempts to access the engineering VM. However, the other administrators can access it without issue. Which of the following is the best way to identify the root cause?

A. Rebooting the engineering VM
B. Reviewing the administrator's permissions to access the engineering VM
C. Allowing connections from 0.0.0.0/0 to the engineering VM
D. Performing a packet capture on the engineering VM

Correct Answer: B
Justification: Reviewing permissions ensures the administrator has the correct access rights to the engineering VM.

Question 42
A cloud solutions architect is designing a VM-based solution that requires reducing the cost as much as possible. Which of the following solutions will best satisfy this requirement?

A. Using ephemeral storage on replicated VMs
B. Creating spot VMs in one availability zone
C. Spreading the VMs across different regions
D. Using provisioned IOPS storage

Correct Answer: B
Justification: Spot VMs are cost-effective as they utilize spare capacity with lower pricing compared to on-demand instances.

Question 43
A critical security patch is required on a network load balancer in a public cloud. The organization has a major sales conference next week, and the Chief Executive Officer does not want any interruptions during the demonstration of an application behind the load balancer. Which of the following approaches should the cloud security engineer take?

A. Ask the management team to delay the conference.
B. Apply the security patch after the event.
C. Ask the upper management team to approve an emergency patch window.
D. Apply the security patch immediately before the conference.

Correct Answer: C
Justification: An emergency patch window balances security needs and operational requirements with management approval.

Question 44
A cloud engineer has provisioned a VM for a high-frequency trading application. After the VM is put into production, users report high latency in trades. The engineer checks the last six hours of VM metrics and sees the following:
- CPU utilization is between 30% to 60%.
- NetworkIn is between 50kbps and 70kbps.
- NetworkOut is between 3,000kbps and 5,000kbps.
- DiskReadOps is at 30.
- DiskWriteOps is at 70.
- Memory utilization is between 50% and 70%.

Which of the following steps should the engineer take next to solve the latency issue?

A. Move to a network-optimized instance type as the network throughput is not enough.
B. Modify the disk IOPS to a higher value as the disk IO is being bottlenecked at 100 IOPS.
C. Increase the memory of the instance as the high-frequency trading application requires more memory.
D. Increase the instance size to allocate more vCPUs as the CPU utilization is very high.

Correct Answer: A
Justification: A network-optimized instance type will address the high NetworkOut demand causing latency in trading operations.

Question 45
A cloud engineer was deploying the company's payment processing application, but it failed with the following error log:
ERROR:root: transaction failed HTTP 429 response, please try again.
Which of the following are the most likely causes for this error? (Select two)

A. API throttling
B. API gateway outage
C. Web server outage
D. Oversubscription
E. Unauthorized access
F. Insufficient quota

Correct Answer: A,F
Justification: API throttling and insufficient quotas are common reasons for receiving HTTP 429 errors.

Question 46
An organization's web application experiences periodic bursts of traffic when a new video is launched. Users are reporting poor performance in the middle of the month. Which of the following scaling approaches should the organization use to scale based on forecasted traffic?

A. Scheduled
B. Manual
C. Event
D. Load

Correct Answer: A
Justification: Scheduled scaling allows for resource adjustments based on predictable traffic patterns.

Question 47
A critical security patch is required on a network load balancer in a public cloud. The organization has a major sales conference next week, and the Chief Executive Officer does not want any interruptions during the demonstration of an application behind the load balancer. Which of the following approaches should the cloud security engineer take?

A. Ask the management team to delay the conference.
B. Apply the security patch after the event.
C. Ask the upper management team to approve an emergency patch window.
D. Apply the security patch immediately before the conference.

Correct Answer: C
Justification: An emergency patch window balances security needs and operational requirements with management approval.

Question 48
A cloud engineer was deploying the company's payment processing application, but it failed with the following error log:
ERROR:root: transaction failed HTTP 429 response, please try again.
Which of the following are the most likely causes for this error? (Select two)

A. API throttling
B. API gateway outage
C. Web server outage
D. Oversubscription
E. Unauthorized access
F. Insufficient quota

Correct Answer: A,F
Justification: API throttling and insufficient quotas are common reasons for receiving HTTP 429 errors.

Question 49
A cloud engineer has provisioned a VM for a high-frequency trading application. After the VM is put into production, users report high latency in trades. The engineer checks the last six hours of VM metrics and sees the following:
- CPU utilization is between 30% to 60%.
- NetworkIn is between 50kbps and 70kbps.
- NetworkOut is between 3,000kbps and 5,000kbps.
- DiskReadOps is at 30.
- DiskWriteOps is at 70.
- Memory utilization is between 50% and 70%.

Which of the following steps should the engineer take next to solve the latency issue?

A. Move to a network-optimized instance type as the network throughput is not enough.
B. Modify the disk IOPS to a higher value as the disk IO is being bottlenecked at 100 IOPS.
C. Increase the memory of the instance as the high-frequency trading application requires more memory.
D. Increase the instance size to allocate more vCPUs as the CPU utilization is very high.

Correct Answer: A
Justification: A network-optimized instance type will address the high NetworkOut demand causing latency in trading operations.

Question 50
An organization's web application experiences periodic bursts of traffic when a new video is launched. Users are reporting poor performance in the middle of the month. Which of the following scaling approaches should the organization use to scale based on forecasted traffic?

A. Scheduled
B. Manual
C. Event
D. Load

Correct Answer: A
Justification: Scheduled scaling allows for resource adjustments based on predictable traffic patterns.

Question 51
A company uses containers stored in Docker Hub to deploy workloads for its IaaS infrastructure. The development team releases changes to the containers several times per hour. Which of the following should a cloud engineer do to prevent the proprietary code from being exposed to third parties?

A. Use IaC to deploy the IaaS infrastructure.
B. Convert the containers to VMs.
C. Deploy the containers over SSH.
D. Use private repositories for the containers.

Correct Answer: D
Justification: Using private repositories ensures proprietary code is not exposed publicly.

Question 52
Which of the following is an auditing procedure that ensures service providers securely manage the data to protect the interests of the organization and the privacy of its clients?

A. CIS
B. ITIL
C. SOC2
D. ISO 27001

Correct Answer: C
Justification: SOC2 auditing ensures secure data management and aligns with organizational and client privacy needs.

Question 53
A cloud engineer wants to replace the current on-premises, unstructured data storage with a solution in the cloud. The new solution needs to be cost-effective and highly scalable. Which of the following types of storage would be best to use?

A. File
B. Block
C. Object
D. SAN

Correct Answer: C
Justification: Object storage is scalable, cost-effective, and ideal for unstructured data in cloud environments.

Question 54
A security analyst reviews the daily logs and notices the following suspicious activity:
The analyst investigates the firewall logs and identifies the following:
Which of the following steps should the security analyst take next to resolve this issue? (Select two)

A. Submit an IT support ticket and request Kali Linux be uninstalled from John Smith's computer
B. Block all inbound connections on port 4444 and block the IP address 201.101.25.121.
C. Contact John Smith and request the Ethernet cable attached to the desktop be unplugged
D. Check the running processes to confirm if a backdoor connection has been established.
E. Upgrade the Windows x64 operating system on John Smith's computer to the latest version
F. Block all outbound connections from the IP address 10.150.71.151.

Correct Answer: B,D
Justification: Blocking malicious connections and investigating potential backdoors mitigate immediate threats.

Question 55
A security analyst confirms a zero-day vulnerability was exploited by hackers who gained access to confidential customer data and installed ransomware on the server. Which of the following steps should the security analyst take? (Select two)

A. Contact the customers to inform them about the data breach.
B. Contact the hackers to negotiate payment to unlock the server.
C. Send a global communication to inform all impacted users.
D. Inform the management and legal teams about the data breach.
E. Delete confidential data used on other servers that might be compromised.
F. Modify the firewall rules to block the IP addresses and update the ports.

Correct Answer: A,D
Justification: Notifying customers and management ensures compliance and accountability during data breaches.

Question 56
Which of the following types of storage provides the greatest performance advantage for a traditional relational database?

A. File
B. Object
C. Block
D. Ephemeral

Correct Answer: C
Justification: Block storage offers low latency and high IOPS, making it suitable for relational databases.

Question 57
Which of the following is used to detect signals and measure physical properties, such as the temperature of the human body?

A. Beacon
B. Transmission protocols
C. Sensors
D. Gateways

Correct Answer: C
Justification: Sensors measure physical properties, including temperature, and are used in IoT environments.

Question 58
A company wants to combine solutions in a central and scalable environment to achieve the following: control, visibility, automation, and cost efficiency. Which of the following best describes what the company should implement?

A. Batch processing
B. Workload orchestration
C. Containerization
D. Application modernization

Correct Answer: B
Justification: Workload orchestration centralizes control, enhances visibility, and supports automation in scalable environments.

Question 59
Which of the following requirements are core considerations when migrating a small business's on-premises applications to the cloud? (Select two)

A. Availability
B. Hybrid
C. Testing
D. Networking
E. Compute
F. Logs

Correct Answer: A,D
Justification: Availability and networking are crucial to ensure reliable access and connectivity post-migration.

Question 60
The performance of an e-commerce website decreases dramatically during random periods. The IT team is evaluating available resources to mitigate the situation. Which of the following is the best approach to effectively manage this scenario?

A. Migrating to a dedicated host
B. Purchasing additional servers
C. Scheduling resource allocation
D. Configuring automatic elasticity

Correct Answer: D
Justification: Automatic elasticity adjusts resources dynamically to match fluctuating demand, improving performance.

Made in United States
North Haven, CT
05 November 2026

21760250R00183